PARENTING ADHD POWER PACK 3 IN 1 BUNDLE

UNLOCKING YOUR CHILD'S FULL POTENTIAL BY MASTERING SPECIAL EDUCATION, DEFUSING EXPLOSIVE BEHAVIORS, AND CREATING A DRAMA-FREE HOME

ROSE LYONS

CONTENTS

PARENTING A CHILD WITH ADHD
How to Prepare Your Child for School Life,
Integrate Executive Functioning Skills, and
Foster Successful Friendships

DEFUSING EXPLOSIVE BEHAVIOR IN CHILDREN WITH ADHD

Peaceful Parenting Strategies To Identify
Triggers, Establish Emotional Response And
Create Structure For A Drama Free Home

THE SPECIAL EDUCATION PLAYBOOK

The Ultimate Guide to Empower Parents in the 504/IEP Process to Unlock Your Child's Unique Learning Profile

Free for you!

As a thank you for reading this book, download this BONUS GUIDE to teach your child how to keep their room tidy and functional in 7 steps!

Check out my other books and follow me on Amazon to get updates of when I have new publications! Click here to Follow Me Rose Lyons Author Page

PARENTING A CHILD WITH ADHD

HOW TO PREPARE YOUR CHILD FOR SCHOOL LIFE, INTEGRATE EXECUTIVE FUNCTIONING SKILLS, AND FOSTER SUCCESSFUL FRIENDSHIPS

INTRODUCTION

One thing that hinders communication, especially between parents and their children, is a simple fact that no two people are alike. To illustrate this, think about the people (or person) in your life whom you believe are your opposites. As friends, family members, or colleagues, we all have people whose interests, personality traits, and perspectives sharply contrast with ours. Now, imagine being responsible for raising them as your children.

For parents raising children with Attention Deficit Hyperactivity Disorder (ADHD), this is more than just a visualization exercise; it is a daily reality. Children are typically poor communicators, and it is even more challenging to understand and help them when they also have ADHD.

The most apparent symptoms of this disorder are impulsivity, inattentiveness, and impatience. Unfortunately, since this behavior is not learned but is a result of nature, there is not much the affected child can do about the disorder to just stop the negative behaviors. Indeed, children are often unaware that they have a condition and that issues must be addressed.

Parents, however, are usually quite observant, and they can see that their child's behavior is not just problematic now but may also be derailing in the future. So before they put the pieces together, they may ask questions like, "Why doesn't he listen to me?"; "What do I do to make her sit still at the dinner table?"; "How am I failing my child?"

You are not alone in this worry. About 2.2% of children worldwide struggle with ADHD (ADDitude, 2022). In the United States alone, 6.1 million children have been diagnosed with the disorder (CDC, 2021). Nevertheless, it is essential to remember that your children are having a rough time too. As children grow older, they will notice the effect that their behavior has on other people, as well as on themselves. However, as mentioned before, children can do little or nothing about this condition unless they are helped by their parents (or any other type of guardian). What they need more than anything else is your love and support.

The fact that you are reading this book shows that you are heavily invested in your child's well-being. You want them to be successful in various areas of life, including socially and educationally. So it can easily be deduced that you are ready to learn how to make your child with ADHD comfortable and happy. This willingness to make the right choices for your child is an important step.

The first task this book undertakes is the correction of a common misconception that people have regarding ADHD. Although it is a disorder, it is not a life sentence. Your child who has the condition of this disorder is not destined for a failed future, and the first chapter of this book will show you why. How you perceive this condition will inform how you interact with your child and the measures you can take to help them.

Because of the problems associated with ADHD, many people are often quick to describe it as a curse. This sentiment may even be shared by adults diagnosed with the condition. Although this perception is erroneous, we should not be quick to dismiss it, as it may not be the result of malice or prejudice. In truth, ADHD *can* be hard to live with.

For one, success in any endeavor requires focused attention. Without this, your high IQ and talent may not count for much. One of the most common symptoms of ADHD is a seeming inability to keep one's mind focused on a single task for a meaningful length of time. People with this condition tend to be quickly and more frequently distracted than neurotypicals.

However, it should be noted that this distraction typically happens when the affected child has little interest in a particular task. Therefore, on those activities that they do not find boring, people with ADHD may become *hyper-focused* (Low, 2021).

If your child is also hyperactive, their behavior may be described as unruly and, at the worst, wild and disorderly. You can imagine the impact this could have on the sociability of your child and all the ways it may affect their emotional and mental development. As such, we should forgive those who declare ADHD a curse.

ADHD is merely a condition that can be managed. Indeed, your affected child has every chance to foster meaningful and long-term relationships. In addition, they can succeed at any task and become valuable members of society despite their ADHD.

Need proof? You may not know this, but several prominent figures, from politicians to scientists, have this condition.

James Carville is a political consultant who has been instrumental in helping politicians—both in the United States and other countries—secure public office. He is famously credited with Bill Clinton's 1992 presidential victory. In 2004, James Carville admitted on CNN that he had ADHD. This condition caused him to drop out of college, but he eventually graduated from law school and found his passion for politics.

How about the Pulitzer prize winner, Katherine Ellison? Although she was not diagnosed with the condition until 2007, when she was 49 years old, Katherine has distinguished herself as an author and journalist.

Sir Richard Branson is another notable figure who has achieved significant and admirable things. You may know him as the founder of the world-class airline Virgin Atlantic. However, did you also know that he has been diagnosed with ADHD and dyslexia? It presented some problems for him, as he recounts struggling in school and being unable to focus on things he did not have a passion for.

However, Sir Richard has used this condition to his advantage. Hyper-focus, which may result from having ADHD, helped grow his business into its current conglomerate. Since people with

ADHD have a 300% likelihood of starting a business, we may conclude that this condition compelled Branson to found his first business at age 16.

There are many other famous names whose exploits disprove the notion that ADHD is a curse. The founder of IKEA, Ingvar Kamprad, and superstar musician, Justin Timberlake are a couple of other examples.

This book, *Parenting a Child with ADHD*, has been painstakingly researched to equip you with the knowledge to help your child achieve their dreams while managing their ADHD. This book is 15 years in the making and is the product of personal experience and professional study.

Rose Lyons, the author of this book, has two lovely children, both of whom were diagnosed with Attention Deficit Hyperactivity Disorder. Her journey in helping her children has provided her with first-hand knowledge on how to deal with the condition. Rose has also carried out several studies on not just ADHD but other mental health conditions. She has gone on to help other parents successfully confront and overcome the challenges posed by ADHD. She hopes to make even more people aware of the mental health needs of children and adults.

Before now, parents dismissed the symptoms of ADHD as nothing more than childish exuberance or laziness in the case of an inability to focus. Nevertheless, of course, parenting is by no means an easy job. It definitely can be challenging in both standard and unique ways. For Rose, the position of parenting is the most delicate and important one in the world, and she wants to help everyone become more successful at it. This book is an extension of her compassion toward every parent who struggles with the challenges of ADHD.

This book will give you the tools you need to create a supportive and nurturing environment for your children with ADHD. Regardless of their diagnosis, you can raise them to be independent and confident.

Prepare to discover more about Attention Deficit Hyperactivity Disorder than you had grasped previously. Prepare to learn about the structure and processes of the ADHD brain and how it differs from a neurotypical one. After reading this book, you will be able to interact more effectively with your child who has this condition. In addition, your parenting strategies will be fine-tuned to accommodate your child with ADHD. You will also learn about modern and effective treatments and medication to manage the condition.

Prepare to become the best possible parent for your child and their number one cheerleader.

1

ADHD—A CONDITION, NOT A CURSE

Meet Christie, a young child in elementary school. She has always been quite different from her peers but in a good way. She is funny, full of life, and brilliant. She is a curious child and loves to learn new things. She is one of the smartest and kindest children in her class. However, there is a flip side to her. She is sweet as sugar one minute, and she can be sour like salt candy the next. She has a temper problem, and even the tiniest things— like someone talking loudly or when she does not get to choose her cereals for breakfast—can set her off. As a result, her mother often has difficulty making her sit through their meals together. Christie is a mess at church, too, as she keeps pushing the other children in her pew.

She was even ousted from her class a few weeks ago for misbehaving and has become the black sheep. Lately, Christie has been having issues sitting straight and focusing on lessons. Her mother does not want her to get on meds, fearing it will turn her baby girl into an addict.

C onfused and frustrated, Christie's mother has come to a dead end. She does not know why her more than capable daughter exhibits odd behavior and struggles with specific tasks. She feels like a bad parent when she has to scold her daughter for wiggling too much, talking excessively, and being so forgetful, even when she is a good child.

UNDERSTANDING ADHD—THE FIRST STEP TO BECOMING A BETTER PARENT FOR YOUR CHILD

Does the above scenario sound familiar to you? Do you feel like you are the one in the story? Do you feel like you are at your wit's end with your child and nothing seems to help?

Chances are, you have not been able to get help or find a solution for your child because you have no idea what is wrong with them. On the one hand, they are perfectly healthy, and you do not see any physical or health challenges with them. But, on the other hand, if your child is anything like Christie, they struggle with a condition known as ADHD.

So, no, they are not just misbehaving because they want to. All the unpleasant attitudes which you notice are a result of ADHD. This can be worrisome, especially if you have no idea what this condition means. Raising children, in general, is a difficult task, but raising a child with ADHD can be an unimaginable challenge. The journey of caring for children with ADHD from childhood to adulthood is rough, punctuated by bouts of success and even more significant failures. It is a challenge that you need to take up fully armed with information.

WHAT IS ADHD?

Demystifying ADHD is the first step for you as a parent in understanding the condition.

So, what is it?

ADHD is an acronym for Attention Deficit Hyperactivity Disorder (ADHD). It is a mental health condition that induces varying hyperactivity and impulsive behaviors. The inability to focus on a particular task or sit still for a long time is a characteristic of a person with ADHD.

People with ADHD are inattentive and suffer fluctuations in their energy levels more often and at more severe rates than those who do not have the condition. The effect of this can usually be noticed in their home, school, and social life.

Past researchers used to refer to the symptoms that cause this condition as Attention Deficit Disorder (ADD). The term ADD has been outdated since 1987. The third edition of the Diagnostic and Statistical Manual of Mental Disorders (DSM-3) used to categorize the condition into two subtypes:

- ADD with hyperactivity
- ADD without hyperactivity

However, after a revision by the American psychiatric association, the two subtypes were merged to become ADHD. ADHD has joined the league of common childhood mental health conditions and is reported to affect around 9.4% of children and adolescents in the United States.

ADHD is a neurodevelopmental disorder that presents early in childhood. Although the average age of onset is usually seven years, diagnosis often comes later, during their teens. Children with ADHD have problems controlling spontaneous responses ranging from movement to attentiveness to speech.

ADHD is not a learning disability, although the symptoms can increase difficulty in learning. There is also a chance for children who have ADHD to have other disabilities such as dyslexia, anxiety, and ODD (Oppositional Defiance Disorder). Even though it is not a learning disability, its effects can still be lifelong.

THE THREE TYPES OF ADHD AND THEIR SYMPTOMS

ADHD is grouped into three types, namely:

- Inattentive type
- Hyperactive, impulsive type
- Combined type

The Inattentive Type

The inattentive type of ADHD borders on inattentiveness. Children with this type of ADHD struggle with focus, task completion, and keeping to instructions. Most researchers believe that children with this type of ADHD may go undiagnosed for a long time or receive improper diagnoses because they do not disturb the classroom. Girls who have ADHD often present with the inattentive type.

Symptoms of the Inattentive Type of ADHD

Children who struggle with the inattentive type of ADHD have the following symptoms:

- Frequent loss of items like books, homework, toys, and clothing
- Easily distracted by little occurrences in their surroundings
- Prone to making mistakes or missing details during study or work
- Difficulty maintaining focus when reading, listening, or having a conversation
- Have trouble paying attention when spoken to

The Hyperactive-Impulsive Type

This type of ADHD manifests as hyperactive and impulsive behaviors like:

- Fidgeting
- Interrupting others when they talk
- Impatience in waiting for their turn

The primary symptoms of this type of ADHD are:

- Excessive talking
- Difficulty playing or doing tasks quietly
- Difficulty sitting still
- Interrupting others when they are talking, playing, or doing other tasks

- Acting without thinking
- Difficulty controlling powerful emotions like anger and often having outbursts and temper tantrums
- Moving around constantly, like running and climbing inappropriately

The Combined Type

This type of ADHD is quite common. Children and even adults who experience this type display conditions of inattentive and hyperactive symptoms. Children often have difficulty paying attention, display impulsiveness, and have unusually high energy levels. A child with this type of ADHD presents mixed symptoms of the other types of ADHD.

Children with ADHD have a more challenging time fitting in than other children. This causes individual problems as well as stress on the family. It is common for parents who have no idea what ADHD is, or do not know how to solve their child's difficulties, to brand it a curse. However, no, ADHD is not a curse. It is just a childhood mental disorder that is manageable. If your child has ADHD, it does not mean they are troubled with an affliction or something metaphysical about their condition.

COMMON SIGNS OF ADHD IN CHILDREN

Regardless of the type of ADHD present in a child, these are the signs that can notify you to take action:

- **Self-focused behavior:** When a child cannot recognize the desires and needs of other people, it could be a sign that they have ADHD. This often progresses to symptoms like interrupting and difficulty waiting their turn.

- **Emotional troubles:** Children with ADHD have difficulty managing their emotions. It is common to find them bursting out in anger at odd times. If they are very young, they may display tantrums.
- **Fidgeting:** If a child has ADHD, they can hardly sit still. When asked to sit, they try to stand up, run around, fidget, or squirm.
- **Problems playing quietly:** Because they are often fidgety, it is difficult for children with ADHD to engage in quiet or calm play.
- **Unfinished tasks:** One of the significant signs of ADHD is leaving tasks unfinished. Children with ADHD often indicate interest in many things but cannot finish them. For instance, they begin projects, homework, or chores, but soon enough, they do something else that has caught their fancy.
- **Lack of focus:** A child with ADHD struggles with paying attention even when they are being addressed directly. After talking to them, they will admit they heard everything but cannot repeat what you said. Often, they hear your words but are unable to process them.
- **Avoidance of tasks needing extended mental effort:** Children with ADHD have difficulty focusing, which affects how they participate in activities that need comprehensive mental effort. These children often avoid mentally tasking activities, like doing homework or paying attention in class.

- **Mistakes:** One common sign of a child with ADHD is being mistake-prone. As they mainly have trouble heeding instructions that involve planning or plan execution, they often make careless mistakes. However, this is not a sign of laziness or unintelligence.
- **Daydreaming:** Although people link noisiness and hyperactivity to children with ADHD, being quieter or more withdrawn than other children can be a sign of ADHD. More often than not, children with ADHD stare into space, daydream, and ignore the things around them.
- **The trouble with organization:** Children with ADHD cannot keep track of their tasks and activities. In school, this makes them get into trouble as they cannot make their homework, school projects, or other assignments a priority. This can make daily routines like getting ready seem like Groundhog's day at home.

SYMPTOMS IN MULTIPLE SETTINGS

When a child has ADHD, the symptoms manifest in different settings. The inattentiveness or hyperactive behavior will be noticed both at home and school.

2

WHAT CAUSES ADHD AND WHAT DOESN'T

A DHD is a common mental condition that is largely misunderstood, which is why scientists are trying to understand why it happens.

Since its first diagnosis and discussions, there have been different theories about why people have ADHD. However, there is no concrete proof of the exact cause of ADHD. Instead, scientists studying it for decades have highlighted some factors that potentially lead to its onset.

SOME POSSIBLE CAUSES OF ADHD

According to the Centers for Disease Control and Prevention (CDC) reports, around 9.4% of children in the United States have ADHD. Still, no scientist has pinpointed the exact cause of this condition. However, it is believed that some factors play a significant role in getting this condition. Some of these essential factors that influence ADHD are listed below:

Genes

Much research has revealed strong evidence linking genes to the development of ADHD. In addition, scientists' research indicates that this condition runs in families. People with close relatives with this condition are likely to have it, and individuals whose parents have the disorder are more likely to have it. However, the same genes that trigger the disorder are yet to be discovered. Ongoing research seeks to study the potential connection between the DRD4 gene and ADHD (Tovo-Rodrigues, et al., 2013). DRD4, also known as the dopamine receptor gene, is responsible for regulating the behaviors affected by the feel-good neurotransmitter dopamine. One typical example is risk-taking. Prior research in 1998 showed that this gene influences the brain's dopamine receptors (Swanson, et al., 1998).

Different gene variations have been observed in people with the disorder, making researchers believe that it is somewhat linked to the development of the condition. Chances are, there are several genes responsible for the condition. Even though genes play a role in the development of ADHD, people with no family history of the disorder have also been diagnosed with the condition. This disorder also depends on other factors, including a person's environment.

Neurotoxins

Some scientists say ADHD can be linked to common neurotoxic chemicals like lead and pesticides. In addition, pesticides containing organophosphates have also been connected to ADHD. Usually, these chemical pesticides are sprinkled on lawns and agricultural products, and children come in contact with them during play or through their food.

Studies have shown that organophosphates negatively affect the neurodevelopment of children.

Nutrition

Although there is speculation that food dyes and preservatives are responsible for causing hyperactivity in children, there is no strong evidence backing it. For example, many processed and packaged snack food ingredients include artificial coloring. In addition, edibles like jams, soft drinks, relishes, and food pies contain sodium benzoate for preservation. Again, however, there is no concrete evidence linking these food ingredients to ADHD.

Smoking and Alcohol

The environmental connection to ADHD in children happens before they are born. For example, pregnancy-related smoking is linked to specific ADHD symptoms in children. In addition, studies have shown that exposing children in the womb to alcohol and drugs increases their chances of having ADHD.

WHAT DOESN'T CAUSE ADHD - DEBUNKING SOME COMMON MYTHS AND FEARS

People think differently when they hear about ADHD, and the lack of understanding of ADHD negatively impacts the treatment of ADHD. In addition, widespread misinformation and myths about ADHD affect the individual's reaction to the condition. Therefore, these myths need to be clear, as they harm the ADHD community and prevent people from seeking diagnosis and treatment.

As such, people need to understand that the following do not cause ADHD:

- **Consuming sugar in excess:** Currently, no verifiable scientific evidence indicates that excess consumption of sugar in children causes ADHD. People often think eating sugar makes children hyperactive, but it does not happen. Studies have not been able to link the two. Even though some studies suggest that children with ADHD can be sensitive to some food substances, there is no solid evidence to back it up.
- **Watching TV:** TV is often given a bad rep for its role in many child developmental problems and some ADHD symptoms. However, it does not directly cause ADHD. One of the main symptoms of ADHD is attention deficiency, and there is proof that watching too much TV reduces attention span. Looking at fast motion pictures for a long time over-stimulates the neurons connected with sound and sight. When these neurons are overstimulated, the neural centers do not respond well to ordinary stimulants.

As a result, concentrating on essential things requires more effort and time. Based on studies, children between the ages of one and three who are exposed to TV can have a reduced attention period by the time they are seven. However, the effects are not harmful enough to develop ADHD.

Some researchers maintain that the effects of TV on ADHD are inconclusive. Anybody who watches too much TV will struggle with attention deficiency, which is not limited to children without ADHD. Studies have also shown that the TV-watching habits of children with ADHD are the same as those without it (McBee, 2021). Many children worldwide watch TV most of the time, but they have never received an ADHD diagnosis. Meanwhile, ADHD has been diagnosed in children who do not have much access to the TV. Even though watching TV does not cause ADHD, parents must regulate how much time children spend watching TV.

- **Playing video games:** Some people think that letting their children play video games can make them have ADHD. The rationale is baseless, as no evidence indicates that playing video games causes ADHD. Like with TV, children and adults who spend more time looking at the screen struggle to maintain attention than others, but that does not lead to ADHD. Researchers suggest that children cannot get ADHD just by spending too much time behind the screen.
- **Poor parenting:** When a child has been diagnosed with ADHD, many parents carry the guilt upon themselves. Their guilt is often borne out of wishing that there was something they could do to make their children manage their symptoms. The myth of ADHD resulting from poor

parenting is why most parents think their child's diagnosis is their fault.

While a person with ADHD benefits from structure, more harm is done in the long run if they are repeatedly punished for symptoms like hyperactivity, restlessness, or impulsivity. However, these ADHD behaviors are often seen as poor manners, and the parents receive the blame for not controlling their child.

Girls Do Not Get ADHD

Usually, young girls are not hyperactive like young boys. Therefore, people rarely detect ADHD in girls because females do not display as many behavioral problems as males. This reduces the chance of referring girls for ADHD evaluation.

As a result of this myth, more girls live with untreated ADHD, which worsens and makes them have issues like:

- Mood
- Anxiety
- Antisocial personality
- Other comorbid disorders in adulthood

Girls *can* be diagnosed with ADHD, and it is just as important to identify their symptoms and provide them with the needed support.

People With ADHD Are Lazy

People who do not understand ADHD think of those individuals with the condition as lazy. As a result, a person with ADHD often feels guilty for being less productive and motivated due to this myth. Generally, people with ADHD require more structure and reminders to make things work, especially if they have to participate in activities requiring extended mental effort.

However, the myth about ADHD being a form of laziness is fueled by some symptoms, which manifest as disorganization, lack of interest, and motivation, with exceptions for activities the ADHD individual truly enjoys.

The truth is that people with ADHD love to accomplish things, but the struggle needed to complete seemingly simple tasks makes people regard them as lazy. They could be overwhelmed by doing things like cleaning their room. Myths like this should be discarded, as they make people feel like they have failed, eventually dropping their self-esteem.

Having ADHD Is Not That Serious

ADHD should be taken seriously, and parents should seek to understand the condition. The condition affects the individual's quality of life. Unlike others, people with ADHD have more chances of suffering from anxiety, mood, and substance use disorders.

Later in life, people with ADHD struggle with meeting work responsibilities and are often monitored or on probation. As a result, they are regularly afraid of losing their jobs and being less capable of fulfilling their financial needs, which can affect their personal life. In addition, although they require more time to complete tasks, educational and employment settings might not accommodate them.

ADHD Is Not a Real Medical Disorder

Some people see ADHD as a fad, but it is as real as it gets. Research shows visible differences between a brain with ADHD and one without it, including how they react with brain chemicals like dopamine, glutamate, and norepinephrine.

The brain sections linked with ADHD are crucial for executive functions, like:

- Planning
- Organizing
- Initiating tasks

ENVIRONMENTAL FACTORS

Parents are often worried when their child is diagnosed with ADHD, as they try to figure out if it is a nature or nurture thing. Some parents begin to feel it is something in them or something they have done that's responsible. These feelings are usually stronger when one parent has the condition, and their child is diagnosed with it.

However, psychologists state that people with neurodevelopmental disorders have neurological differences that they are born with. So people are born with the condition, which does not just start as they grow. Quite a lot of factors contribute to the onset of ADHD, but the impact of the environment plays a huge role.

Some psychologists assert that strong evidence links some environmental risk factors to a future ADHD diagnosis. Some of the environmental factors likely to cause ADHD include:

- In utero exposure
- Exposure to environmental toxins
- Illnesses

In Utero Exposure

According to relevant studies, when a pregnant woman smokes tobacco or drinks alcohol, there is a high chance that the child will eventually have ADHD. In addition, studies have shown that the risk of children having ADHD increases if their mothers are heavy smokers or if they drink more than four alcoholic drinks in one sitting.

Another in utero factor is the maternal diet, infections during pregnancy, and medications used, like caffeine, antidepressants, and antihypertensives. In addition, the American Psychiatric Association suggests the likelihood of developing ADHD increases in babies born early or at low birth weight.

Exposure to Environmental Toxins

Toxin exposure can play a significant role in utero or during childhood. Some toxins are lead, mercury, pesticides, and certain chemical compounds. For example, lead and pesticide organophosphate, which are found in the environment, can affect neurological development in children.

Illness

Some studies indicate that bacterial meningitis, a severe bacterial illness, can pose a risk for ADHD. Bacterial meningitis is transmitted through human-to-human contact and food, making it an environmental hazard. Another illness that places people at risk of ADHD is encephalitis, an inflammation in the brain caused by infection or autoimmune response.

The reality of ADHD, again, is that researchers have not been able to figure out the exact cause of it. Furthermore, this is likely because ADHD is not caused by just one thing. So it is difficult to pin down the cause to just one factor.

However, based on twin and family studies, genetics seems to be one of the significant factors. Unfortunately, though, genetic predisposition is not a surety that someone will have ADHD because of its many other risk factors. Often, ADHD is not caused by just one risk factor but is primarily a combination of genetic and environmental factors, which generally raises the chances of a person having the condition.

Psychologists admit that it is difficult to separate genetic and environmental factors because family members share genetics and lifestyle. Therefore, it is essential to consider all the predisposing factors since ADHD is the outcome of the total of those factors.

Other factors like brain damage have been seen to play a role in developing ADHD. For example, some ADHD diagnoses are often triggered by damage from head trauma, early life injuries, and atypical brain development.

Managing Environmental Stressors

ADHD is a neurodevelopmental condition caused mainly by genetics and environmental factors. Prevention of this condition is futile due to the genetic predisposition aspect of it. However, parents can manage the effect of environmental stressors on the health of their unborn children by taking steps like:

- Getting adequate prenatal healthcare
- Cutting off drug, alcohol, and tobacco exposure during pregnancy
- Reducing contact with environmental toxins like lead and pesticides

Most importantly, as a parent, you must understand that ADHD results from many factors. The debate about the exact cause is still ongoing, meaning you do not have to beat yourself up about your child's condition. There is no way you or anybody else could have prevented it, as there is no definite cause.

Some scientists argue that ADHD has no external cause, and people who have it are born with it, and it just escalates depending on time and their living conditions. Many theories have come up in the past years to explain the condition, but the truth remains that no one has been able to figure out an exact cause yet.

3

THE BIOLOGY OF ADHD AND NON-ADHD BRAIN

ADHD is a confusing and frustrating mental condition that takes a toll on the minds of the people living with it. In addition, they have to deal with an inconsistent way of living, as some days are good while others are shady.

As discussed earlier, scientists have spent their lives researching this condition and have listed dozens of telltale signs of the condition, yet they have not been successful in finding the root cause of it. However, discovering some crucial factors that play a role in aggravating ADHD is the closest anybody has ever come to profiling it.

As science has advanced with time, researchers and medical examiners have found some data on ADHD and its impairments to find a direction to do something about it. One such key study includes the study of the nervous system, explaining the differences between the ADHD brain and the brain without the condition.

THE ADHD VS. NON-ADHD BRAIN

ADHD is an actual condition. Despite what critics say about it, it exists, and there is enough data and real-life stories to support it. Unfortunately, cynics downplay or question its existence by blaming the symptoms on bad parenting or a lack of willpower and motivation from the individual with the condition, which is untrue. These dismissals of what is a real experience can be demoralizing for people with ADHD or their families.

However, people with ADHD can validate their experiences through the research results showing that stark differences exist between the ADHD brain and the non-ADHD brain. The brain of an individual with ADHD has a different structure, chemistry, and function than the normal's.

Brain Structure

The brain structures of people without ADHD have differences that affect many areas of the brain, which link to common ADHD symptoms.

Children with ADHD have noticeably smaller brains than those without. The difference in size can be seen in different brain regions like the amygdala and hippocampus, which connect emotion regulation, memory, and motivation. First, however, you need to know that the brain size difference does not play any role in their intelligence.

The National Institute of Health published a paper in 2007 stating that brain maturity is delayed in certain areas for a child with ADHD. The most notable delay point was the front of the cortex, which manages attention, and cognitive and planning control. The only region in the brain of an ADHD child with a maturation rate that's faster than average is the motor cortex, which connects to symptoms like fidgeting and restlessness.

Some regions in the frontal lobe of children with ADHD mature slower. Furthermore, since the frontal lobe is in charge of skills like attention, social behavior, and impulse control, children with ADHD may struggle with dysfunction associated with these skills. Regular activity in the frontal lobe's premotor and prefrontal cortex regions ensures motor activity and attentional capacity. Still, a person with ADHD has less activity in these brain regions.

The differences between a brain with ADHD and one without are more pronounced in children than adults.

Brain Function

The effect of ADHD on brain functioning is observed in different aspects. ADHD is connected to problems with cognitive, motivational, and behavioral functioning. It destabilizes mood regulation, emotions, and connections within the brain cells. It even disrupts how the brain communicates with its different parts.

The neurons in the brain are a network of nerve cells transporting information from one part of the brain to another. The neurons of people with ADHD develop slower and are not so efficient in sending some messages, bits of information, or behaviors. As a result of the slow development, the neurons may function abnormally in areas like a reward, focus, and movement.

Scientists use MRI and X-ray-based imaging tools to observe slight abnormalities in the brain function and structure of people with ADHD. Results from imaging of people with ADHD show that structural connectivity of the neurons is abnormal. However, the functional connectivity of people with ADHD is increased in some regions.

According to research based on comparisons with brains of people without this disorder, ADHD brains are hyperactive in some regions and hypoactive in others. The implication is that there could be a problem with the brain's computing ability to match cognitive demands adequately.

For instance, people with this condition find it difficult to manage brain activity in the regular attention network, causing distractions.

ADHD causes improper executive functioning skills in areas like:

- Attention
- Focus
- Concentration
- Memory
- Hyperactivity
- Impulsivity
- Social skills
- Organization
- Planning
- Decision making
- Task switching
- Learning from past mistakes

- Motivation

Some of the brain imaging techniques used to observe the functions of the ADHD brain include:

- Functional magnetic resonance imaging (fMRI)
- Positron emission tomography (PET)
- Single photon emission computed tomography (SPECT)

The brains of people with this condition have abnormalities in blood flow to certain parts of their brains, affecting the region's activity. In addition, children with this condition have different connectivities between the frontal cortex of the brain and the visual processing area. Studies and brain imaging techniques show that the ADHD brain does not process information similarly to a non-ADHD brain.

Brain Chemistry

The brain neurons transfer messages across the brain, and there is a gap between neurons, known as synapses. Synapses have to contain neurotransmitters for messages to be transmitted in the brain. Each neurotransmitter or chemical messenger has a unique function assigned to it.

Dopamine and noradrenaline are the major neurotransmitters. However, the brain of an ADHD person cannot properly regulate the dopamine system. For instance, the dopamine level is either too little, lacks receptors, or is not appropriately utilized. In the ADHD brain, having a high level of dopamine transporters without corresponding levels of receptors causes the brain to ignore important messages. This implies that dopamine travels too fast for the messages in the brain to be acknowledged.

The relevance of dopamine lies in managing the brain's reward and pleasure center and the sustenance of motivation and attention. Dopamine triggers children to determine the reward for a task. When a child perceives a reward as important, the dopamine levels spike, and the child takes up the task immediately.

Due to the abnormal dopamine functioning in the ADHD brain, there is little interest in routine tasks with low reward potential. As a result, the child with this disorder finds it difficult to start tasks or continue without distraction, making them lose interest in activities and move on to the next best thing.

An abnormal dopamine system enhances the difficulty for children in waiting for the things they want or taking action to get the reward in the future. It is difficult for them to picture future pleasure; they can only focus on things that have their attention *now*. Dopamine is great for learning, too. Activities that trigger high levels of dopamine in the brain are enjoyable, as the brain changes to recognize it, and the child finds it easier to repeat the behavior in the future.

HOW ADHD IS DIAGNOSED

The diagnosis for this condition is not made through objective tests like a blood test, physical test, or an X-ray. Only qualified doctors, psychiatrists, and psychologists can diagnose this condition using complete evaluation processes like:

- A comprehensive interview with the patient
- A review of medical history and school reports
- Attention, memory, and distractibility measurement tests

The information retrieved from the tests will then be compared with the Diagnostic and Statistical Manual of Mental Disorders (DSM) guideline for diagnosing this disorder. Although PET and fMRI are relevant for research, they cannot be used for diagnosis because they only determine the brain function during the period the test is taken. Brain scans cannot provide information for brain function in diverse situations like a clinical test. Again, scan data is usually based on group averages and does not apply to individuals.

Diagnostic Criteria

When a clinical test is done, the individual has to meet different conditions to get an official diagnosis. This applies to all types of ADHD; inattentive, hyperactive-impulsive, or combined. These are the conditions:

- Patient symptoms must be present before they turn twelve
- Patient symptoms must show up in multiple settings (home, school, work)
- Patient symptoms must interfere with daily activities
- Other mental health issues must not explain away a patient's symptoms

The diagnostic criteria for the three types of ADHD are described below:

Inattentive Type

When diagnosing children with the inattentive type of the disorder, a certain number of symptoms have to be recognized. Six or more symptoms of inattention must be seen in children 16 years old and under, while five or more symptoms need to be present in those 17 and older. In addition, the symptoms must have been observed for a minimum of six months before the test to receive a diagnosis for this condition.

An individual who is to be diagnosed with the inattentive type of ADHD needs to have some or all of these symptoms:

- Regularly making careless mistakes or ignoring details
- Has problems remaining focused on specific tasks or activities
- Hardly listening when spoken to
- Never finishing tasks or heeding instructions
- Problems with organization
- Has deep hatred for long-term tasks
- Regularly misplacing important items
- Very forgetful and easily distracted

Hyperactive-Impulsive Type

The age-based criteria for determining the hyperactive-impulsive type of ADHD is the same as the attentive, but based on the specific symptoms for the hyperactive-impulsive type of ADHD, which are:

- Constant fidgeting and squirming
- Continuous movement or restlessness in inappropriate places
- Inability to remain seated or stay in one spot
- Excessive talking
- Cannot remain quiet during leisure activities
- Has problems waiting their turn
- Responds before a question is finished being asked
- Regular interruption into other's conversation

Diagnosing a person with this condition is not the last stop. First, the health professional has to determine how severe it is by using this criterion:

1. Mild: The individual shows minor impairment in functioning but has enough symptoms to reach the diagnosis criteria
2. Moderate: The impairment is more pronounced
3. Severe: More than the minimum number of symptoms for diagnosis are present, as well as major impairment from the symptoms

Why Is an Accurate Diagnosis Important?

Due to the myths surrounding this condition, some parents might not be open to getting an official diagnosis for their children. Some are not interested in pursuing the potential medication needed, and others are worried about the stigma attached to having this disorder. However, getting an ADHD diagnosis is advantageous, and parents must shun hearsay if they suspect their children have the condition. Receiving an accurate diagnosis for this disorder boosts your chances of getting help, even if you do not show interest in using the medication as a treatment method.

Besides the apparent reason that a diagnosis is the first step to getting treatment, there are subtler benefits. It benefits you and your child emotionally because now you can put a name to the symptoms which your child has been presenting. ADHD symptoms can cause shame, embarrassment, and guilt. Most parents blame themselves and worry about their child's underperformance. It is natural for you or the child to get frustrated over the long periods it takes them to finish their tasks. Having a diagnosis keeps those emotions in check and keeps you from throwing the blame around.

Moreover, having written evidence of an official diagnosis can help get accommodations for the child with ADHD at school or in the workplace. Diagnosis for this condition is followed by a treatment course that enables you to manage the symptoms better.

Professionals Who Diagnose ADHD

Professionals qualified to diagnose this disorder include psychiatrists, psychotherapists, psychologists, neurologists, and some physicians. However, do not book an appointment with a health care provider until you find out if they have experience diagnosing this disorder.

If you do not know where to start with the assessments, discuss this with your family doctor so they can refer you to a qualified health care provider to do the assessments. Sometimes, pediatricians and general practitioners diagnose this condition, and when they suspect your child has it, they might provide you with a reference to see a specialist for extensive assessments.

Attempting to diagnose ADHD online is not ideal. While some quizzes and questionnaires online can be great as a self-screening process, they cannot act as an official diagnosis. The quiz, however, might be the force that propels you to reach out to a qualified medical examiner for that official diagnosis.

What to Share With Your Doctor or Medical Examiner

When diagnosing this condition, provide the doctor copies of relevant medical, school, or employment records. In addition, remember that you must provide a comprehensive family and social history. Some examiners send out questionnaires that will be completed before the appointment, so you must ensure that you present them at the appointment. Although a parent's consent is often needed before it is done, children's teachers or daycare providers sometimes get a copy of the questionnaires.

The Assessment Process

The duration of an ADHD assessment is dependent on the health care provider, but on average, it lasts for three hours. The methods are specific to the practitioners, but an in-person interview is inevitable. The topics discussed during the consultation include family, health, development, and lifestyle history.

Depending on the initial findings, the clinician may ask to interview other people who are closely related to the subject. For example, the clinician might request to speak with a teacher, daycare provider, or coach for children.

The ADHD assessment can include questionnaires, intellectual screenings, rating scales, and sustained attention and distractibility measures. In addition, the medical examiner might want to find out the following about your child:

- How often do they quit a task before eventually completing it?
- How often do they misplace items?
- How often do they forget essential things or instructions?
- Do they have problems with sitting still?
- Do they struggle to relax?
- How often do they get distracted by things around them?

The evaluation for this condition requires a medical history. If a medical exam has not been done recently, the examiner might suggest one ensure the symptoms do not have medical causes. The examiner may also recommend psychological testing to support conclusions and give a more thorough assessment. In some cases, the examiner screen for learning disabilities.

Solution for this disorder, but getting an early diagnosis and treatment is a significant step to improving the lives of the children with this condition and making them have a better experience at school and in life.

4

TALKING TO YOUR CHILD
ABOUT ADHD

When your child is diagnosed with ADHD, it is easy to be confused and begin pondering their whole life from that moment. It is also natural for your mind to be worked up with multiple questions about how your child will cope with life's challenges. But every minute you ponder these questions you cannot answer is time wasted, time that would be better put to use in spending quality time with the child, convincing them that their life is not to be derailed by the diagnosis.

Being a parent is enough hard work in the first place, and dealing with this disorder does not make it any easier. But even when faced with this, the responsibility should not be a nightmare. There is enough information and systems to ensure that your child has a good life, but it is up to you to quit worrying and start talking.

At this stage of their life, it is essential to lay down a firm communication structure that allows you to speak to the child about the condition while assuring them of their ability to live a happy, quality life. This is not about lying to them; instead, it is about helping them feel comfortable in their skin, regardless of their condition. Your words and actions have to line up for the conversation.

Understandably, it will be hard to find the right words, and you may struggle with anxiety about discussing this subject with them. However, the child deserves to know why they have struggled emotionally, socially, and academically. They need to understand that it is not their fault they forget things quickly or have no recollection of certain things. You owe it to them to explain why it seems like their life is unmanageable and their affairs are all over the place.

You are the one shot they have at living life as close to normal as possible.

EXPLAINING ADHD TO YOUR CHILD

On average, children are typically diagnosed with ADHD around the seven-year mark. Explaining such a complex topic to a child of that age will be difficult, no doubt, but it is also a crucial step in the right direction for both parent and child.

For starters, you want to speak in a language they will understand. Your vocabulary may be too complex for their reading level, so be sure you are explaining in an age-appropriate way. Avoid the unnecessary details and go in for the age-relevant ones.

You should know that this conversation is not a one-time thing. You must keep updating your child as they mature until they fully grasp the condition. So, please do not rush in with all the details; take your time to deliver it. Not only does this help the child deal with what is happening around them, but it also stokes their curiosity to learn more about themselves.

Here are a few talking points to start with when having the ADHD talk:

- **People with this disorder can also be successful:** Just because they have ADHD does not make them impervious to success. Matter of factly, there are many positive role models making waves with this disorder and carving a niche for themselves. You could start with someone they know, like a family member, friend, or neighbor. Then you could point them to a celebrity, like Jim Carrey, Michael Jordan, Will Smith, Justin Timberlake, Emma Watson, and the list goes on.
- **Having ADHD does not make them flawed:** This disorder should not be seen as a flaw or weakness. It is not a sign that a child is weak or will never amount to anything. The list of celebrities with the condition above demonstrates that success is possible and that these people also lead everyday lives.

The condition makes them a little different from their peers, but it is not a distinguishing flaw. Like any other condition, people with ADHD can have positive experiences and outcomes if given the right support system. Assure them of your presence each step of the way.

- **It is not just them:** ADHD is not a super rare condition that makes your child a unicorn. Not one bit. Over one in every ten children in the United States lives with this disorder. Some sources suggest that the statistics could be 20 percent of the population or one out of every five people.

It can be isolating to think that you are different; hence, alone. But you want to prevent this in your child. Reach out to groups specializing in children with this condition, and help them make friends with other children like them.

An after-school program or summer camp for children with this condition is an excellent place to start. Look for one within your locale so you can still show up for them if they struggle to fit in. In addition, your child will feel less alone in such environments tailored to develop their social and emotional well-being.

- **Having ADHD does not make them dumb:** Granted, they may struggle academically. But this does not mean they are not as bright as their siblings or peers. If the conditions were right, many ADHD children are pretty smart. For example, Thomas Edison and Albert Einstein were two geniuses who contributed to advancing technology and society. Both men had ADHD all their lives but were still regarded as geniuses of their time.

TIPS FOR STARTING THE CONVERSATION

Here are a few tips for a healthy and impactful conversation about ADHD with your child:

- **They may not be interested:** You would expect that, since it is about them, your child would be interested, right? No. They may stare at you blankly or just indulge themselves without paying you any heed. This is especially the case for younger children.

Rather than giving up and leaving them to figure it out on their own, you need to keep trying until they pay attention and are willing to have the conservation.

- **Pick your time well:** Timing is crucial when trying to have a conversation about ADHD. You want to aim for periods when they are less likely to interrupt you. Avoid times when they are interested in other things, like playtime, dinnertime, or bedtime.

Even after finding the right time to impart them, give some time before starting the next conversation. You want them to digest what you spoke about and come up with questions or show understanding in their actions.

- **Avoid dwelling on negatives:** It is easy to get caught up and only focus on the negatives of this condition, but that will not help your child. Instead, play to their strengths and capabilities. Whether it is their involvement in arts, sports, and science, be willing to give your support and show interest in helping them accomplish more.

- **Open communication is vital:** One conversation is not enough to inform your child about the complexities of ADHD, so do not limit it to one moment. Keep a continuous, open dialogue involving other life areas such as extracurricular activities, friends, school, and homework.

- **Learn more:** If you do not know about ADHD before the diagnosis, you should do your research and learn more about it. Speak to your doctor and get in touch with support and advocacy bodies. Doing so helps you to get in touch with other parents with children like yours, allowing you to learn from them and exchange ideas. It could also be an excellent way to monitor your child's progress through how he interacts with other children.

- **ADHD is not an excuse:** This condition can be made into an excuse for anything, which will only make your child put off things rather than be accountable and deal with them. You want to teach your children that the condition is not a leeway for destructive behaviors or refusing to put in the work.

TALKING ABOUT THE BRIGHT SIDE

ADHD has various symptoms that interfere with or even disrupt different areas of your child's life. Nonetheless, not all of these symptoms have adverse effects and can be helpful in positive outcomes. This shows that you are getting a mixed bag with the condition.

ADHD has three subtypes, which provoke different symptoms in a child. Some children may only experience impulsive and hyperactive symptoms, others may have inattentive symptoms, and some may have a combination of all three.

Most of the time, we tend to focus on the problems these symptoms cause, and we forget about the unique skills and qualities that trigger in the child. Studies on the subject of this condition show that there are some positives to the condition (Sherrell, 2021). However, these studies were derived from the experiences of people with this condition and not actual scientific studies. Some people involved in the study reported favorable outcomes since their diagnosis.

The Child Neuropsychology journal published a small study in 2006, which identified that sample groups made up of people with this condition were more creative when carrying out specific tasks than other groups without this condition. The task was simple: The researchers asked each participant to draw animals that could be found on another planet that was not Earth. The idea was to create a new toy.

In 2017, another study attempted to examine adults with ADHD and analyze their creativity. The participants were asked to devise new ways of using towels, books, belts, and tin cans.

After the study, both people with and without this condition came up with many ideas. However, the most stunning result was that the people on ADHD medications and those without the disorder showed no differences in creativity.

But it gets interesting.

When the participants were informed that a bonus was at stake for whoever devised the most ideas, people with this condition came out on top. This outcome is not unfounded, as other prior studies also show that competition and rewards hugely influence people with ADHD.

These findings are helpful for several reasons. Most importantly, they enforce the narrative that people with this condition are just as innovative and creative as others without the condition, if not better.

That said, here are some benefits of this condition, as garnered from research over the years:

BENEFITS OF ADHD

- **Increased self-awareness:** People with ADHD often have to monitor their behavior for changes, and most develop a heightened sense of self-awareness. Monitoring their behavior is a crucial part of their day as they manage their disruptiveness.

The negative part of this hyper-self-awareness is that having to do it regularly may reduce their ego and tire them out mentally. However, on the flip side, to prevent this fatigue, they develop a coping mechanism to check and balance themselves effectively.

For people with ADHD, a higher sense of self-awareness helps them understand their needs and feelings while also seeking better ways to properly manage their reactions and behaviors at any given time.

- **Spontaneity:** Impulsivity is one of the critical factors in ADHD. Although it can be a negative behavior that pushes people with the condition to be impatient, cut off others, and act rashly, it is not always a bad thing. People with this condition get progressively better at managing their impulsivity, focusing it instead on new areas and experiences requiring spontaneity.

For these people, finding the balance between boredom and hyperarousal is imperative. So, not only does spontaneity help to spice things up, but it also provides them with enjoyable experiences that take their minds off other distractions.

- **Hyperfocus:** Hyperfocus is another experience for people with this condition. It revolves around channeling all their focus into a subject or task. This behavior can go either way. For one, if they are overly focused on one thing at a time, other areas of their lives may suffer. On the other hand, having hyperfocus ensures that they stay on task, concentrate better, and are more capable of learning better.

Think of this behavior as a "state of flow." Mihály Csíkszentmihályi, a psychologist, defined it as a time of immense focus, absorption, and attention to a task, producing an intense enjoyment.

- **Resilience:** It can be challenging to manage children, more so one with this disorder. So, you must be prepared for the day to face challenges that affect how much they can focus at school or on tasks, manage time and procrastination, take their medication, and manage symptoms that influence their socialization.

Even though it can weigh heavily on you, remember that the challenges are first-hand for your child. But again, that does not make them weak; children with this disorder show remarkable resilience and strength. Resilience has the mental aptitude for dealing with hardship and stress without relying on coping mechanisms, especially negative ones.

A study highlighted that teachers and parents found many children with this disorder to have high resilience in the face of setbacks (Dvorsky, 2016). This makes them more likely to stay on task and achieve their aims, despite difficulties.

- **High energy levels:** Children with this condition are often perceived as rambunctious, especially ones with diagnosed hyperactivity. These high energy levels often manifest as excessive talking, restlessness, and fidgeting. However, being energetic is not altogether problematic because it can be profitable if used right.

High energy levels are only a problem when unfocused. Otherwise, it is an excellent source of motivation for managing how children with ADHD pursue their goals and stay productive.

Another essential benefit is that children with this condition are better suited for multiple activities (like sports and physical activities) than their peers. They also feel younger, which gives them a positive outlook on life and general well-being.

- **Creativity:** Although children with ADHD may suffer from inattentiveness and distraction, they are not simpletons. As we found from the studies above, they are widely creative, and that is due to their divergent thought processes. Rather than sticking to conventional methods and fixed patterns of problem-solving, they prefer to devise innovative solutions and ideas.

A different study discovered that people with ADHD see themselves as naturally curious, which they consider an upside of the condition (Cherry, 2021). And since curiosity is a crucial part of creativity, curious people are more open and desiring to learn. This way, they can explore newer paths and unique ideas for solving problems.

PUTTING THESE BENEFITS TO GOOD USE

It is not enough to know the benefits. You also want to help your child see these strengths and understand how to use them in the right situations. For example, when they feel very energetic, they can channel their time and effort into a productive venture, like arts and crafts, writing, and exercising. This way, they can flex their minds and bodies while using excess energy. Alternatively, they could try to achieve their goals at school or around the house.

On the other hand, when your child is experiencing hyperfocus, that is the best time to work on a new skill, like learning to code or playing an instrument. Or, you could indulge them in a project, like building a treehouse or redesigning a room around the house; anything to help them channel that focus and find great solutions. It is best to gear them towards activities that promote their creativity, such as talking to a friend, listening to music, or making arts and crafts.

In conclusion, when your child is diagnosed with this condition, it is not the end of their life or normalcy as they know it. Furthermore, the condition does not hamper their chances of success or subsequent growth. On the contrary, if properly managed, ADHD can help your child become one of the best, most successful people on the planet. We have seen this countlessly in the people we celebrate and look up to, from entrepreneurs to media personalities to athletes.

What is more, with advancements in science and the creation of new technologies, ADHD is not as unknown as it used to be. The condition is more manageable now, and there are many resources to improve your understanding of the subject. You can also choose from a range of treatment options for your child. We will get into more details on this in subsequent chapters. This condition is no longer a stumbling block to having a decent and prosperous life.

5

SELF-CARE WHILE DEALING WITH ADHD CHILDREN

As a parent, helping your child overcome challenges is a requirement for the role and an inherent inclination due to your ties with them. This parenting role does not change because a child is diagnosed with ADHD. However, it is crucial now, more than ever, to ensure they have an everyday life. Therefore, many parents are willing to go the extra mile to provide a haven for growth and understanding for their children.

However, while these sacrifices are all well and good, it is easy to forget another person in the picture—*you*. Yes. Even though your child has the condition and not you, it is still imperative that you take good care of yourself. Otherwise, you will not be able to show up for your child as much as they need. And in your zeal, you would have failed them. To take care of your child, you must first be in a great mental and physical position.

To do this, you must set a structure that allows you to catch your breath now and then. Just a moment to reflect and take care of yourself so that you do not let yourself go is critical. You also deserve a happy and fulfilling life, which could double as a great source of motivation for your child.

EFFECTIVE SELF-CARE TIPS FOR PARENTS OF ADHD CHILDREN

When dealing with children with ADHD, life gets cranked up a notch higher. As a result, your well-being can be jeopardized, and you will struggle to maintain both sanity and physical health.

As a result, self-care is key to staying healthy and having your affairs in order before rendering help to your child. This section will go through some effective strategies for safeguarding or restoring your spiritual, physical, and mental health while maintaining healthy living.

Take a Walk

Working out is a great way to keep your mind and body active and fit. However, you will not always have the time to go to the gym or try an intensive workout routine between catering to your child and your other responsibilities. Thankfully, you can still take a walk. A brisk walk or long stroll can help you clear your head and get some air.

It does not matter what you are doing as you walk; you could use the time to get groceries or take your pets for a walk. The goal is to get some energy from being in a neutral setting.

Meditate

A five-minute meditation routine is enough to help calm your body and mind and revitalize your spirits. If you have not tried meditation, you can start with some guided meditation websites or apps. Depending on your device and what you are into, there are several options.

Try breathing exercises to help you manage stress levels as you exercise. This way, you can improve your relaxation without taking too much time by having to nap. Even though taking a few deep breaths does not seem like much, they effectively calm the body and mind.

You can rope your child into some of these activities if you can manage it. For example, meditation can help tone down their high energy levels and improve focus.

Splurge on Yourself

As a parent, it is easy to get caught up with your child and forget that you must be treated right. Do not neglect yourself. The money you make should also go into making you feel good. So, take the time out to splurge a little on yourself.

Get that jacket you have always thought about getting. Change or freshen up your hairdo. Take yourself out to eat. The idea is to do something for yourself, however small. Do not take the liberty to spend more than you should. To ensure you do not exceed any limits, consider adjusting your budget to allow room for saving towards this activity. You deserve to be treated right, so make an effort to do so.

Get Your Laughter On!

Despite how wholesome it can be, laughter is an underrated part of our society. Your child is going through a lot, and you may be dealing with it regularly, but do not let that rob you of your joy. Laughter helps to improve your immune system and lower stress levels.

So, whip out your phone or laptop and look up some cute and funny videos or memes. Alternatively, watch a comedy show. Just do whatever gets the laugh out of you.

Play Some Music

Music is another part of our culture that plays a role in how we interact with one another or feel. It is a relieving medium of expression for both the singer and listener. In itself, music can be therapeutic.

Create time to listen to music or search for new songs that align with your tastes. Not only is this a great relaxation activity, but it also helps you understand more about yourself.

What's more, music can be enjoyed privately or shared with others. It could be a bonding medium with your child, like when you both have the same favorite song. So kick off your shoes, snuggle into the couch, turn up your music, clear some space, and create a dance floor.

Get a Hug

Hugs are therapeutic and can help to relieve stress and tension. But, of course, not everyone is a hugger. However, we cannot deny that hugs feel good, especially when they are genuine, given, and from people we care about, who also care about us.

So, look around you; walk up to your partner, friend, parent, or child, and give them a good old bear hug. They might not get it at first, but they will hug you all the same.

Practice Mindfulness

To be mindful is to be aware of everything going on around you. Unfortunately, between caring for your child and other life responsibilities, everything outside the fire of your mind can easily blur out. This is not great, as it might relegate other essential things to the background. As a result, practicing mindfulness can help you better delegate your attention to your affairs. Also, it allows you to enjoy the moment better instead of questioning what could have been or the future. This way, you can enjoy what is in front of you and give your child a good life.

Make a Smoothie

Smoothies are great and provide the body with tons of nourishment and fuel, thanks to their protein, greens, and fruit content. Having one can be an excellent way to wind down and get back on track before returning to other activities or caring for your child. It is also a healthier alternative to beverages like coffee or soda.

Get Some Alone Time

For some parents, the only time they are alone is when they use the restroom. This can be a sobering reality, and you do not want that to be your case. Hence, it is recommended that you take some time out to enjoy your own company.

Depending on your spare time, it could be as little as five to ten minutes or as long as several hours. Try not to do anything that does not make you feel relaxed at this point. Now would be a good time to try that smoothie, do some breathing exercises, and practice mindfulness and meditation. The goal is to recharge before delving into work again.

Play Games

Games are great for unwinding, whether mobile games, video games, or board games. Immerse yourself in a game to get your creative juices flowing and enjoy a bit of your competitive edge.

There are many ways to enjoy a game, from playing virtually, by yourself, or playing against family and friends.

Take the Time to Enjoy Nature

Studies identify that spending time in the natural environment improves our psychological health. As little as a hike on a trail, a walk around the park, or just gardening around your yard can make you feel relaxed and rested.

A study was conducted on patients admitted to hospitals with rooms that overlooked green spaces. These patients got better significantly faster than others not placed next to windows with such views. Not only that, but they also reported feeling less anxiety and pain (Ulrich, 1984). This shows that exposure to natural landscapes can offer relief on both mental and physical levels.

Alternatively, you can bring nature into your home with some indoor plants. These plants can be challenging to look after, so be sure about the commitment. Also, if you live along the coast, it could help you visit the beach and splash around.

Savor Something

There is so much to do, and time seems to fly quickly. This rush could likely make you savor things less, so take some time out of your days to savor something. Make it a habit, from little things like having your first cup of Joe for the day to having breakfast with your family. Learn to live in those moments and enjoy them to the fullest.

Keep a Gratitude Journal

Focusing on everything going wrong with you or your child's condition can sometimes make it challenging to be thankful. However, gratitude is not without pay. Studies reveal that people with gratitude journals enjoy better and longer sleep. As a parent, sleep is a precious resource you want to enjoy.

The upside of keeping a gratitude journal is that you do not have to make an entry every day or at defined times; it can be as short as a line of words on any day of the week. In addition, it does not cost a thing and can help you refocus on your prerogatives.

You can make an entry just before bedtime, listing some things you are thankful for. It could be the simplest things or the most sophisticated situations, whatever you want. The general idea is to remind yourself that life is beautiful and there are things to feel good about and be thankful for. This could even be added to your child's bedtime routine to get them to say what they are grateful for.

Make a Retreat in Your Bedroom

Clutter in your bedroom can make you less relaxed and more on edge. So it is understandable if you sometimes feel lazy about putting the clothes away after laundry or cleaning and storing shoes properly.

However, caring for yourself also means preparing your living space to facilitate relaxation. As such, your bedroom is an excellent place to start. Turn it into a retreat that makes you want to come back every time. Throw on those comfy sheets and do a bit of decorating. Place that cozy chair near the window, pry apart the curtains, and settle in with a good book and a glass of wine.

With the room decluttered and aired out, you will find yourself nodding off in no time.

Hold the Electronics

These days, our lives are more digitized than at any other time in history. You could do many things with your gadgets, including surfing the web, browsing social media, or binging shows or streams. While these activities can sometimes be relaxing, they can also lead to more stress and anxiety. This is because digital devices curate pressure, which compels you to do specific tasks, like replying to messages before bedtime or reading those "per the last emails" from work.

While these are not the most arduous tasks, they are mentally tasking. Moreover, they could culminate in a more significant problem over time. So, as a rule of thumb, try a digital detox, in which you steer off of electronics for a bit from time to time. Doing this can help with addiction and be a model for guiding electronic inclinations in your child. Studies show that people who sleep away from their phones get better rest and are generally happier to cement the upsides of the digital detoxification.

Join or Start a Book Club

Book clubs serve myriads of purposes. They can be an excellent medium for meeting other people and starting a social support structure. On the other hand, it could also be the driving force you need to take time to read. Another benefit is that it helps to get you excited for something every other week.

You can start a book club with friends or visit your local library to join one in your locale. There are also online book clubs that you can join, although they are not always great replacements for physical book club meetings. In addition, online book clubs often miss out on traditional book clubs' intimacy and personal touch, making you less motivated to join or keep up.

Create and Achieve a To-Do List

When we talk about caring for ourselves, doing chores does not seem like a relaxing activity. Running errands and cleaning does not seem high up the list of recreational activities, and we understand why. However, checking off items on your to-do list has a lot of relief and is unburdening.

It does not matter what the task is, whether it is decluttering your room, cleaning your bathroom, or booking an appointment for your child. The idea is that making and ticking off your to-do list gives you a sense of accomplishment and something to be thankful for. Moreover, you can go about your to-do list daily, weekly, or monthly. In doing so, you will find a sense of calm in finishing your tasks, rather than procrastinating and leaving them to pile up.

Indulge Your Senses

Life happens whether you are too busy or lazy to bother with it. So, you might as well engage your senses and find inner peace to last you.

Take a long bath, play soothing sounds, light some scented candles, and drink herbal tea. Anything to engage your different senses and bring you to the point of zen, away from the hustle and bustle of day-to-day life, will allow you to relax and decompress.

Spend Time With Family and Friends

Focusing all your time and effort on your ADHD child could rob you of precious moments with other family members and friends. Finding the balance between self-care, caring for your child, and hanging out with family and friends can be challenging. But you owe it to yourself and them to try.

Including me time in your schedule is essential. This way, you can plan toward it without compromising other essential things. This is a great self-care tip for balancing your affiliations and avoiding the stress of strained relationships.

PARENTING TIPS FOR SINGLE PARENTS ON RAISING ADHD CHILDREN

- **Do your homework:** ADHD can be a genetic matter sometimes. If your child has the condition, there is a 30 to 40 percent chance that either you or your partner has ADHD. If left untreated, the condition can make effective parenting difficult, if not impossible, especially in the case of single-parent households. The symptoms of untreated ADHD make it hard for the child to be organized, keep to a schedule, and maintain consistency. If you are concerned about your ADHD status, consider talking to your primary health care provider for diagnosis and advice.

- **Schedule family meetings regularly:** Plan for weekly family meetings with your children. The assembly aims to discuss a specific topic. Encourage your family members to make conscious decisions to contribute to the creation of the agenda, and put rules in place to ensure everyone gets some time to air their views. You want the meeting to be solution-centric and productive, and it is best when everyone is a part of the process.

- **Highlight everyday stressors:** We all have unique stressors that impact our quality of life. You must avoid or limit your stressor to make the most of your time. For instance, a stressor may involve taking on other people's tasks because you cannot say "no." While you cannot control how they will respond to being denied, you must also look out for yourself to avoid burnout and overwhelm.

Granted, there will be stressors that you cannot just nope out of. However, in such cases, it helps to refocus on the positives and identify helpful coping mechanisms to deal with the stress. For example, start with some deep breaths, and delay your response to avoid impulsive reactions. You can also try meditative and relaxing routines or exercises that reduce stress levels.

- **Talk about chores:** As a single parent, it is easy to be caught up in household chores every other day without delegating. But it does not have to be so. Involving your children in chores can be a positive experience for bonding and skill acquisition. Not only do they get practical life skills, but they also develop good work ethics and a sense of responsibility.

On the other hand, delegating chores will open up more time for you to focus on other things. Also, over time, your child will get used to the routine and not require oversight anymore.

- **Get the proper support:** It takes a lot of effort to raise a child, so you may want to get a solid support structure around you. Identify key family members, support groups, friends, and babysitters who will help you nurture your child properly.
- **Create some one-on-one time:** Finding the time to squeeze another appointment or task into your already crammed schedule may threaten to send everything

flying. However, it cannot be helped that your child requires some one-on-one time with you to reconnect and develop your relationship. This time spent together is especially crucial for children with ADHD, who could sometimes experience negative spells in which they feel unwanted or low on confidence. You could build up their self-esteem with one-on-one time and teach them to feel better about themselves.

- **Create to-do lists:** Every day is an excellent day to make and follow a to-do list. However, in making plans for the day, learn to be reasonable in your expectations. Do not expect to summit Everest and make it in time for dinner on the same day. Leave enough room for unforeseen contingencies.
- **Create routines and set clear rules:** Create house routines and follow them religiously. Not only will this make your days more predictable and easy to follow, but it will also help your child follow instructions better. This benefit is especially helpful for children with ADHD, as they perform better in situations with consistent and straightforward rules.

When devising rules and routines for your household, it is best to partner with your child. First, discuss possible repercussions for certain behaviors if your child's other parent is still in the picture. Then, partner with them to create a consistent environment geared towards the convenience of both parties and the child. This way, everyone knows visiting times and can plan their schedules around it, making room for contingency.

Otherwise, if the other parent is not involved, you may want to bring your child's doctor into the picture. Plan around hospital visits, checkups, and other health plans.

HANDLING MARITAL LIFE

Raising a child with ADHD can make you feel disconnected from many things, including your marriage, which can strain your relationship with your significant other. Hence, it is crucial to take some time out to focus on your marriage. Remember that raising a child is the job of both parents, so you do not want to commit too much and go in alone. This will save you unnecessary marital problems.

Also, as much as your friends will understand not reaching out consistently, you should try to reciprocate the gesture by sending out a message often. It does not have to be anything special or nifty; just checking up on them and listening to the goings-on in their lives can keep the friendship going for longer. Your child's condition is not enough reason to abandon all forms of normalcy in your life. If your child is to believe that their life is still on track, you cannot afford to let yours get derailed.

That said, here are some practical tips to help you maintain your marriage when dealing with children with ADHD:

- **Take turns:** As a couple, taking care of your ADHD child can be easier if you go in turns. This way, everyone gets a break at some point from the child and one another. Understanding how this sounds, you could mistake it for troubling signs, but it is not. Too much of everything is bad, even the company of someone you truly care about. You are taking the time to refresh both mind and body, providing you with much-needed balance, which can be hard to come by in a family setting.

- **Do not fly solo:** Just as you both have to take turns with your child, you also have to split parenting responsibilities. Doing so makes things easier on both parents and reduces the risk of resentments and conflicts, which could sour relationships.
- **Adaptability is key:** Your child's ADHD status will not change in a heartbeat, so it would help you learn to cope. Find ways around the suitable condition for the child, your partner, and you.
- **Streamlined intents:** It is challenging to raise a child with ADHD, and you do not want to add marital problems to the list. Working together instead of trying to one-up each other provides the best chance of helping the child have a better life. So, try to avoid blaming each other for shortcomings. In the end, you are both ordinary people just trying to do right by your child, however tasking it seems. The odds of success are way better when there is coordination and unity of efforts.
- **Set clear house rules:** Plan and agree on house rules with your significant other. Being on the same page creates a better avenue for raising your children, including ones with and without ADHD. Clear-cut rules also help to prevent a clash of interests, as everyone knows, understands, and accepts the rules of engagement.
- **Go on a vacation or take an extended break:** Fit in some couple time into your schedule. You and your significant

other must grow your relationship away from the children.

In conclusion, raising children with ADHD is tasking and affects your physical and mental health. From their impulsiveness to their reluctance to obey, it can make it frustrating to perform your responsibilities, and you may sometimes be seething in anger. Other times, you may feel guilty for going hard on them, especially as the condition has a hand in their behavior. It is for this reason that you ought to practice self-care. The pressure gets intense sometimes, and you need an outlet to de-stress and refocus your priorities. However, to be there for your child, you first have to be responsible for yourself.

Furthermore, in your quest for self-care, do not forget to practice your virtues. For example, love and compassion are crucial when dealing with children with ADHD. Because when all else fails, these virtues will help you through.

A WELCOME BREAK

"Be kind to others, so that you may learn the secret art of being kind to yourself."

— PARAMAHANSA YOGANANDA

Let's take a break.

It feels good, doesn't it? Just a moment to take a breath without taking in any new information or having to handle a situation with the kids.

You probably don't get many of these moments... Not many parents of children with ADHD do. So it's important that you *do* give yourself a break – both in terms of how much you expect of yourself, and in the practical sense. Those self-care tips in Chapter 5 are important... don't be tempted to skip them because they don't seem to directly relate to your child.

Take a moment, too, to acknowledge the extra work you're putting in to help your child and your own journey as a parent. You don't have a lot of time, but you're here now, with this book. Don't be hard on yourself if you can't read the whole thing. Your life is full, and you're doing everything you can.

Nonetheless, if you'd like to make this break last a moment longer, you have a glorious opportunity to help out other parents of children with ADHD.

By leaving a review of this book on Amazon, you'll help other parents who are looking for this guidance to find it quickly and easily.

No matter how much you've read, sharing how it has helped you and what information you've found here will signpost to other new readers with limited time and energy where they can find the help they're looking for.

You're doing an amazing job. Thank you for helping me to make sure other parents know they are too.

6

PARENTING STRATEGIES FOR HELPING YOUR ADHD CHILD - AT HOME

At this point, it is pretty clear that raising children with ADHD is a different ballgame from raising children without the condition. The challenges are more severe and require carefully crafted strategies for navigating the child's day-to-day life and how they turn out. However, even at that, knowing what to do is the easiest part.

For starters, you must understand that there are biological differences between the brains of a child with and without ADHD. Of course, your ADHD child can comprehend discipline and learn to organize themselves and their affairs, but that does not make them any less susceptible to impulsive behaviors. On the contrary, the condition makes them likely to do things on a whim or without care or focus. Furthermore, if you think that will not bother you, you lie.

As discussed in the previous chapter, self-care comes first in raising a child with ADHD. It helps you be there for them at all times. However, that is not the end of it. You also need to know the dos and don'ts of parenting ADHD children so that you do not complicate things for them or yourself.

PRO-PARENTING TIPS FOR RAISING ADHD CHILDREN

As the parent of a child with ADHD, one word you repeatedly hear is structure. But why? What has structure got to do with a cognitive condition? Simple: Structure provides a predictable and organized environment—two critical factors in raising a child with ADHD. Creating an organized environment involves planning a schedule and daily routines for your child. However, on the other hand, a predictable environment has expectations, rules, and repercussions that are known and understood by the child through positive reinforcement.

Think of a structured environment like scaffolding. Every limit, reminder, and routine you set up contributes to the upward growth of the building, which, in this case, is the child with ADHD. Scaffolding may not be the prettiest sight, but its importance to the solidity of the structure cannot be understated.

A structured environment is ideal for children with ADHD because they know what to expect at any one time. It is this understanding that provides them with a sense of security. The result of such an environment is evident in children with and without ADHD because they grow up with better self-awareness and knowledge of how the world works.

However, this does not mean that children are incapable of self-structuring; far from it. Many children devise their structure for tasks, chores, and schedules and exhibit good behaviors without being prompted. Things are different for children with ADHD, though. Self-structuring is more challenging due to the disorders of the condition. They struggle to regulate their emotions and responses and have poor organizational skills. For them, maintaining focus and avoiding impulsive behaviors is a chore, especially with the many distractions begging for their attention.

ADHD symptoms are primarily connected to their problems with self-control. Therefore, children with ADHD require better external structures or control systems to manage their symptoms, stay grounded at all times, and serve as a stepping stone for other helpful strategies.

That said, here are some tips for creating an effective and lasting structure:

- **Manage their sleep cycle:** Children with ADHD have a problematic bedtime routine, no thanks to their condition. The inability to fall asleep quickly worsens other symptoms of the condition, like recklessness, hyperactivity, and inattention. As such, it is vital to help your child navigate sleep. You must remove potential inhibitors, such as caffeine, sugar, and screen time to do that. Create a bedtime ritual that calms their senses and helps them relax.
- **Decide on acceptable and unacceptable behaviors:** A structured environment aims to help your child understand the consequences of their actions and manage their inclinations to act impulsively. Creating one requires strength, affection, empathy, energy, and

patience. Start by deciding on behaviors that may or may not be tolerated. Ensure the child is aware of these behaviors, and do your best to enforce them.

Punishing ADHD children is complicated as many do not mind having things taken away from them. When your child breaks the rules, talk to them first and ask questions such as, what rule is it that you broke? Why did you break this rule? What can you do next time to avoid breaking this rule? This is not to say that you should care for your child with an iron fist. Instead, it is to ensure consistency and safeguard the child's improvement.

Certain behaviors should not be excused, like refusing to turn off the TV, staying off screens before bedtime, or being reluctant to get up in the morning. Of course, it would take some getting used to for the child to internalize all the rules, but they will over time. To further aid this process, make the rules as clear and straight-forward as can be, with rewards to foster good behavior.

- **Have faith in your child:** Create a list of everything you find unique, positive, and valuable in your child. Have faith in them that regardless of their condition, they are capable of changing, succeeding, learning, and maturing. Moreover, as you wake up and prepare them for the future daily, reaffirm this belief and help them believe it, too.
- **Tone down distractions:** Children with ADHD are often subject to distractions around them, such as video games, computers, or television. These gadgets encourage them to be impulsive and must be regulated. Start with some

decreased screen time while subsequently increasing their time on other engaging activities with family and friends or outside of the home. The goal is to help them use pent-up energy.

- **Deal with aggression:** Children with ADHD often experience aggressive outbursts, which can be challenging for parents. Instead of clapping back at them, consider other healthier alternatives, like a time-out to help calm both parties. Acting out is not limited to home life alone and could sometimes happen in public. In such a case, removing them calmly and quickly is imperative. Explain what time-out means, and teach them to ruminate on their actions.

Only consider time-outs for negative behaviors, as mild disruptions may be a means of releasing built-up energy. Also, when they behave destructively, intentionally, or abusively, it goes against the rules and demands to be addressed.

- **Encourage them to voice their thoughts:** Self-control is a problem for many children with ADHD and makes them prone to impulsive actions and utterances long before considering the aftereffects. As a result, asking your child to voice their thoughts when they feel the urge to act disruptively could help. Doing so will better comprehend their thought processes and help them work out positive coping mechanisms.
- **Make your child's life organized and simple:** Design a little quiet area where they can indulge themselves, do homework, or take a break when things become

overwhelming for them. Think of it as their special place. Also, keep the house clean and organized, so the child knows the location of whatever they need. Doing so can also help lessen physical distractions around the house.

- **Make the rules clear, but do not be too rigid:** One way to help your child adapt to rules is by regularly discouraging negative behaviors and rewarding good ones. In doing so, do not forget that children with ADHD do not have the same adaptability as other children. So, be flexible enough to allow room for mistakes and learning on the go.

If they exhibit odd behaviors that do not impact them negatively, accept them as some of the influences of their condition. However, on the other hand, discouraging quirky behaviors you do not understand because they do not seem "normal" to you is pretty harmful.

- **Encourage physical activities:** Engaging in physical activities is suitable for using excess energy. It also allows the child to channel their focus into well-defined movements that could bring about low impulsive reactions. Exercising also boosts concentration, improves brain function and memory, and lowers the risk of anxiety and depression. There are many professional athletes with ADHD, but the condition does not get in their way. Experts suggest that children with ADHD learn to focus their energy, attention, and passion by exercising.

- **Get personalized counseling:** It is impossible to be everything your child with ADHD needs. Sure, you can provide for and nurture them, but you cannot also offer the professional help they require from time to time. It is time to get a therapist for your child who will give them a new outlet to let off steam. It can be challenging dealing with the fact that you cannot come through in every way for your child, but seeking assistance is not a weakness.

A therapist will also come in handy for lowering your anxiety and stress levels by providing you with professional insights. You can also join local support groups for parents of ADHD children.

- **Split tasks into smaller bits:** Map out a plan for the activities delegated to your child. Use a large calendar and color coding to highlight chores and when they are due. Doing so gives your child the predictability of knowing what to do next. It also helps bridge their focus and channel it into their day-to-day routines.

WHAT PARENTS SHOULD NOT DO

- **Please do not give in to the child or the condition:** As a parent, allowing your child to get away with everything because they have ADHD can start a slippery slope. You need to set rules for acceptable behavior and enforce them. This is not to say that all nurture, care, and patience go out the window. Not at all. Instead, it is simply that you should not set the bar so low that your child becomes a nuisance.

- **Avoid overwhelm:** Keep in mind that ADHD influences how your child behaves. So, even though the condition is not visible, it is still a disability that affects them and their choices. When things get heated, it is time to take a deep breath and remember that your child is not deliberately trying to push all your buttons.

- **Relax on the little details:** Do not be too rigid with your child. Allow room for some flexibility or "bending" of the rules. For instance, if they had done three of the five chores, do not come down hard on them to finish the remaining two in record time. Remember, they are learning to live within a structured environment, and every step in the right direction is progress. Remember to praise them for what they did accomplish. You can certainly talk to them about the remaining two chores and ask for a plan for when they will be done. Everyone needs skills in life, so treating your child with respect and having an open line of communication is a great building block for them.

- **Avoid negativity:** As simple as it sounds; you may sometimes feel tempted to rush through things. Avoid such inclinations. Take things one at a time to avoid losing sight of what matters: Your child's healthy development. Anything embarrassing or stressful that they did today will not matter tomorrow.

TEACHING HYGIENE TO YOUR ADHD CHILD

Just because a task does not seem like a big deal for you does not mean your child is living the same experience, especially when they have ADHD. Getting children with the condition to do basic hygienic tasks like helping with the dishes, taking out the trash, or tidying up their rooms can be challenging. You may be torn between deciding to let them off easy without chores or wondering why they do not bother to help at all. Neither option is good. Understand that your child is looking for guidance, and it may be that they just need your help to stay focused. So while you may not be doing the chore, you are there to guide or help keep them on track. For example, leaving a child to clean their room will likely make it messier. What if you were in the room, hanging out on the bed, talking to them, and guiding them on how to clean their room appropriately? Or understand that asking for an entire room to be cleaned in one set without breaks or even broken up in multiple days is not the best of ideas. Remember, ADHD children do not have a long attention span for things that do not interest them.

Not letting them participate in chores disrupts the structure you are trying to build around them. On the other hand, their refusal to help is not necessarily born out of disregard, so remember that. You need to adjust how you approach the subject of chores. For starters, always be direct and specific with whatever tasks you want them to do, and state any incentives that might bolster their cooperation.

Another thing you want to incorporate is listing. Lists help children with ADHD track their activities and give them the predictability of knowing what to do next. So, instead of just stating what you want them to do, make a to-do list and paste it on a wall. Now, they do not have to deal with trying to remember the chores. Furthermore, you can break down each task into smaller components. For example, instead of just writing, "tidy your room," try "fold the laundry into the drawers," "bring dirty clothes to the laundry room," or "make your bed." The details here make it much easier to work with.

A chore chart is another technique that can help familiarize your ADHD child with household activities. Unlike the to-do list, a chore chart involves chores, a breakdown of each one, the time of completion, and what they can expect to get. Think of it as a mini treasure map with tasks to access the gold. For smaller children, stickers or points further drive home the idea of chores and makes them even more interested. A behavioral contract may be more beneficial for older children (including teenagers) than a chore chart. The difference is that they are involved in the creation process. Call a meeting to review acceptable and unacceptable behaviors and rewards and punishments. Agree, and sign it.

Stickers, points, and rewards are all incentives to guide your child down the right path. For example, with a point system, the child accumulates them from performing assigned chores. In turn, they are rewarded with outings, privileges, or activities agreed upon prior. Also, decide on how much they can use these points. For children under seven, two to three times a week is excellent.

For children between seven and ten, once a week works fine. The goal of the reward system is to provide a positive incentive for the child's behavior. It is better to reward well-done jobs than punish incomplete ones. For every task completed, tick the chart or place a star on it to remind your child of what they stand to gain for good behavior.

Lastly, do not hover around eager to help when setting up tasks for your children. Sometimes, let them figure things out on their own. Of course, be within reaching distance for when they need your help and ensure they do not get distracted and steered away from the task at hand. However, do not interfere too much and make them dependent on your presence. One way to help them grow independent is to take a picture before and after doing a task, like cleaning up their room. It could also help them become more confident in their abilities.

In conclusion, making plans for regulating how your child behaves is an essential step in creating a support system that facilitates growth and organization. It will not be easy because children with ADHD often prove challenging to manage. However, you should be okay with the proper behavioral techniques and structure.

7

PARENTING STRATEGIES FOR HELPING YOUR ADHD CHILD - AT SCHOOL

ADHD plagues focus and attention, making children more susceptible to impulsive and destructive behaviors. In turn, these behaviors lead them into trouble, which is why many children with ADHD struggle to have good relationships with their peers. Unfortunately, their conditions also make them prime targets for classroom nuisance, even when they are relatively quiet and innocent.

But all is not lost. Here are some strategies for aiding your child to improve at school and rise to the occasion when called upon.

EXECUTIVE FUNCTION

An executive function is a series of cognitive skills needed for discipline and self-control. It is also a cognitive process responsible for managing tasks and thoughts, decision-making, prioritizing activities, and effective time management. Executive function skills aid in establishing strategies and skills for handling projects. It also determines how we act to move forward with each task. People without executive function struggle with organizing, analyzing, scheduling, planning, completing tasks—or working with deadlines. They quickly lose track of time, misplace things, suffer overwhelm from tasking projects, and prioritize the wrong things.

There is confusion surrounding this subject and how it concerns people with ADHD. For example, an ADHD be classified as an executive function disorder? Or are all executive function disorders ADHD? The answers to these questions depend on how we define executive functions and their role in self-regulation.

Karl Pribram first used executive functioning in the 1970s. His studies suggested that the prefrontal cortex is primarily responsible for mediating executive functions. Traditional medicine has seen the subject applied immensely in clinical psychology, psychiatry, and neuropsychology. However, executive functioning has evolved into a broader topic discussed in education and general psychology. It has been integrated into classroom accommodations and teaching strategies.

There are seven core self-regulation types affiliated with executive functioning. They include:

- **Self-motivation:** Pushing yourself to accomplish things without extrinsic motivation or consequences
- **Nonverbal working memory:** Making mental notes for behavioral guidance

- **Emotional:** Integrating images, words, and self-awareness to influence your feelings on certain subjects
- **Problem-solving and planning:** Identifying new and innovative solutions and paths
- **Self-restraint:** Constraining yourself
- **Verbal working memory:** Maintaining internal dialogue
- **Self-awareness:** Turning the spotlight on yourself

The Four Circuits of Executive Function

Looking at ADHD from these circuits' perspectives helps us understand the origin of specific symptoms. Variations in symptoms affecting a child with ADHD depend on the level of impairment seen in these circuits. For example, some children have higher emotional regulation issues while others have higher working memory deficits. Some may experience challenges with time management but are much better at other things. Whatever the case, each of these circuits explained below comes into play:

- **The Who Circuit:** This circuit covers the area stretching from the frontal lobe to the back of the hemisphere. It is responsible for self-awareness and regulates the goings-on around us, how we feel, and what we do, both internally and externally.
- **The When Circuit:** The when circuit connects from the prefrontal areas of the brain to one of the oldest areas, known as the cerebellum, which is one of the backmost parts of the brain. This circuit is responsible for timing and regulates the sequence of behaviors and how seamlessly they are performed. It also coordinates the

timeliness of actions and the decisive time of doing anything. A dysfunction in the when circuit, especially in people with ADHD, is responsible for their inability to manage time judiciously.

- **The What Circuit:** This circuit runs from the frontal lobe's outer surface to the brain's area known as the basal ganglia—or, more precisely, the striatum. This circuit is responsible for working and adequate memory, so it manages the thoughts that guide our actions. This is especially the case for making plans, setting goals, and cogitating about the future.

- **The Why Circuit:** This circuit also begins from the frontal lobe and passes through the central area of the brain called the anterior cingulate. It ends in the amygdala, the limbic system's primary gateway. The circuit is considered the "hot" circuit because it is directly in charge of emotions. It regulates how our thoughts influence our feelings and vice versa. It is also primarily responsible for decision-making, particularly in planning. When deciding between several options, the why circuit comes into play to help single out an option among all others based on their motivational and emotional properties and how they make us feel.

The Development of Executive Functions

Abilities linked to executive functioning develop at different paces from one another. The development process is sequential, with one skill developing off the back of another. Every type of executive function interacts with one another. It plays a role in the regulation of behaviors in individuals to lead to desired outcomes in the future.

The development of executive functions begins at age two and continues until age 30 when they become fully developed. However, people with ADHD often experience delayed development by 30 to 49 percent, making them more inclined to be driven by short-term goals instead of long-term ones.

The back regions of the brain are in charge of information storage about everything one learns. On the other hand, the front area is where the stored information is used for social effect and success in life. This shows how the prefrontal cortex mediates executive functions through the four primary circuits.

People experiencing executive functioning challenges—especially those with ADHD—may suffer impairments in one or more of the discussed circuits. As a result, such people may experience dysfunction in terms of social skills, planning, touch memory, and emotional regulation.

To better understand the executive dysfunctions in your child, do your homework on the subject and find out the best interventions and therapies that could help. Also, get in touch with your child's doctor once you begin noticing symptoms, including, but not limited to, the ones discussed below.

Symptoms of Executive Dysfunction

People with executive functioning difficulties may be subject to any or several of these symptoms:

- The trouble with creating schedules and organizing things
- Poor time management, or the inability to make plans while also taking cognizance of future activities
- Problems with processing and analyzing information
- Challenges with coordinating actions to achieve long-term goals
- The trouble with managing impulses and emotions

On the other hand, when there are no defects in executive functioning, people tend to:

- Complete activities in a timely fashion
- Coordinate the steps necessary for performing tasks
- Effectively analyze and process tasks
- Make adjustments or shifts as needed to complete activities
- Make plans for addressing goals
- Create timelines for achieving goals

How Executive Function Impacts Children With ADHD

The connection between ADHD and executive functions is that the latter develops as a result of impairments in the former, which is the self-management module of the brain. So, while people without ADHD can suffer from impairments in executive function, people with the condition suffer from several executive function impairments.

These six clusters of executive functions are often impaired in attention deficit hyperactivity disorder:

- **Action:** Tracking and managing physical activities
- **Emotion:** Dealing with frustrating and regulating feelings
- **Activation:** Organizing activities and materials, time management, and starting tasks
- **Effort:** Analyzing speed, maintaining driving force, and managing alertness
- **Memory:** Accessing recall and using working memory
- **Focus:** Identifying, maintaining, and alternating attention when necessary

Executive dysfunctions are sometimes hereditary, especially in children with ADHD. Nevertheless, there is also a chance that damage could cause in the prefrontal cortex, severe neglect, in vitro exposure to harmful substances, and trauma. One study discovered that people susceptible to impairments in executive functioning typically suffer from injuries, disorders, damage, or disease to the same area as the brain.

Managing Problems With Executive Function

Executive function problems can also stem from learning disabilities and disorders in executive function. Whatever the case, the reason for managing issues with the condition is to help strengthen executive function skills, which are otherwise deficient in the affected individual. Put simply: The primary goal is to work out the problem.

The management process is individualized and dependent on the areas that require more attention and the underlying reason for the dysfunction. However, according to the National Center for Learning Disabilities (NLCD), here are some general tips to help improve problems with executive function:

- Create routines and plan shifts and transition periods for activities
- Set up visual task aids or visual schedules, like a flow chart of activity milestones, and go over them multiple times daily
- Use a step-by-step approach to work by splitting tasks into more minor activities.
- Ask for written guides or oral guidance as much as possible.
- Use tools like alarm watches, computers, or organizers to track time and stay on course

Using these strategies can help you manage the issue in your child before, during, and after seeking medical counsel. Not only will it make their life much easier, but they will also not be easily overwhelmed with little tasks.

PARENTING TIPS FOR HELPING YOUR ADHD CHILD
AT SCHOOL

- **Please do your homework:** It is crucial to know the
  policies, regulations, and laws safeguarding the health of
  your child, as well as the rights the child has. Two federal
  laws ensure that children with disabilities receive "free
  and appropriate education." The first is Section 504 of the
  Rehabilitation Act of 1973, and the second is the
  Individuals with Disabilities Education Act (IDEA).

Both rules require schools to provide the necessary
infrastructure and services to aid learning. There may even be
other laws unique to your state. Find out about them; you want
the law on your side.

- **Learn about the Individualized Education Program
  (IEP):** If your child with ADHD needs something
  different from what is taught in school, or a new way to
  learn things, it is best to give them an IEP. Not only does
  an IEP satisfy these needs, but it also shows you how to
  track their progress offering insights on the type of
  service to expect from the school. The school is expected
  to meet with parents twice a year to review the IEP. The
  first review is establishing the IEP and what needs to be
  included. The second meeting is to review the goals and
  how your child performs. You must stay very involved
  with the IEP and ensure that all teachers adhere. An IEP
  can follow your child through college and update

throughout the school years, but it is imperative to remain involved, so your child has their needs met.

- **Find out the policies and support that apply to your child at their school:** Send a written note to the principal of your child's school requesting an evaluation of their services and policies. If you want to learn more about how to go about this letter, consider visiting the Children and Adults with Attention Deficit Hyperactivity Disorder (CHADD) website for samples.

Some schools, especially public ones, offer social skill groups—small gatherings of two to eight children led by a speech therapist or the school's psychologist. The group teaches children to manage specific social situations and connect with their peers.

- Know the 504 plan: If an IEP is unnecessary for your child—who will remain in the same class as other students on the same grade level—you might need a 504 plan. This document shows how the school supports your child, with each plan designed to meet the child's needs. While class lessons will remain relatively unchanged in this case, you can expect the following privileges for your child:
- Counseling, occupational therapy, or speech therapy
- Providing verbal answers in a test as opposed to writing them down
- Getting more time to complete schoolwork and tests
- Attempting tests in a different room than others or with fewer students to limit the chance of distractions

- Having the option to skip reading and use audiobooks instead

However, there are no rigid laws on obtaining a 504 plan, so it is up to your child's school. If you feel the plan would be helpful for your child, reach out to your local school district and learn the terms involved.

- **Speak to teachers:** Regularly meet up with your child's teacher to discuss their goals and needs and how best they can be helped in class. This could mean relocating your child's seat from the windows and doors to the front of the course. This way, they can remain focused and avoid distractions. The teacher can also come in to offer a little help. Request access to the school schedule, so you do not catch the teacher at the wrong time.

This is also handy for tracking your child's progress. If you can help it, getting another set of books for your child to use at home can help. In doing so, you can learn how best they learn and relay it to the teacher.

- **Work together:** It would help to work with your child's teacher instead of trying to impose on them. Your child will take it as a sign that the adults in their life want the best for them.
- **Be coordinated:** Parent-teacher meetings are often kept short so parents can ask questions. When attending, come prepared to ask vital questions. Organize all the

necessary details, including test results, teacher notes, and report cards, in a binder for easy reference.

- **Do not get offensive:** Occasionally, you may be called about your child not paying attention in class or disrupting class activities. It is easy to give the caller a piece of your mind at that moment. Instead, reach out to them about your child's condition. Explain that you know how much of a handful your child can be, and suggest possible solutions. Simply providing the child with directions for a task or changing their seating setup can help.

- **Speak regularly:** Keep in touch with your child's teacher by mail, phone calls, and in person. By doing this, you can find out how your child is progressing, how they deal with schoolwork, and if they are adjusting to changes. You could also learn about the assignments your child brings home and ask for help. This way, you can ensure that your child can go through the homework independently or request extra time on tests.

Visit the teacher's website to learn about projects, upcoming tests, and exams. Seek the teacher's advice on how to help your child prepare for the due dates and organize their stuff outside the classroom. This can save you from dealing with meltdowns at the last moment.

- **Approach cautiously:** Be careful how you approach teachers to avoid putting them on the defensive. For instance, rather than asking, "Why don't you help John Doe when he struggles with classwork?" say, "I fear that

John Doe may be struggling to finish classwork. How can we help him stay focused so he does not fall behind on his studies?"

- **Create mutual goals:** Your child manifests and is influenced by ADHD symptoms in and outside school. So, say they struggle to follow directions; try discussing with the teacher some new means of keeping the child grounded and onboard. The solution must be practical both at home and in school.

- **Express gratitude:** When teachers go out of their way to understand your child and aid them in learning, be appreciative. Send a note to express your appreciation or visit in person.

- **Discuss in person:** Plan your schedule to include meeting times with your child's teacher. Each meeting should be set up around the early stages of the school year. Stick to the plan and meet up to discuss your child's situation. During the meeting, remain courteous and cheerful. Do not focus on the problems alone.

Instead, talk about creating solutions. For example, do not say, "Jane Doe, she is headstrong." Instead, say, "I have noticed that Jane Doe does not like to ask for help if others are around but will ask if she can talk quietly with someone." Any other educational plans or reports should also be shared in the meeting.

- **Join the conversation:** Volunteer at the school, chaperone an event, attend back-to-school events and offer to help with the library. Little pitching-ins show the school and the teacher that you are committed to your child's growth. You will also get insights into how your child interacts outside the home.

- **Please keep your child's teachers informed:** Since you are bringing them into the process, there is no need to cherry-pick the details that teachers should know. Inform them if your child starts or changes ADHD medications. This way, they can look out for side effects and provide you with feedback on whether or not the meds are helping the child. You also want to keep them in the loop on significant household changes that could affect your children, such as the birth of a baby, a death in the family, or divorce.

- **Getting started at a new school:** As mentioned above, children with ADHD are often hardest hit by significant changes. So, whether relocating during the summer or beginning the first year of middle or high school, you want to ease the burden on them. For a start, reach out to the school beforehand. This way, the new school can pair your child with teachers and classes suited to every learning style and ability.

- **Learn more:** Call the school early on and plan to send your child's report cards, notes, and test scores from the previous school. Schedule a meeting with your child's teacher and the guidance counselor. At the same time, go over the IEP or 504 plan to see if you need a new one.

- **Petition the guidance counselor to give you and your child a tour of the school:** Get to know the school nurse, the teachers, the principal, and other vital people your child will meet. Help your child get used to the roads by walking them around the premises. If you can manage it, arrange a hangout or playdate with another student from their new class.

- **Create plans and routines:** Create plans, routines, and practices to help your child adjust to the changes and feel better on their first day.

HELPING YOUR CHILD WITH THEIR HOMEWORK

Not many children are huge fans of homework. And rightly so, too. For children with ADHD, homework routines seem monumental. It is enough hard work writing down the assignment and bringing home the necessary information to accomplish the task. As a result, they tend to lose some papers either on their way home, at home, or on the way to school.

Sometimes, it is a different ball game, and they do not even bother attempting the assignment. For example, suppose the homework makes it home in one piece. In that case, they find the effort needed to focus on the work, recall the instructions, and understand the assignment hard to come by. Moreover, with all the distractions floating around, there is much to focus on. As a result, much homework does not get turned in, and the ones that attract poor grades. This can lower the self-esteem of the child, making them feel incompetent. They also start to despair and are easily hurt by criticisms for their behaviors.

As a parent, we want to help them do better. So here are some simple but practical tips for getting around this hurdle:

- **Color coding:** Color coding is a great way to help organize and can go a long way with ADHD children. So, the next time you are getting them an assignment notebook, get different colored book covers, pens, notebooks, and folders. Designate each color to a specific subject. Finally, get another lockable folder for storing homework papers. This way, your child will have a permanent location for accessing homework files. It will also improve their organizational skills and make them less likely to lose assignments.

- **Offer support and tools:** Take your child shopping to pick a notebook of their choice for writing down homework assignments from school. Get in touch with their teachers to issue verbal reminders about the assignments and give them time to take notes. Furthermore, you could inquire about how homework is issued. You can solicit the teacher to begin doing so if it is not written on the board. Such a change will benefit both your child and the entire class.

You can also prime the teachers to look out for your child and ensure they maintain focus and take down assignments as instructed. Moreover, when they are distracted, a quick tap on the shoulder should be enough to redirect their attention without embarrassing them. Teachers could also go through the assignment notebook by the end of class to ensure the accuracy of the writing. Finally, you could ask for a weekly schedule of the assignments at home as a backup.

- **Acknowledge efforts:** As your child goes through their assignments, endeavor to be relaxed and positive all the way through. The time is right to offer feedback on their hard work and efforts. During mealtimes, compliment them before other family members. It is easy to get caught up with the negatives of ADHD and forget that your child is also human and in need of acknowledgment. Do not hesitate to point out when they are doing well. If they behave well until the end of the week, you could even take them out to someplace special to celebrate.

- **Arrange their backpacks:** Join your child in arranging their backpack. As they offload their books for assignments, teach them how to clean their bags. Start with old, unnecessary items they hoard in some areas. This way, you will not have to deal with moldy leftovers or snacks they forgot to eat several weeks back. Doing so also helps to organize the items in the bag, which makes for fewer distractions for the child. While this activity may appear trivial, offering your child with ADHD extra guidance and support goes a long way for them.

- **Be your child's advocate:** Do not be afraid to set up meetings with your child's teachers to talk about any concerns you may have about their homework. Granted, it will not always be possible to see all teachers attend to your child. For such cases, use other means, like phone calls or emails.

If possible, teachers may be willing to reduce the assignment workload your child has to deal with. Of course, the change will be subtle, so their peers do not see it. For instance, if a mathematics assignment requires the class to attempt 30 questions, your child may only have to do 15. To set this up, get in touch with their teachers and speak about giving the child extended time or reduced workloads.

- **Medication:** If your child is on meds, remember that the drug may have worn off towards late afternoon, which is usually the time for homework. Consult your child's doctor to find out if you can withhold one of the medication dosages until homework time. Ensure your child does not get the medicine too late, as it could affect their sleep.
- **Maintain a pseudo library at home:** Reach out to the principal of your child's school and find out if you can get another set of school books to keep at home. For children experiencing ADHD, taking home the right books for assignments is challenging. So, having a backup set they can fall back on at home can be life-changing on the worst days.
- **Plan homework time:** Starting homework immediately after returning from school is a good habit much miss out on. Of course, it seems like no fun, especially after a whole day of learning. However, that is not half of it. Having a snack before plunging back into school work is advisable for some children. At the same time, their break could be some minutes of playtime or exercise.

If you try this break time after school, note how your child reacts. If they need the time to let off pent-up energy and regain their focus, it is a worthwhile addition to your schedule. First, create a designated homework area. It does not have to be anything fancy; your kitchen island, or the dining table, could suffice.

Alternatively, you could use your child's room. However, there are drawbacks to this option. For one, they are in their own space and may be more prone to distraction. Furthermore, it helps to be within reaching distance from them to answer questions and provide prompts as necessary. Moreover, since their bedrooms are often more isolated, this approach may not work correctly.

Some children prefer the quiet when doing homework, while others enjoy some background music at home. There are even children who prefer to work intermittently with little short breaks in between. Speak to your child and find out their preferred environment.

Finally, prioritize ease and predictability over sophistication in creating a homework routine. Once homework is completed, review it to ensure it has been done right. Then, help them put it away in their homework folder and return all the other items they use to their respective places.

STRATEGIES FOR ADHD CHILDREN AT SCHOOL

When pairing up with your child's teachers, it helps to give them some tips about engaging with your child. Doing so could make tutoring much more manageable while creating a safe space and structure for your child outside the home.

- **Be flexible with rules:** Children with ADHD often experience restlessness. So, while standard classrooms have rules about students staying in their seats for lessons, children with ADHD may struggle with this rule. Instead, they could focus better by standing or pacing.

For the children who get fidgety, palming a tiny Koosh ball or something easy to maneuver in their hands helps with stimulation without causing disruptions. Some studies claim that chewing gum could even help boost the concentration of some students with ADHD. However, the research was pretty inconclusive. Furthermore, given how many schools frown on chewing gum, it is unlikely such changes may be allowed.

- **Acknowledge and reward positive behavior:** Incentives and rewards should always take center stage in motivating students instead of punishment and criticism. Changing rewards often could spice things up and create healthy competition to avoid boring the students. Children should not be prevented from going to recess as punishment for bad behavior.

Children with ADHD are, in fact, better able to focus after physical activity in a gym class or outdoors. In all, prioritizing rewards and incentives gives the school or classroom a favorable structure for children with ADHD.

- **Allow them some leeway:** Children with ADHD find it difficult to sit still for an extended period, so giving them room to leave their seats and move around the class could help them immensely. This subject should be handled cautiously so as not to disrupt the type or cause other students to want the same leeway.

Find creative ways to help them, like asking them to collect the notebooks of their peers, fetch materials from the storage closet, take a note to another official in the building, or wipe the board. Even something as minor as creating a little break time in between classes to let everyone get a drink of water at the fountain or from their lunch boxes helps a lot.

- **Encourage children to seek support:** children with ADHD require more help in class than other children, but it is unlikely that classroom aids are always available, in the same way, that academic support services for ADHD in schools may not be in place. So, while it could help for the child to be given a one-on-one audience with an adult, it is sometimes best to pair them up with their peers.

This pairing brings a child with ADHD into a group with another kind, mature classmate. The outcome is beneficial for both parties in terms of academics and socializing. For the child with ADHD, they have the chance to grow a relationship with their peers, improve their social skills, and show commitment. On the other hand, the study buddy makes a new friend, regularly reminds the student with ADHD about schoolwork, offers encouragement, and helps them stay grounded until a task is complete.

- **Maintain a consistent level of expectations:** The classroom engagement rules should be simple to understand and straight to the point. They should also be reviewed and updated regularly to stay abreast of changes. Rules should also be highlighted in an area of the classroom where they can be easily accessed.

It helps children read the rules and what is expected of them. This way, teachers can determine their understanding of it. Students can read the rules without understanding their meanings or implications.

For students who experience difficulty switching between tasks or lessons or managing time in general, having a schedule in hand and going over it regularly can ease them into the transition process better. Alternatively, you can use verbal cues, time signals, or timers to alert them of the duration of activity at any given time.

- **Give feedback regularly:** Both children with and without ADHD can benefit from regular feedback about their behaviors in class. In the same way, consequences for behavior, whether positive or negative, should also be meted out quickly.
- **Tone-down distractions:** Children with ADHD are often prone to distractions, so it could help to seat them away from potential sources of disruptions, such as windows, pencil sharpeners, doors, and cubby areas. Also, tone down the distractions in the classroom, including visual stimuli like clutter or sound stimuli like noise.

Putting on white noise or soft music to play in the background can help improve concentration and focus in children with ADHD. However, there is a tendency for it to be distracting for other children without the condition.

- **Avoid overloading them:** children with ADHD are easily prone to overwhelm. To counter such occurrences, consider breaking down the total workload into smaller bits for easier assimilation. Also, children are more likely to consider smaller micro-tasks easier to navigate than the same tasks lumped into one big whole.

Furthermore, children with ADHD may also experience sleep problems, which affects how much attention they pay in class and their overall behavior. Younger students are generally better prepared for learning earlier in the day when energy levels are high. However, you may experience a slump in productivity and energy after lunch. For older students, though, like teenagers and college students, morning classes are a chore.

That said, create a system that allows the class to handle more challenging and pressing subjects and schoolwork during the most engaged, alert, and productive periods.

In conclusion, remember that children with ADHD may struggle with attending school, staying focused in class, and doing after-school tasks like homework or projects. As a parent, show support by being compassionate about their struggles and helping to create a stable structure that eases the pressure on them. To do this, you need effective strategies that help your child improve at school and schoolwork while also imbibing necessary life skills. Finally, do not be afraid to reach out to the school and collaborate with teachers to create healthy and helpful structures for your child.

8

ADHD MEDICATION AND TREATMENT

A DHD can get frustrating to manage, especially at the onset of the diagnosis. In addition, you are usually torn between grief and anxiety, making the process all the more frustrating. However, you can take respite in the fact that there are prescription medications to help with the condition. While these drugs may not outrightly heal your child, they can help manage symptoms and give them a more normal life.

MEDS ON, MEDS OFF – WHEN AND WHEN NOT TO TAKE MEDICATION FOR ADHD

Usually, when your child requires ADHD medications, the signs are clear as day, with impairments in executive functions being the most prevalent symptoms. But how do you know these symptoms and tell them apart from youthful exuberance? Here are some signs to look out for:

- The child struggles at school and is often behind on schoolwork
- They find it challenging to develop and maintain friendships
- They exhibit behavioral problems both at home and at school
- They struggle with sports and after-school activities

ADHD medications—stimulants- typically—are the recommended treatment methods for children manifesting any of these signs because they address the core symptoms of the condition. Alternatively, you could take the path of behavioral therapy or combine it with the recommended stimulants.

When you are sure that their behavioral issues are more than childhood shenanigans and have got a diagnosis to back it up, you might want to start ADHD medications. But before you do, speak to the child and consult a medical professional.

Stopping Medications

Nevertheless, just as it is important to know when to start medicating, it is also crucial to know when to stop. Knowing when to stop medicating is not as clear-cut as knowing when to start, especially when the child is doing much better than beforehand. It makes you wonder if they should not continue the medication for life.

While it might seem like a reasonable proposition, there are a lot of other factors to consider. Here are some to take into cognizance during decision-making:

- Hesitation on your part, say, during the start of a new school year, to see how they fare without the medication
- Side effects. Many ADHD medications come with several adverse effects, including but not limited to moodiness, loss of appetite, or insomnia
- Children may begin rejecting medications, especially as they mature into teenagers

Although these reasons are not unfounded, they are not good enough to justify stopping ADHD medications. For instance, if the child is experiencing frequent side effects of the drugs, changing the medication or lowering the dose may bring better results than quitting altogether.

But another caveat is that many pediatricians and parents are skeptical about halting a good run of form and will likely keep the child on medication regularly without considering necessity. Nevertheless, whatever the case, you should continue to track your child's progress even after adjusting the dosage or changing medications.

When deciding to stop medicating, collaborate with your child's doctor to look for signs suggesting that moving past medications may be okay. That said, here are some reasons to consider:

- On days that the child is not on the medication, or when they fail to take it, symptoms are unnoticeable
- You had maintained the exact dosage over time, even when the child grew older and added a few pounds

- Your child has been doing well, with controlled behavior, and no symptoms of ADHD in the past year since beginning medication

TIPS FOR STOPPING ADHD MEDICATION AND MINIMIZING SIDE EFFECTS

Do not just quit the medication for the child. Instead, speak with the child and consult your doctor like when you started it. Then, let it be a unanimous decision to try stopping the medication.

Take cognizance of the possible risks of quitting ADHD medications and how they can affect the child. You want to ensure a safe transition for your child. For instance, non-stimulant meds like clonidine should not be stopped cold turkey. Doing so could lead to spikes in blood pressure. Professional medical guidance and oversight are needed for this process.

Time the process to coincide with low-stress periods of the year, such as when the child has adapted to school routines or after tests or exams. Waiting for holidays or vacations can also be a bad idea, as the child is not under the duress of schoolwork and might be less oversaturated. Instead, you want to find a time when everything is balanced and just a little easier.

After you stop medicating, schedule regular checkups at home and school to ensure that the child is still performing well, do not wait until the report card comes in to find out or for the teacher to ring you up. Instead, provide your child's teachers with a questionnaire to complete over several weeks, like the Vanderbilt Assessment Follow-Up form. There is also a form for parents, which should be forwarded with the teachers' form to your child's doctor. It is not up to their medical eye to decide if quitting the medication has been working fine for the child.

Compliance with ADHD Medication

Since stimulants like Adderall and Ritalin are widely abused and used outside the medical context, especially by teenagers and young adults, many parents do not imagine their child will have a problem taking ADHD medications. However, many children struggle with compliance as they enter teenagehood, whether they have taken the medications before or are just starting. This stems from their growing sense of independence, which makes them more likely to resist being medicated for chronic conditions.

Here are some tips to help win the compliance battle:

- Adjust the dosage or change the medication if the sole reason for noncompliance is side effects. You could even suggest lower symptoms in contrast to abandoning medicating altogether.
- Consult your child's doctor to find out if something else is going on with the child, like oppositional defiant disorder, depression, substance use, and anxiety that may fuel their resistance.
- As in the beginning, get your child involved in the decision-making process. Instead of imposing it on them, try to find their reasons for noncompliance.

- Consider letting the child stop medicating during the weekends and other school breaks or holidays to see how they fare.
- Solicit help during and after school hours when switching ADHD medications to ensure your child is being monitored.
- Open a dialogue with your child and ensure they understand that the medication is neither a crutch nor a cure. It is like medicating for any other chronic condition, like how a person with insulin problems uses an EpiPen.

MEDICATION FOR TREATING ADHD

Stimulants

Stimulant medications are often prescribed to people with ADHD due to their effectiveness in improving symptoms of the condition. How it works is that the stimulants in the medication boost neurotransmitter levels in the brain. As such, the brain receives a shot of norepinephrine and dopamine, improving symptoms like hyperactivity, impulsivity, and inattention in people with ADHD.

Although stimulants are often the go-to medications for treating ADHD and are backed by the Food and Drug Administration (FDA) for use by children, many who use them do not respond to treatment or simply cannot tolerate stimulant therapy. There is also the case of people responding better to one form of stimulant over another.

When using stimulants, here are some of the most common side effects you can expect to experience: Irritability, dizziness, lower appetite, increased anxiety, and insomnia. Other side effects are not as widespread as those mentioned above, such as tics, blurry vision, mild stomach aches, increased heart rate and blood pressure, and nausea.

It helps to know and expect these side effects since they influence how willing you are to take or adhere to the medication. If your child experiences side effects from stimulant medications, consult your doctor. Do not leave anything to chance. This is so that you can safely quit or adjust the dosage of the medication under medical supervision.

The most common stimulant medications used for treating ADHD are Focalin (dexmethylphenidate), Adderall (amphetamine and dextroamphetamine), Dyanavel XR (amphetamine), Vyvanse (lisdexamfetamine), Daytrana or Concerta (methylphenidate), Zenzedi or Dexedrine (dextroamphetamine), Ritalin, Methylin, Metadate CD (methylphenidate), and Desoxyn (methamphetamine).

Non-Stimulants

Although stimulants are the typical first choice for many people treating ADHD, other non-stimulant medication options are also available. The entire premise of these medications is as follows:

- When stimulants cause too many side effects
- For people with a history of drug use
- When you do not respond to stimulants
- For people with a history of specific heart conditions

- For people with a history of bipolar disorder

Here are some non-stimulant medications you can use for your child:

- **Strattera:** Strattera (Atomoxetine) is one of the first medications outside of stimulants that the FDA approved for treating attention deficit hyperactivity disorder in both adults and children above age six. Some potential side effects of this medication are vomiting, fatigue, agitation, irritability, dry mouth, decreased appetite, stomachache, increased blood pressure, dizziness, nausea, and increased heart rate.
- **Tricyclic antidepressants (TCAs):** Tricyclic antidepressants are not technically ADHD medications and are used off-label for treatment. Some of the commonly used drugs in this category are Tofranil (imipramine), Norpramin (desipramine), Amitriptyline, and Pamelor (nortriptyline). These drugs may cause side effects such as vivid dreams, drowsiness, dry mouth, insomnia, constipation, headaches, stomachache, and blurred vision.
- **Effexor:** Effexor (venlafaxine) is another off-label ADHD medication that is an antidepressant. It helps to improve mood and boost concentration. Common side effects of the drug include tremors, anxiety, nausea, sleep problems, dry mouth, and sexual problems in adults.
- **Wellbutrin:** Wellbutrin (bupropion) is another form of antidepressant medication. It has been found to lower depression symptoms in many users and ADHD

symptoms. However, some side effects of Wellbutrin include insomnia, irritability, worsening of existing tics, and weight loss caused by reduced appetite.

- **Anti-hypertensive drugs:** Other medications used for treating ADHD are heart blood pressure drugs, like Tenex (guanfacine) and Catapres (clonidine). They help to manage symptoms of ADHD but may cause side effects such as fatigue, stomach pain, decreased blood pressure, nausea, dry mouth, insomnia, dizziness, and drowsiness.

Of the non-stimulant medications mentioned in this section, Strattera is the most studied for use as ADHD treatment in children and adults. As a result, studies show fewer side effects when using it compared to others, like TCAs. Strattera is also more effective for ADHD than Wellbutrin.

Other Medications

Some people fail to respond to stimulant and non-stimulant medications or experience intolerable side effects. When that happens, medical professionals may offer other medications, such as guanfacine or clonidine, which the FDA approves for use by adolescents and children for managing ADHD symptoms. For people with no problems using stimulants, guanfacine or clonidine could also be administered to boost the effects of the medication.

Less common alternatives are often antidepressants like Wellbutrin (bupropion), although it is not FDA-approved for managing ADHD symptoms.

COPING WITH SIDE EFFECTS OF ADHD MEDICATION

Below are some common side effects of ADHD medication and how to treat them:

- **Headaches:** You can alleviate headaches in your child by administering the medication during or after mealtimes. However, there are times when headaches stem from deficiencies in vital minerals. This situation is noteworthy because some children with ADHD have magnesium deficiencies, which can lead to headaches.
- **Problems with sleeping:** Children with ADHD may face sleep problems regularly. Often, the medications they take may affect their ability to fall asleep. Other times, the restlessness symptom of ADHD comes into play, making it harder to go to sleep.

To combat this problem, you must set up a good sleep routine for your child. Make the time memorable for them, and put them in the mood for bedtime. Here are some helpful tips:

Start preparing them for sleep some 30 minutes before their bedtime. Although it may not be time to go to sleep, it helps to engage your child in quiet activities. For instance, switching from a fast-paced video game or sport to bedtime in minutes can cause sleeplessness. So, you want to steer the child towards activities like coloring, piecing together puzzles, or reading.

Work on their hygiene routine by encouraging them to use the bathroom, brush their teeth, wash their hands or take a bath, change into pajamas, turn off bright lights, and get into bed. Stick to this routine religiously, and try to get your child in and out of bed, as this will help you create a wake-up and bedtime routine.

- Reduced appetite: Feed your child healthy snacks rich with calories across the day. Some foods to try are:
- Toast and a hard-boiled egg
- Crackers and cheese
- A muffin served with a glass of milk
- A banana or apple served with peanut butter
- A protein bar

Consult your doctor for advice about administering medication after mealtimes.

- Stomach aches: Only administer medications during or after meals to reduce the likelihood of stomach problems.

CONTACTING THE DOCTOR

If these strategies discussed so far have failed to improve side effects in your child, consult your doctor immediately. In addition, seek advice on other side effects, such as tics (involuntary vocal or motor movements like throat clearing, muscle tensing, excessive eye blinking, coughing, or facial grimaces), irritability, and increased anxiety levels.

ADHD medications also have potential risks that you should discuss with the doctor. For example, non-stimulant medications like Qelbree (viloxazine) and Strattera (Atomoxetine) warn about triggering suicidal behaviors and thoughts. Therefore, you want to monitor your child using these medications to track changes in their behaviors or mood.

Do not fail to bring up potentially serious side effects and your child's medical history. These factors play a role in determining the best medication for the child and give you insights into what to consider when a situation arises.

PHARMACOGENETIC TESTING

Since ADHD is a complex condition, finding the best combination and volume of medications can be a chore. Depending on genetic makeup, some people metabolize medicines faster or slower than others. As a result, medications linger in the body for extended periods, leading to side effects. On the other hand, when they go through the body too quickly, their effectiveness wanes.

Thankfully, advances in technology and genetic testing provide people with ADHD with new knowledge about the type of medicine and the proper dosage to achieve the best results for treating the condition. In some instances, gene-based testing removes the need for trial and error, which is both expensive and frustrating.

Gene-based testing analyzes how medicines are metabolized in the body, showing the types of drugs that will give you the best results. This helps you avoid unpleasant side effects and guides the doctor in finding the proper dosage for your child. For example, many people who take amphetamines like Adderall suffer from nausea. A genetic test will show how your child's body reacts to this drug. With that knowledge, your doctor can begin lowering side effects through altered dosage or medications.

For instance, with a non-stimulant like Atomoxetine, the medication goes through the body faster. However, since some percentage of the population have a slower metabolism for such drugs, the Atomoxetine may linger in the body for 24 hours. This could make the treatment ineffective and trigger frequent side effects. Whatever type of medication you choose for your child, ensure that they are backed by a medical professional, including dosages. Having your child undergo gene-based testing before you begin medicating for the best results is also essential.

Although not everyone will love the process, it provides valuable information about well-being and treatment options crucial to lowering side effects and improving drug effectiveness.

9

NATURAL REMEDIES FOR TREATING ADHD

Although prescription medications are the way to treat attention deficit hyperactivity disorder, other natural remedies work well to reduce symptoms of the condition. For many, these natural remedies mean fewer side effects triggered by pharmaceutical concoctions. Natural remedies, also known as complementary and alternative medicines (CAM), typically revolve around lifestyle and dietary changes.

NATURAL STRATEGIES AND REMEDIES FOR TREATING ADHD

- **Sleep:** Helping your child nail down a good night routine is critical to quality sleep. Getting the recommended hours of shut-eye helps to reduce ADHD symptoms. For instance, if your child procrastinates on homework until the last minute, they may go to bed late. And that means little sleep, as their busy minds will keep them up longer than necessary. In turn, they will wake up groggy in the morning and still tired from not getting enough rest. ADHD affects your child's ability to concentrate or focus, and poor sleep only worsens that. If it continues, their mood and overall well-being will suffer, too.

- **Exercise:** Exercise helps with improvements in ADHD symptoms, mainly executive functions. Many studies have attempted to identify the different forms of exercise and their impact on ADHD. The final verdict is that all exercise types work just as well for the condition.

So, rather than focusing on type, the main objective should be to select an exercise routine your child enjoys. Ridiculous as it seems, enjoyment is a major driving factor in forming habits. Moreover, since a healthy habit like exercising helps with ADHD, it is worth cultivating. The workout routine does not have to be fancy; it could be simple exercises like martial arts, spinning classes, running, or yoga. To avoid boredom, you could even diversify the routine with multiple activities.

Some studies suggest that taking some time to enjoy the outdoors could help boost ADHD symptoms. Exercising can be an excellent way to combine physical activities and outdoor time.

- **Energetic play:** Exercise affects two significant symptoms of ADHD the most: impulsivity and hyperactivity. While children can have fun with organized physical activities like martial arts or sports, they may also benefit from energetic play several times a day. Active play can be anything from biking to playing on a trampoline, hopping with friends, or running around the yard with siblings.

- **Nutrition:** Diet is another aspect of your child's life affecting ADHD symptoms. Making conscious plans to feed them healthy foods, reduce junk food, and find food intolerances can help immensely.
- **Clean eating:** Some studies show that specific food additives and ingredients could exacerbate ADHD symptoms. For instance, sodium benzoate, found in many common drinks and foods, has been linked to some of the highest ADHD rating scales. Another is monosodium glutamate, a flavor enhancer in many foods, such as baby food, bouillon cubes, and salad dressing. Some studies even report unhealthy cognitive reactions due to MSG.

Caffeine also enters the fray. As a stimulant, it worsens ADHD symptoms while improving dopamine flow, increasing alertness and focus. This complex trade-off results from side effects such as insomnia, nervousness, and anxiety. Caffeine is also known to impact stimulant medications negatively. There have also been studies linking additives and food coloring to hyperactivity symptoms in children.

- **Food intolerances:** Some studies suggest that people with ADHD are more likely to experience food intolerances and allergies than others. Common symptoms of intolerance are swelling of the tongue, hives, problems with breathing, or itchiness. A simple blood or skin test can diagnose your child with food allergies.

Food intolerances, on the other hand, are not so easy to diagnose. For instance, they may not be detected in blood tests, and the side effects of eating a specific food may not come immediately. However, intolerances gravely affect the quality of life. For instance, they can lead to decreased energy levels. They could also increase the likelihood of impulsiveness in your child and lower cognitive clarity or their ability to focus.

- **Protein:** Adding protein to your child's meal can help them to deal with symptoms of ADHD. Proteins have immense effects on neurotransmitters, like norepinephrine and dopamine, which are essential chemicals in managing ADHD symptoms. Neurotransmitters are biochemical communication links through which brain cells interact.

On the other hand, protein also helps to regulate blood sugar levels, which helps with brain function. Stimulant ADHD medications replicate these effects by boosting the flow of neuro-transmitters in the brain's synapses. Therefore, having enough protein in their meals could help improve the function and efficiency of neurotransmitters. This could mean better performance for your child throughout the day. Therefore, making an ADHD meal for your child should consist of a decent balance of fiber and protein sourced from oatmeal, unprocessed fruit, and vegetables.

- **Blood sugar:** Although the study on the link between ADHD symptoms and high-sugar dietary patterns was somewhat inconclusive, some evidence shows that diets rich in sugar may worsen specific ADHD symptoms. If your child overeats sugar, the glucose level in their blood will fluctuate, and they may experience energy crashes. These changes can exacerbate ADHD symptoms in focus, memory, and activity levels.

Rather than encouraging your child to eat unhealthy snacks and junk food, turn their attention to foods rich in fiber and protein. Go for snacks loaded with these natural ingredients to leave them feeling fuller for extended periods. Protein and fiber also help to regulate the movement of blood sugar levels.

- **Elimination diet:** An elimination diet can be done in two main ways. For one, you can remove the top causes of allergies from your child's meal, including chocolate, eggs, dairy, soy, peanuts, corn, shellfish, wheat, and yeast. Alternatively, you could take them out one by one and track whether or not your child's symptoms reduce.

The first method is likely unadvisable because taking out so many foods from your child's diet grossly reduces their options. Instead, they end up with a restrictive diet, which is challenging to keep up with. There is also the likelihood that your child will suffer from nutritional deficiencies. Therefore, the best way to begin eliminating foods from their diet is to consult a dietician. This way, you have medical professionals offering guidance on how to proceed.

BEHAVIORAL THERAPY AND ADHD

Behavioral therapy is an umbrella term for types of therapy that treat mental health disorders. This therapy seeks to identify and help change potentially self-destructive or unhealthy behaviors. It functions on the idea that all behaviors are learned and that unhealthy behavior can be changed. Therefore, the focus of treatment is often on current problems and how to change them.

Types of Behavioral Therapy

There are many different types of behavioral therapy:

▷ **Aversion Therapy**

Aversion therapy is often used to treat substance abuse and alcoholism problems. It works by teaching people to associate a desirable but unhealthy stimulus with a highly unpleasant one. The unpleasant stimulus may be something that causes discomfort. For example, a therapist may teach you to associate alcohol with an unpleasant memory.

▷ **Cognitive Behavioral Play Therapy**

Cognitive behavioral play therapy is commonly used with children. By watching children play, therapists can gain insight into what a child is uncomfortable expressing or unable to express. For example, children may be able to choose their toys and play freely. They might be asked to draw pictures or use toys to create scenes in a sandbox. Therapists may teach parents how to use play to improve communication with their children.

▷ System Desensitization

System desensitization relies heavily on classical conditioning. It is often used to treat phobias. People are taught to replace a fear response to a phobia with relaxation responses. A person is first taught relaxation and breathing techniques. Once mastered, the therapist will slowly expose them to their fear in heightened doses while they practice these techniques.

▷ Cognitive Behavioral Therapy

Cognitive behavioral therapy is viral. It combines behavioral therapy with cognitive therapy. Treatment is centered around how someone's thoughts and beliefs influence their actions and moods. It often focuses on a person's current problems and how to solve them. The long-term goal is to change a person's thinking and behavioral patterns to healthier ones.

BEHAVIORAL THERAPY FOR CHILDREN WITH ADHD

Applied behavior therapy and play therapy are both used for children. Treatment involves teaching children different methods of responding to situations more positively.

A central part of this therapy is rewarding positive behavior and punishing negative behavior. Parents must help to reinforce this in the child's day-to-day life. It may take children some time to trust their counselor; this is normal. However, they will eventually warm up to them if they feel they can express themselves without consequences. Children with autism and ADHD often benefit from behavioral therapy.

BEHAVIORAL THERAPIST - WHY YOU NEED ONE AND HOW TO GET ONE

Finding a therapist can feel overwhelming, but many resources make it easier. When finding a provider, you can choose from:

- Social workers
- Faith-based counselors
- Non-faith-based counselors
- Psychologists
- Psychiatrists

You should ensure that your chosen provider has the necessary certifications and degrees. Some providers will focus on treating specific conditions, such as eating disorders or depression.

If you do not know how to get started finding a therapist, you can ask your doctor for a recommendation. They may recommend you to a psychiatrist if they think you might benefit, as psychiatrists can write prescriptions for medication.

Most insurance plans will cover therapy. Some providers offer scholarships or sliding-scale payments for low-income individuals. A therapist will ask you many personal questions about yourself. You will know you have found the right therapist if you feel comfortable talking to them. You may have to meet with several therapists to find the right one.

In conclusion, prescription drugs are the obvious way to treat a condition like ADHD. However, they are not always good as they have side effects that may be much more severe in different people.

Thankfully, some natural remedies and therapies have proved quite effective in treating ADHD. You can get in touch with a qualified professional who will be able to guide you more on the therapies and bring in better results.

Luckily, you do not need professional support for using natural remedies, as it is doubtful they have any adverse effects.

SUPPORT RESOURCES FOR PARENTS

G iven a choice, many parents would not choose to raise children with ADHD. Not because the children are a curse to be shunned, but due to the sheer effort that goes into it. But over the years, the pressure of raising children with the condition has lessened thanks to increased awareness and improvements in treatment methods. ADHD is no longer the dreaded and misunderstood condition it once was.

With the myriad of help available, you just have to find the right resources to help you cope in your journey to provide your child with a normal life.

BEST ADHD PODCASTS

- **The Faster Than Normal Podcast**: This podcast relays the success stories of people living with ADHD. From CEOs to rock stars to everyday people, guests come on to speak about finding success in work and day-to-day life, regardless of their condition. This podcast might be the pick-me-up you need to change your mindset about how you see ADHD and its impact on your child's future.

- **I Have ADHD**: Kristen Carder, an ADHD life coach, hosts this podcast. She dedicates the show to teaching people with ADHD vital organizational and time management skills. Listen to this podcast daily if you need practical tips to help your child set goals and be productive.

- **CHADD**: CHADD is an acronym for Children and Adults with Attention Deficit Disorder. The organization was created in 1987 to create awareness for people with ADHD. CHADD is a network of volunteers who help to teach, encourage, and support people living with ADHD, including teachers and parents.

- **Distracted**: Mark Patey is the founder of this podcast. He was in fifth grade when his diagnosis turned up as ADHD. Afterward, he was placed in a special education class with children considered troublemakers and others with severe disabilities. Regardless of the difficulties ADHD created for him, Mark grew up to become a businessman. And a successful one, too. On Distracted, he talks about what the diagnosis means and how it should not be the trigger for a negative spiral.

- **ADHD reWired**: Eric Tivers, founder of ADHD reWired, is a coach, therapist, and Licensed Clinical Social Worker (LCSW). His approach to the podcast is different from most on this list. He does not just bring on experts on the condition; he also reaches out to regular folks living with

ADHD. His listeners benefit from listening to relatable stories from relatable people and hearing actionable strategies from experts.

- **Adult Attention Deficit Disorders Center of Maryland**: This podcast is a collaborative platform shared by Valerie L. Goodman, a clinical psychotherapist and LCSW-C, and David W. Goodman, a medical doctor, and professor of psychiatry and behavioral sciences. The duo offers various resources, from practical to educational, for helping people with ADHD. Their audio interviews and podcasts aim to tackle common problems encountered by people with the condition, like being diagnosed with another mental health issue besides ADHD.

- **Parenting ADHD**: Penny Williams hosts the Parenting ADHD podcast. She is a mom who took it upon herself to find out every last detail about ADHD when her son was diagnosed. This is the closest relatable podcast of the lot. So, you can start from here, if you would like. Penny is now a coach and author who partners with parents to teach them about their children's condition. Her podcast has several episodes that discuss all the necessary details on parenting ADHD children, including relaxing activities, homework, and positive parenting.

- **ADHD Experts**: On this podcast, high-profile experts on ADHD are brought in to help discuss issues on work life, family life, and education. Unlike other podcasts on this list, ADHD Experts uses a more interactive format. Questions are collected from parents with ADHD children and adults living with the condition. To participate in the show, simply register for the live webinar.

- **More Attention, Less Deficit**: Ari Tuckman, the host of this podcast, is a psychologist, MBA, and PsyD, who prioritizes the diagnosis and treatment of adults, teenagers, and children living with ADHD, including other related conditions. He wrote a book titled "More Attention, Less Deficit" to aid adults with attention deficit hyperactivity disorder. He goes over various issues per episode on the podcast, providing practical steps to creating positive changes.

- **ADHD Support Talk Radio**: Tara McGillicuddy is an ADHD expert and the creator and director of ADDClasses.com. Her podcast focuses on important challenges and problems people with ADHD experience. She pairs up with other experts to discuss several issues on ADHD, including future planning, stress management, and financial management, among other things.

- **Practical ADHD Strategies**: Laura Rolands was a human resource professional with over 15 years of experience. In 2009, she became an ADHD coach and created MyAttentionCoach.com. In this podcast, Laura shares some great tips for managing the condition. She also conducts interviews with experts in fields like mindfulness and time management.

- **Adulting with ADHD**: This podcast is designed for a specific audience: Women. Sarah Snyder, the host, goes over personal stories of her experiences with the condition. Other times, she brings on other women with

ADHD to talk about relevant subjects such as menopause, pregnancy, and postpartum depression.

- **Taking Control: The ADHD Podcast**: This podcast was created by Nikki Kinzer, PCC and certified ADHD coach. She helps her listeners develop helpful strategies for dealing with stress, improving productivity levels, organizing, and managing time. On the show, Kinzer looks at some of the specific areas in which people with ADHD find trouble. Afterward, she provides practical tips for solving the problems.

BEST ADHD APPS

When picking an app for your child with ADHD, consider its ease of use, its vital features, and its availability on Android and iOS. The apps highlighted in the section are selected for their high ratings and glowing reviews, ensuring that they were used by actual people and worked as intended. This way, you can get good value for your resources.

Some of the best ADHD apps are Bear, Evernote, Asana, Due – Reminders and Timers, Trello, Remember the Milk, Clear Todos, Brain Focus, SimpleMind Pro – Mind Mapping, Todoist, and Productive – Habit Tracker.

Facebook Support Groups

Facebook is easily one of the largest social media networks for connecting with communities that matter to you. From groups to pages, there is something for everyone, including people with ADHD or parents of ADHD children.

Joining one of these groups may seem daunting, as you do not know anyone there. But do not despair; everyone in such a group is united under the banner of ADHD. The community is vital because it makes the condition relatable and much easier to deal with now that it is clear you are not alone.

Here are some of the reasons to join a Facebook group about ADHD and what you stand to gain:

- **Vent:** Dealing with ADHD is so challenging that parents battle depression, anxiety, or OCD when caring for their children. Facebook groups allow you to vent about your challenges each day and get the frustration off your chest, knowing fully well that you are surrounded by folks who understand.
- **Ask questions:** Pose questions to people with ADHD and parents with children with a similar condition. Ask them if they forget to do their hair before driving the children to school or if they fell asleep at work from overworking the previous day. Ask everything and anything.

Consider joining Parent Support Group for ADHD/ODD and Autistic children. Alternatively, you could just enter "ADHD" into any old search engine and find groups or pages that work for you.

In conclusion, whether you need some strong tips to deal with the condition or want to know more about ADHD for the sake of your child, using any of the support or resources discussed in this chapter can help greatly. Your child can live a normal life with hopes for future success.

MAKING AND KEEPING FRIENDS

Making friends is a big deal for children. Although children experience trouble making and keeping friends, the social difficulties children with ADHD face must be expertly managed. Children with ADHD struggle more with building friendships for many reasons connected to their ADHD symptoms. The symptoms of ADHD make proper engagement with others a herculean task for the child, causing frustration. Although parents would love to address the bad behavior resulting from that frustration, addressing the root cause is better.

Making and maintaining friendships requires tons of skills like talking, sharing, listening, and being empathetic, which children with ADHD do not acquire naturally. As a parent, this can be a constant source of worry. Children with ADHD cannot pick up social skills that other children assimilate at a higher rate.

Because their symptoms make them neglect social cues, children with ADHD potentially drive others away from them.

Before a child is diagnosed with ADHD, the social isolation from other children can be unexplainable and worrisome, as it seems the ADHD child has a wrong air around them, which other children seem to avoid. They may attend a few playdates but never get invited back.

When children are much younger, it is difficult to detect their lack of social skills because other children might only wonder why they display such an attitude but might not take offense. Again, when children are much younger, their playdates have the presence of a parent or caregiver. But the lack of social skills becomes much more noticeable as the child grows, causing alienation during playtime because now other children can take offense.

Children with ADHD need help to learn how to build and maintain friendships. The bulk of the work lies on parents, who have to make this work without upsetting their children. If your ADHD child struggles with making friends, you have a lot of work cut out for you.

HELPING YOUR ADHD CHILD WITH BUILDING FRIENDSHIPS

- **Guide your child to overcome impulsivity:** Children with ADHD can not effectively control their impulses. They often interrupt their friends or have difficulty keeping up with the conversation flow. When this happens, their friends can become frustrated and may leave them behind or ignore them.

Although it will take time, regular practice will help your child interact better with others. Introducing children with ADHD to yoga or meditation can help them weigh their actions and initiate the best response. If the child is not old enough for yoga, getting them to sit still may be hard, but you can convert mindfulness into a game to help them practice.

Teach your child to pause and think about their options before deciding. Then, help them determine which choice will provide a positive response. When your child learns this at home, they will replicate it in their relationship with friends.

- **Guide your child to stop hitting:** When a child cannot control their impulse, their conversations with friends might not be the only thing affected. The impulsivity may make the children with ADHD hit others due to their anger and frustration. You can help them stop this act by determining exactly why it happens.

Usually, children react when they are put in a position they want to end. For example, they will react if your child's friend takes their toy or calls them a name. The best way to address this issue is to consider why the action happened—solving the why will prevent your child from hitting.

Children with ADHD should be shown ways to cope with anger and frustration, and exemplary action is the best way to do that.

Whenever you negatively show anger to your child or partner, offer an apology.

This helps your child learn. Guide your child through ways to avoid confrontation, for instance, taking short, calming walks or taking several deep breaths. Children with ADHD are impulsive, so your child needs to learn to channel their impulses into other activities, like jumping jacks or running, until they are calm.

- **Guide your child to stop using rude words:** Parents of children with ADHD understand and excuse some of their children's behaviors because of their condition. However, if these children say rude or hurtful things, other children can label them as mean or bullies. As a parent, you can prevent name-calling when they use rude words by teaching your ADHD child empathy.

An angry response whenever your child uses rude language, will only escalate the situation. The best way to react to this will be to let them know how you felt about their comment. Doing this helps the child to understand that words can be impactful, helping the child be conscious and empathetic to others.

This same strategy can be applied when your child is rude to their friends. It will help them understand that their rude words were hurtful and initiate the process of mending the relationship. Most importantly, understand that your child cannot learn all these instantly, which will take quite a long time. Therefore, you have to apply patience as you help your child practice.

- **Helping your child to keep friends:** Children are likelier to keep friends when they have frequent playdates. A child of school age can develop socialization skills and build friendships if they interact with others outside of school. ADHD children benefit from playdates because you can make the environment safe for them to practice positive skills. The following tips will help you guide them to maintain friendships.
- **Teach your child to resolve conflicts:** During playtime, it is normal for children to have conflicts. However, conflicts are more frequent for children with ADHD due to impulsivity. When conflicts occur, teach your child that their actions can hurt their friends. A good way to make children with ADHD remorseful is to let them step into the shoes of the offended. Ask them how they would feel if they were in their friend's position. Then, ask them how they will want their friend to apologize. Get them to say or do those things to their friends to fix the conflict and rebuild the friendship.
- **Teach your child to prevent future conflicts:** It might take a while before you can get your ADHD child to avoid future conflict. However, you must ensure there is constant improvement. When there is a conflict, let your child practice resolution skills. Constant practice improves their confidence.

Ensure you remind your child to continue practicing "stop and think" skills so they can become an automatic part of your child's instincts. Then, as time goes on, they will impulsively stop, think, and respond instead of reacting.

- **Teach your child to avoid triggering situations:** Your child can maintain friendships by learning to stop triggering situations. While teaching your child how to manage their social skills and control their impulses, teach them, as well, to keep off from environments that cause conflicts.

When playing, they can avoid activities like roughhousing on the playground or at birthday parties. Although keep in mind that getting them off activities like this will help them manage their reactions, you should not restrict them from these activities forever. When the child's impulse control improves, allow them to use their "stop and think" skills to understand and predict situations that can trigger a physical conflict.

With increasing confidence levels, children with ADHD can understand their emotions and how they affect their interactions. Eventually, they will learn signs that show a situation will cause conflict and learn to steer clear before their impulse takes over.

- **How to achieve a successful playdate:** Having established that playdates are great for children to make friends, you need to have a plan to make it work. First, invite a playmate to whom your child is close. Ensure that the playmate has things in common with your child. Without shared interests, it will be difficult to have a successful date. Before the date, it is better to filter play activities to remove physical activities requiring high energy or physical contact. For instance, you can remove touch football from the playlist if your child cannot stop touching others.

TIPS TO HELP YOU PREPARE YOUR ADHD CHILD FOR A PLAYDATE

- **The guest gets to choose:** Let your child learn to step back for their guests. When a child visits, let your child know that a friend is welcome in the house as a guest while they play host. Although your child can suggest activities for playtime, the final decision lies with the guest.
- **Accept the guest completely:** Help your child remember not to criticize if they dislike their friend's method of doing things because everyone has a different pattern.
- **Be kind to the guest:** Avoid inviting more than one friend at a time. Even though your child might know many other children, the others may not know or be friends. This could spark conflicts, putting your child in a position they cannot handle.
- **Avoid hovering, but be alert for intervention:** As long as you have taught your child good social skills, trust that they will use them. Encouraging your child to use healthy skills is a good way to reinforce them. It is good to be nearby but stay in another room so you can observe your child's reactions to potential conflict.

You cannot wholly erase disagreements from children's playdates. Instead, it would be best if you strived to help your child react better when they happen.

EXPLAINING YOUR CHILD'S ADHD BEHAVIOR TO OTHER PARENTS

One of the most challenging aspects of parenting a child with ADHD is explaining your child's behavior to other parents. For example, you probably have had to explain every time your child hit a friend or said rude things to them.

Many times, children with ADHD lose friends because other parents do not want their children to interact with them. This can cause pain for you and your child and fuel a continuous cycle of making and losing friends. Instead of watching your child grow lonely from not having friends, try to explain ADHD behaviors to other parents as much as possible. The following tips can help you:

- **Do not wait until a conflict happens:** Talk to the parents of your child's friend before any incident happens. Make them understand your child's behavior and let them know how you address it. This way, the other parents can handle your child's emotions without prejudice, and you can make them your allies in making a better life for your child.
- **Actively resolve conflict:** When there is a conflict, make an effort to resolve it to prevent escalation. Step aside with your child and discuss their behavior. Offer

encouragement for the things that were done well and share ways to improve them in the future.

- **Reach out after a conflict:** Address the conflict when the parent of the offended child arrives and ensure they know it has been resolved. Share the steps you took to achieve resolution. Listen to the other parent, so they know their concern about protecting their child is valid. This helps everyone part on a good note.

However, you must remember that even though everything is done right, parents may want to avoid future playdates. Let your child know that they do not have to be discouraged if this happens.

Most importantly, you and your child must understand that childhood friendships are fickle. They change often, and your child's friends will change while improving social skills. Help your child build self-awareness by discussing the playdates and determining which friend they would like to see more frequently. Monitor your child's behavior during playdates and use it as a learning experience. Do not send them to a friend's house for a playdate until conflict management skills are built. Helping a child with ADHD develop their social and friendship skills might be tasking, but it helps them have a better quality of life.

CONCLUSION

The reaction of many parents upon learning that their children have Attention Deficit Hyperactivity Disorder may range from despair, and anger, to apathy. In fact, some parents do not bother to learn why their children behave differently than others. You, who have made it to the end of this book, do not fall into either of those categories. Instead, you are not only eager to learn about your child's diagnosis but are also committed to finding the correct ways to parent your ADHD child. This is certainly commendable.

This book must have impressed you that ADHD is not a curse, if nothing else. This condition need not determine your child's future. Instead, they can attain greatness in whichever area of life interests them.

The first chapter of this book undertook the job of demystifying ADHD. The prevailing reason why people think this condition is unmanageable is ignorance. If such parents know anything about the condition, that knowledge most likely comes from unreliable sources. This book has strived to be empathetic because, without a doubt, ADHD can be challenging to deal with. But it also explained, in great detail, what the condition is.

For instance, Chapter One revealed the three types of ADHD. Your child who has this condition may either be hyperactive and impulsive, or they could be inattentive. The third type is a combination of inattentiveness and hyperactivity. As such, you should be careful not to assume that your child is incapable of or has difficulty paying attention simply because of their proclivity to be hyperactive.

Chapter Two continued from where the preceding chapter left off. It dispelled the myths and stated the facts regarding the causes of ADHD. Although genes, alcohol and substance abuse, and poor nutrition have been linked to ADHD, there is no proof that video games, TV, sugar consumption, and gender are causal factors of this condition. Unfortunately, some people still believe that girls cannot have this disorder, and misconceptions like that can be especially dangerous. It may lead to depression and suicidal ideation for girls whose claims are disregarded.

The third chapter of this book took us into the brains of people with ADHD. We learned, in this chapter, how the brains of people with this disorder differ from those of neurotypicals. This book section was important as it conclusively did away with the notion that ADHD may only exist in the imagination of those diagnosed with it.

With the necessary foundational knowledge of ADHD carefully described, the succeeding chapters of this book, *Parenting a Child with ADHD*, focus on solutions for parents with children with the disorder. From learning how to talk to your child with ADHD to effective parenting strategies, this book equipped you with the skills to provide adequate care for your child living with this disorder.

Nothing truly is worse than feeling guilty for being unable to help your child when you are certain they need it. And ADHD, especially for parents dealing with the disorder for the first time, can feel like a hopeless situation. But, thankfully, hope *does* exist.

This book is packed with carefully researched solutions and true and relatable anecdotes that'll guide you from despair to triumph. If you apply the knowledge in this book, your child will become more sociable, successful, and confident. Feel free to highlight the points in this book that you found important. Then, go back and reread what stuck out to you, and make notes or set reminders to enable you to consistently practice the solutions shared in this book.

Do not feel discouraged or disheartened if some solutions fail to produce the desired results quickly. If your will is strong and you are determined to help your child shine in ways you know they can, this book will surely work for you.

Parenting is a grueling job, and it is even tougher when ADHD is thrown into the mix. However, with the right resources, like this book, you will find that raising a great child into a stellar adult can be fun.

If *Parenting a Child with ADHD* has been helpful to you, please leave it a favorable review!

Just click here to leave a quick review!

A SHINING OPPORTUNITY TO HELP ANOTHER PARENT

You're doing a remarkable thing, and everything you've learned here will make your journey that little bit easier. Now you have the perfect opportunity to give that chance to other parents!

Simply by leaving your honest opinion of this book on Amazon, you'll show new readers where they can find the guidance they're looking for – no matter how little time they have.

WANT TO HELP OTHERS?

Thank you for your support. The parenting journey can feel terribly isolating at times… but when we share information, we see that none of us is really alone.

This is the beginning of your exciting journey with your child! If you'd like more awesome content and support from other parents just like you, then I invite you to join the

Parenting A Child With ADHD Facebook Community here:

REFERENCES

Cherry, K. (2021). What are the benefits of having ADHD?. Verywell Mind. https://www.verywellmind.com/adhd-benefits-advantages-challenges-and-tips-5199254

Dvorsky, M. R., & Langberg, J. M. (2016). A review of factors that promote resilience in youth with ADHD and ADHD symptoms. *Clinical Child and Family Psychology Review, 19(4)*, 368–391. https://doi.org/10.1007/s10567-016-0216-z

Locke, L. (2022, August 4). Best be kind to yourself quotes for 2022. Routinely Nomadic. https://routinelynomadic.com/be-kind-to-yourself-quotes/

McBee, M. T., Brand, R. J., & Dixon, W. E. (2021). Challenging the link between early childhood television exposure and later attention problems: a multiverse approach. *Psychological Science, 32(4)*, 496–518. https://doi.org/10.1177/0956797620971650

Sherrell, Z. (2021). *6 strengths and benefits of ADHD*. Medical News Today. https://www.medicalnewstoday.com/articles/adhd-benefits

Swanson, J. M., Sunohara, G. A., Kennedy, J. L., Regino, R., Fineberg, E., Wigal, T., Lerner, M., Williams, L., LaHoste, G. J., & Wigal, S. (1998). Association of the dopamine receptor D4 (DRD4) gene with a refined phenotype of attention deficit hyperactivity disorder (ADHD): a family-based approach. *Molecular Psychiatry, 3(1)*, 38–41. https://doi.org/10.1038/sj.mp.4000354

Tovo-Rodrigues, L., Rohde, L. A., Menezes, A. M., Polanczyk, G. V., Kieling, C., Genro, J. P., Anselmi, L., & Hutz, M. H. (2013). DRD4 rare variants in Attention-Deficit/Hyperactivity Disorder (ADHD): further evidence from a birth cohort study. *PloS one, 8(12)*, e85164. https://doi.org/10.1371/journal.pone.0085164

Ulrich R. S. (1984). View through a window may influence recovery from surgery. *Science (New York, N.Y.), 224(4647)*, 420–421. https://doi.org/10.1126/science.6143402

DEFUSING EXPLOSIVE BEHAVIOR IN CHILDREN WITH ADHD

PEACEFUL PARENTING STRATEGIES TO IDENTIFY TRIGGERS, ESTABLISH EMOTIONAL RESPONSE AND CREATE STRUCTURE FOR A DRAMA FREE HOME

Join our Community!

Hosted by Author
Rose Lyons

This is the beginning of your exciting journey with your child! If you'd like more awesome content and support from other parents just like you, then I invite you to join the Parenting a Child with ADHD Facebook Community

I dedicate this book to my amazing family who have been nothing but supportive. My kids are my inspiration for wanting to help more parents in navigating their path of parenting children with ADHD. And a huge thank you to my husband who has believed in me and continued to push me when things got hard. I love you all.

INTRODUCTION

 If you are patient in one moment of anger, you will escape a hundred days of sorrow.

— CHINESE PROVERB

Being diagnosed with a neurodivergent disorder like ADHD opens the door to various challenges, especially for children who are still dependent. ADHD is not, however, a sign that someone is broken. Rather than attempt to fix it, it is in your child's best interest to focus on managing their disorder and becoming the best version of who they already are.

A couple of years back, I was at a parent-teacher meeting on behalf of my daughter when a child who looked about the age of six suddenly entered the room, her eyes searching for her parents. She seemed upset about something, and as soon as her eyes landed on her mother, she threw a fit and yelled at the top of her lungs, explaining how a classmate had taken her pencil case. The child was experiencing an outburst, and when her mother tried to soothe her by getting down to her level to speak with her, the child screamed. Her mother made other attempts to rein in her daughter's outburst, but it was to no avail. The child was determined to say everything she had to without any awareness of the environment. Moreover, based on her mother's embarrassed expression, it appeared this wasn't a first-time incident.

When a child has ADHD, their behavioral patterns can stress out family members, especially the parents. Your child's symptoms may vary from mild to extreme, depending on the severity of the disorder. Every parent loves their child and will always have their best interests at heart, but regardless of this honest intention, parenting children with ADHD can seem frustrating and make you question the depth of your love for them.

You are not alone. This is a familiar feeling of anxiety among parents of children with ADHD. Often, your child may have emotional outbursts, breakdowns, fits of anger, and moments of depression. These are events, amongst many others, that you have been unable to manage appropriately. It is understandable because children with ADHD can be challenging. It is not your fault, and it is not your child's fault, either. Your child's behavior is not an attempt to push your buttons to the extreme, nor is it a result of something you did wrong as a parent.

Children with ADHD should not be written off as children with unsolvable behavioral issues, as they can grow to become successful individuals in society. You will have numerous struggles as you go through life's hurdles with your children who have

ADHD. But it would help if you always thought about this analogy. You know how your dog gets so excited because you enter the room? Be that way with your child. Show them that you are excited to see them and show them attention. Doing this will help them know how much you care and are there for them. Your love and support of your children, even in the most challenging moments, will help shape them into successful individuals. There are many incredible stories of children with ADHD growing up and succeeding in their lives, and all those troubles they had as a kid has subsided. For example, Olympic swimmer and gold medalist Michael Phelps grew up with ADHD. His symptoms included anxiety and behavioral issues. He was inattentive and would grab papers from his classmates. Some people in his entourage even said that he'd never amount to anything. Thankfully his mother advocated for him, and despite his challenges, he found passion and success. Having a child with ADHD does not mean they cannot become amazing members of society. We are focusing on the approach to help them get there.

Understandably, as a parent, you are at that point in your life where you'd like to know that there is hope to get through each hurdle of this parenting marathon, which sometimes leaves you feeling disheartened. It would help if you had all the pointers and practical solutions to alleviate your problems with managing your child and restoring balance to all that has been out of proportion in your relationship. This book provides many possible answers to your questions and gives you a deeper understanding of your child's struggles with their emotions and how much you need to be a safe space for them as a parent. We are especially focusing on children who experience explosive behavior as part of their ADHD symptoms to assist parents with defusing these behaviors before they occur and how to handle them during. However, the book can also be used by any parent with ADHD children as a tool to add to their parenting toolbox.

The book further explores concrete solutions to modify your parenting methods and prevent you from constantly feeling on edge with your children. Children with ADHD need parents who lead by example and help them manage behaviors through principles rather than uncontrolled emotions.

Leading by example can be extremely helpful to your children's development.

It is important to remember that you are human, too, and your children need to see you being accountable for your actions. So if you were to lose your cool and snap or yell at your child, apologize.

I have compiled factual information through experience with two incredibly beautiful and energetic ADHD-diagnosed children and intensive study of this disorder of others for over fifteen years. I aim to help parents better deal with and manage children's behaviors with this diagnosis while negotiating the challenges of running a family and career. The knowledge in this book represents my foray into sharing with parents who need expertise and support to raise great children irrespective of their disorder.

Before discovering new information, successfully parenting children with ADHD was extremely difficult. There was no guide or support, and parenting was mostly done through guesswork and the hopes that one was making the right decisions. However, the emergence of new findings and solutions alleviates the uncertainties and mental pressure of parenting children with ADHD. So, rest assured; I can guide you through this turbulent stage of parenting by sharing personal experiences you will find relatable and proven solutions you can rely on.

1

DEMYSTIFYING ADHD

WHAT IS ADHD?

Attention-deficit/hyperactivity disorder (ADHD) is a chronic medical disorder that includes persisting behavioral problems like acting on impulse, being hyperactive, and having difficulty sustaining attention. Many children have this disorder, and they may continue to manage it into adulthood. However, children with the disorder might experience low self-esteem, trouble sustaining relationships in the home and beyond, and poor academic performance. Your child's symptoms may decrease as they age. However, they will never wholly transition out of their ADHD symptoms and become neurotypical. Don't be alarmed, though. The disorder can be managed. Through your help and guidance, your children can learn strategies to become successful and productive individuals.

It is essential as a parent to have an in-depth understanding of what ADHD entails and to be well-equipped with information that will support the process of applying life-changing measures. For example, you might have realized that treatments can help manage symptoms but will not cure ADHD. Treatment for ADHD in children and adults typically involves medications and behavioral management interventions by professionals. However, an early diagnosis and the treatment you apply can significantly affect how your child manages ADHD.

TYPES OF ADHD

ADHD characteristics can differ according to gender, with the diagnosis occurring more often in male children than in females. Although boys usually exhibit more hyperactivity, which a disorder like ADHD can amplify, it may differ completely from girls, who are more likely to show traits of being quietly inattentive. Hyperactivity and inattentiveness are two major features of ADHD present before the age of 12. There is no stipulated age for when ADHD traits in children can appear; oftentimes, you might even find them present in a three-year-old, depending on how mild or severe the disorder may be in your child.

There are three widely known types of ADHD:

- Predominantly inattentive: Children with predominantly inattentive symptoms usually have difficulty staying focused during playtime and when performing tasks. They have trouble following simple instructions you have laid out for them, as they are easily distracted. To understand what kind of ADHD symptom is predominant in your child, look into how often they lose tools needed to perform tasks—like pencils, toys, and books—and whether they avoid tasks that require organizing and mental effort. If your child reflects these characteristics, they are predominantly inattentive. You should note that this does not mean other symptoms are not evident; they are simply minimal.

- Predominantly hyperactive/impulsive: Hyperactivity and a pattern of impulsive behavior in children can be evident when they always seem on the go, constantly moving and running around when inappropriate. Hyperactive children usually have difficulty waiting their turn and seem fidgety, tapping, squirming, or making other body movements that imply they are unsettled. Your child may have a habit of interrupting your conversations with your partner or other people and seem to need a keen eye for when they should or should not engage, despite being old enough to understand this. In these circumstances, refrain from responding harshly since they simply do not know better.

- Combined: Some children have a mix of inattentiveness and a hyperactive or impulsive behavioral pattern. You can tell your child has a combined type of ADHD when most of the inattentive and hyperactive symptoms are evident in their behavior. That is, both types are predominant.

IS SOMETHING WRONG WITH MY CHILD?

There is absolutely nothing wrong with your child. Most children are typically inattentive, impulsive, and hyperactive in the early stages and even later in their development. Healthy children —especially preschoolers—are energetic and often full of life even after they've worn you out as a parent. For older children and teenagers, the length of their attention span during an activity solely depends on their interests. Therefore, you should never classify your child as having ADHD when they are just children or because they are quite the opposite compared to their calm and reserved siblings. Your child's hyperactivity or inattentiveness could be natural, as some children are more outgoing and eager to engage in activities than others. If your child has difficulty socializing or getting along with peers in school but seems to do fine at home with their siblings, this might result entirely from something else, not necessarily ADHD.

If you ever feel overly concerned that your child may be displaying core symptoms of ADHD, you must consult your family doctor or pediatrician. Diagnosing a child with ADHD can only be done by a specialist in children's development and behavior, a psychiatrist, or a pediatric neurologist. Seeking a medical evaluation is crucial and might reveal other potential medical disorders that could explain your child's struggles and difficulties. In circumstances where a diagnosis is made, you will receive the support needed to manage your child effectively.

CAUSES OF ADHD

The causes of ADHD remain unknown, and research is ongoing. However, existing studies indicate that causes could be linked to genetics, environmental factors, or central nervous system problems during a child's essential stages of development. For example, exposure to environmental toxins like lead may influence the emergence of ADHD; this toxin can be found in older homes and buildings that contain lead pipes or lead-based paints. Other theories that could make a child more likely to have ADHD include:

- Premature birth: Children born prematurely have less time for brain development during the gestational period. This has been linked to ADHD.
- Genetics: Children who have parents, siblings, or other blood relatives with ADHD or similar mental disorders are more likely to have ADHD themselves. Chances are that one of your children will have ADHD if you or their other parent has it; the chances of inheritance are slimmer but not written off if a distant blood relative has been diagnosed.
- Alcohol and tobacco use during pregnancy: The abuse of alcohol and tobacco during pregnancy is generally bad for a child's cognitive growth and development. One of the adverse effects of abuse could be ADHD.
- The brain's anatomy: Lower activity levels in the parts of the brain regulating focus could lead to a disorder like ADHD.

ADHD in children is not caused by poor parenting or too much screen time. Unfortunately, most parents tend to believe that their poor parenting results in children's impulsive behavior or inability to pay attention or excel in academics. Another common misconception is that hyperactivity stems from consuming too much sugar or food additives, receiving immunizations, or being exposed to environmental factors such as poverty or chaos in the family. While these factors can feasibly contribute to certain behavioral patterns in children, there is no evidence that they cause ADHD.

WHAT TO EXPECT

ADHD can be an extremely difficult medical disorder for most children to manage at the early stages. If your child has been diagnosed with ADHD, you can expect the following:

- Children with ADHD often struggle in social places; they have difficulty interacting with their peers and will continually strive to find acceptance from adults and their playmates.
- They daydream a lot, which causes them to be inattentive and unable to focus for too long. Depending on the predominant symptom in your child, they might talk too much for your liking. This could be a result of being hyperactive or impulsive.
- They usually seem forgetful and confused, lose track of the order of things and situations, and have difficulty resisting temptation. This is why they might do the opposite of what you have instructed.

- They tend to have minimal self-esteem and doubt their capabilities; this may reduce their chances of succeeding if the disorder is undiagnosed or unattended.
- Teenagers who have ADHD may struggle academically or find it challenging to keep up with lessons because they are inattentive and can barely exert focus when it comes to doing assignments, studying, and performing tasks effectively.
- They are more easily prone to accidents and sustaining injuries compared to children who do not have ADHD.
- They might forget the common protective measures you taught them.
- The peak severity of hyperactivity and impulsive behavior in children with ADHD is usually at seven or eight. However, there is no age range for peak severity in children with predominantly inattentive behavior.
- Some children with ADHD can experience explosive behavior. Explosive behavior means they can experience outbursts or extreme meltdowns in the snap of a moment. It can be a result of overstimulation, frustration, or an inability to express themselves. It is an overreaction to the situation, and the correct measures must be applied to defuse it.

When unaddressed, ADHD in teenagers can lead to depression, worsen the family conflict and their relationships with others, induce stress, affect their chances of getting a job, and lead to other serious issues like substance abuse.

FAMILY LIFE FOR CHILDREN WITH ADHD

An ADHD diagnosis doesn't imply the end of your child's life. By contrast, they can always go on to lead a normal, long, and fulfilling life. But, at the same time, their behavior might make you feel they are too difficult for you to manage. After all, you are human and can become emotionally overwhelmed when your limits are tested.

Imagine you have had a long day as a caregiver performing domestic duties and are looking forward to finally getting some rest after your adolescents return from school and settle in. However, when they arrive, they will not stay put; they are everywhere, exhibiting excessive physical movement and acting without thinking. It sometimes feels almost impossible to parent them because they do not seem to be listening to you. You spent so much time trying to catch up on laundry, clean up the kitchen, maybe tidy their rooms and in a blink of an eye, it's all destroyed. This kind of situation can be exhausting to keep up with on a daily basis. However, it is possible to work on this with time and effort. When you work with your children, you can help them learn how to manage situations, make decisions, and be accountable instead of attempting to make them conform. And by doing this at home, you are also helping to set children up for success in other areas of their lives.

The behavior of children with ADHD might also impact other family members, like their siblings or your partner. Everyone will always seem to be on the lookout for them because they might be engaged in activities that could put them in physical danger. This pattern of behavior can make you inadvertently shift your focus to the child with ADHD and give less attention to the other children because they aren't as hyperactive or do not demand as much attention.

The siblings may feel ignored and uncared for in such cases, causing jealousy, resentment, and hatred. As a family, the demands of monitoring a child with ADHD are exhausting and overwhelming; you always seem to be repeating the cycle of being frustrated by your child's inability to listen to instructions, snapping at them out of anger, and then feeling guilty about your harsh reaction.

When your child with ADHD has moments of explosive behavior, this can make family life even more difficult. That is why learning to defuse and deal with a situation is important for the entire family. While you need to work with your ADHD child to establish coping methods for explosive behavior to reduce it, it is also necessary to communicate with your other children so that they can understand what is happening and not fear their sibling.

Neurotypical children can be difficult enough to manage; having one or more children with ADHD under your care can be even more challenging and emotionally taxing. Their behaviors can disrupt family life and make overcoming family conflict and disorganization difficult. However, has it ever crossed your mind that your children's behavioral deficits are not intentional? Children with ADHD wish to be calm and collected, to be able to clean and tidy up their rooms, to put toys away, to function normally in social gatherings, to have high self-esteem, and to be able to listen attentively in class and excel in their academics. They simply do not know how.

When you understand that ADHD is just as frustrating and challenging for your children as it is for you as a parent, you will be one step closer to responding positively to them instead of being harsh or passively aggressive. Further, understanding how much ADHD impacts your child's future, their tendency to succeed, and the family will take you another step closer to being supportive and prepared to help them live a better lifestyle. The best kind of home for helping a child with ADHD lead a normal and successful life is one with structure, compassion, love, and a strong support system.

Even though parenting children with ADHD can be a struggle, remember to tell your kids you love them. You need to tell them you love them when they make the right decisions and even when they make the wrong decisions. Let them know that you love them on their good and bad days. Show them that you love them if they're happy and smiley, and you still love them when they are angry. Ensuring your children know that there is nothing that could ever take away the love that you feel for your kids is important. You need to tell your kids that you enjoy being around them. Ensuring you express all this love to your children is imperative because it can help them feel safe and cared for. It can also help your children know you are there for them no matter what happens. It may seem like a given to them, but words and actions are necessary to ensure your children know you love them. This is something that all children need but especially for children with ADHD who struggle in so many parts of their lives, it is vital. You are your children's rock. You are their safe haven, and they have to know that.

Family life, when you have a child or children with explosive behavior as one of their ADHD symptoms, can be even more complex. However, there are numerous ways that this behavior can be defused, and the goal of this book is to assist parents in this process. In turn, parents can work with their children on this. Building a solid foundation is the key to helping the child be successful in dealing with their ADHD and the behaviors that accompany it.

This book teaches a lot about ADHD and parenting children with this disorder. This book will focus on defusing explosive behavior in children with ADHD, although it can be a beneficial tool for anyone parenting a child with ADHD. But, if you're looking for a book to provide you with a deeper understanding of ADHD, you can also read my first book, **Parenting a Child with ADHD: How to Prepare Your Child for School Life, Integrate Executive Functioning Skills, and Foster Successful Friendships, by Rose Lyons**.

2

EMOTIONAL REGULATION

H ave you ever seen a friend's child, for instance, fighting or throwing temper tantrums? Perhaps this is all new to you, and you see your friend's embarrassment when she sees you watching. She asks her daughter Becca to share her toys with your daughter who has come over for a playdate but instead the child, who was content a minute ago, takes it badly and screams at her friend, "I hate you!" You may be surprised to see such behavior in a five-year-old, especially if your child doesn't act this way. However, that is the explosive behavior typical of children with ADHD. Upon seeing such behavior played out, you might think, "oh, teach that disrespectful child some manners!" But if your friend hasn't filled you in on her child's condition, you aren't aware of all the facts and how hard the mother has probably been working with her child. What happens next between the mother and her child is a reminder that we shouldn't be judgmental towards other parents.

Your friend does not ground the girl or take away her toys. Instead, she asks Becca to come sit with her and begins singing to her. You're surprised because you've never seen such methods used when a child misbehaves. Instead, you see singing as a reward. However, like magic, Becca is calm and no longer experiencing a tantrum or destroying things and apologizes to her friend for saying something so hurtful. In your mind, you say, "what just happened?" Later, when you talk to your friend about it, she explains how Becca has ADHD, and this method is what works for her. While you have never seen these de-escalation methods, you are amazed by how well they work and are proud of your friend for her efforts to help her child in such a unique way.

Raising children is draining enough, from preparing them for school to fixing their lunch, doing their laundry, and ensuring they are prim and proper for a school day. However, think about parents who must ensure this is on track while also dealing with children with explosive behaviors. That is too many irons in the fire and could make a parent delve into phases of depression. Children with ADHD are prone to explosive behaviors as a result of the characteristics which come with the disorder. It is not uncommon to see a child with ADHD have emotional dysregulation, poor impulse control, and mood disorders. According to the Medical Director of Saranga Psychiatry in North Carolina, Vinay Saranga, some children with the disorder cannot control their emotions and have poor frustration tolerance, resulting in them lashing out (Schuck, 2022). Many parents try different coping mechanisms to manage their child's outbursts. While such methods may succeed, in many cases, it would seem as though the child in question eventually outgrows each solution.

WHAT ARE EXPLOSIVE BEHAVIORS?

In an article on explosive behaviors, Dr. Carlson concluded that explosive behavior is like a fever, a symptom of many illnesses (Carlson, 2022). You know your child is sick but cannot pinpoint their suffering. It can result from ADHD, ODD, mania, anxiety, depression, autism, and Intermittent Explosive Disorder.

Although this book focuses on explosive behavior as a symptom of ADHD, it is important to note these other psychological problems that could result in explosive behavior.

If a child has Intermittent Explosive Disorder (IED), they display sudden and extreme anger. They may also tend towards violence. These children, usually in the age bracket of late childhood to early teens, get into fights and are generally seen in the middle of some confrontation or outburst. Consequently, this affects their relationship with family and performance at school.

HOW CAN PARENTS EMPLOY EMOTIONAL REGULATION?

The ability to regulate your emotions will help you process complicated feelings without getting triggered. This skill relies on emotional intelligence, the ability to express and manage emotions and relationships. Emotional regulation allows people to avoid overreacting. While emotional regulation will help you correctly align your feelings to your goals, emotional dysregulation, as you can imagine, does the opposite.

There are methods you can employ to manage your child's temper. One method with a high success rate with explosive children is PEACE, which stands for Pause, Emphasize, Avoid/Aware, Calm, and Expectations.

HOW CAN PARENTS USE PEACE TO REGULATE EXPLOSIVE CHILDREN?

Parents, teachers, or guardians whose children exhibit violent behavior should, first and foremost, understand that these children act in that specific way due to their disorder. It is not entirely their fault that they lash out and get physical with people and things. Research has shown that children with explosive disorders reflect on their actions and feel guilty after causing problems. Some even break down and cry, while others get confused. Here is how you can handle situations without harming your child and avoid being harmed yourself:

- Pause: Yes, pause. It is an innate characteristic in humans to counterattack when faced with violent situations, but one should understand that they are dealing with children. Stop whatever you are doing. These children only mirror what has been displayed to them by older people. You want to avoid gestures that could startle the child and not look down on them; instead, get down on their level and maintain eye contact with them (Doddson, W., 2022). Pausing is a valuable measure to keep yourself from reacting immediately without listening.

- Empathize: This method should be carried out before or after an outburst. This serves as a self-awareness mechanism passed from parent to child. It would help to tell your child that aggressiveness should not be used to escape a difficult situation. Talk to them repeatedly about recognizing their unique stressor and getting themselves out of their situation. Even if they have another outburst, keep practicing. With time, they will learn and get better. It is unrealistic to think they will not have another outburst, so try to create realistic goals instead and prepare for them.

- Aware/Avoid: You should be mindful of the situation and avoid making things worse. Do not raise your voice, do not tell your child you do not care and do not shut down. However, you should not walk away in the heat of the moment and leave your child to deal with their emotions alone. Be aware of how your child does best in calming down. Do they prefer to sit down in a corner with you in a room to regroup? Do they prefer to sit by you and have you hug them? Avoid arguing with or yelling at the child. Rather than resolving problems, this would only compound them and have an adverse effect. In addition, arguments distract you from the issue at hand.

- Calm: Being calm during an overwhelming situation for your child helps defuse their outburst. You must be able to listen and understand the problem. Do not belittle or write off their feelings as invalid; be careful with your language. Validate their feelings and avoid making them feel stupid. All of our emotions form who we are. According to Dr. Miller, validation means showing acceptance and being nonjudgmental, and this is important because when a child feels understood, they tend to let go of powerful negative emotions (Miller, 2022).

- Expectations: This refers to the conversations that ensue after the situation is resolved and emotions have settled. Let your children know that it is not okay to yell at people, throw things, or display other negative behaviors that may put others in danger. You may set such expectations as "I want you to come to talk to me when you are upset about something so we can figure it out together" and "It hurts my feelings when you say you hate me, so please do not say it anymore."

Every parent with an ADHD-diagnosed child should understand the PEACE strategy so they can apply it when needed.

OTHER METHODS FOR ACHIEVING EMOTIONAL REGULATION

The following list provides additional methods to help your child regulate their emotions:

- Create diversion. Please understand your child's narrative and why they act as they do, and listen to them. Knowing their narrative helps them feel heard and regain their sense of control. Ask questions but know when is the right time to ask those questions.

- Use body contact. Body contact creates an intimate relationship between people. Never underestimate how powerful a hug can be during a meltdown. You could hug your child and steady them when they have outbursts. This simple gesture could help cool their temper. This can create a negative emotion for some children, so again, know if your child would benefit from a hug or a soft touch.
- Put emotions into words. They say evil thrives in secrecy. When a comment or activity is out in the open, its effect is reduced. Teach your children how to put their feelings into words. Whenever they feel angry, let them say, "I am angry." The difference between children who put their emotions into words and those who do not is the chaos resulting from poor communication. A child who does not tell anyone about their anger may have more outbursts than those who do. When children can vocalize their feelings, it helps to prevent violent tendencies (Hallowel, 2022).
- Using words or pictograms, work to determine what your child is feeling. Doing so may help you to pinpoint the cause of the emotions. Since experiencing regular emotions is normal for development and happens to anyone, it is a balancing act to determine if your child's reaction is due to usual emotions or emotional dysregulation. Feeling sadness and anger is just a child finding their boundaries, which is okay. When it is explosive, and the child cannot express themselves except in negative ways, there is an issue. Overall, we do not want to tell our children not to feel these things but

instead teach them how to cope and manage them appropriately. Developing the right strategies to help your child manage their emotions might take time. The important thing is that you do not give up when working through their feelings.

- Reward good behavior. Parents should learn to be positive when disciplining a child. For instance, research has shown that rewarding a child for their good acts is more effective than punishing them for bad behavior. When little Becca gets cotton candy or toys for being good to her siblings, she would most likely do good things to earn rewards. However, parents should be creative in rewarding children so they do not feel entitled when doing good (Bertin, 2022).

In the end, parents and teachers need to understand that although a child will not outgrow ADHD, this disorder can be managed so that the child has healthy relationships with others. In addition, managing ADHD goes a long way in positively shaping a child's development. The difference between a child with ADHD who grows up to become a successful adult and one who throws tantrums and gets in trouble at the adult stage all boils down to how their ADHD was managed when they were younger. Therefore, parents, guardians, and teachers of children with explosive behaviors should pay attention to these children and fortify their quivers with peace arrows.

3

THE ROLE OF PARENTS

P arenting a child or children with ADHD can be very challenging, and you hold a great deal of responsibility in raising them. Caring for them will seem almost impossible because they tend to engage in behavioral patterns that negate your teachings and expectations. ADHD can be managed with the right treatment and support, and you are saddled with the responsibility of helping your child manage their struggles. Your positive influence on your child makes a big difference in their academics. You assist them in acquiring important life skills and, most importantly, making family life easier to manage. It all begins with you – the caregiver. You can apply many methods to help your child become a better version of themselves. For parents of children who exhibit explosive behavior as one of their ADHD symptoms, parenting is even more difficult. There may be days when you feel like you cannot succeed, but we are here to tell you that you and your child can overcome all the hurdles you will face. In this chapter, we are going to provide you with some tips on how you can use your role as a parent to help your child while ensuring that you are caring for yourself and the rest of your family at the same time.

DEALING WITH YOUR EMOTIONS

Emotions are an integral part of human functioning. While your role is to keep the family in good shape and help your child grow into a healthy and responsible adult, it is understandable if your emotions sometimes slip out of control. Parenting a child with ADHD will test your patience, exhaust you physically, mentally, and emotionally, and might also subject you to judgment from others who assume you lack parental skills.

You must never ignore or downsize the ways circumstances impact your well-being. Instead, you should recognize that there will be moments of emotional outbursts. Finding support or strategies for dealing with emotions is imperative, so you do not inadvertently take it out on your child.

Everyone needs "me time" to detox from negative emotions and recharge for better performances. Take a break if you ever feel overwhelmed with responsibility or like you are moving at the speed of light. Ask your partner or child to pitch in with chores and errands. Participating in fun and stress-relieving activities like reading a book, soaking in the bathtub, walking, or watching your favorite TV show can help you regulate your emotions.

If you are married or in a long-term relationship with your partner, spend exclusive time out together to unwind and discuss your emotions. You can steer clear of conversations around your children and catch a break. Instead, attend events, perform yoga and mindfulness meditation, exercise often, go on vacation, have dinner together, or go on dates. At the same time, the children are in the care of a babysitter. Invest in self-care because you can only support your children when you are in the right mind.

ENACTING BEHAVIORAL CHANGE

Encouraging a shift in your child's behavior requires that you have the parental skill and knowledge to influence positive changes strategically. You can apply many methods to support behavioral change in your child's life.

Set Boundaries and Have Expectations

Rules hold great importance for humans. For example, if your community sets a rule to behead any thief caught, the crime rate will most likely decrease in the community. People fear consequences, and children are not left out of this math. They need to know what you frown at and what grants them a "well done" pat on the back, a head rub, or an extra scoop of ice cream. You must state these boundaries and expectations simply, concisely, and clearly, so your child fully understands them.

Write your rules and expectations on a poster board and fix it on a wall in a part of your house that's noticeable. The following are some examples:

- Be kind
- Pick up after yourself
- No yelling

- Do not leave your things lying around

You can write these rules and expectations in colorful letters for your child to follow. You can also add a graphic if this is helpful for your child when it comes to remembering things. Then, when they perform these tasks without being reminded, praise them for their efforts and encourage them to do more. Feedback is important; children must feel recognized and encouraged to change positive behavior. You can also use rewards and incentives to stimulate and promote positive behavioral change. For example, instead of telling your child their mistakes every time they act against the rules, try prompting them, "Do you remember what we discussed as a consequence if you continued to leave your toys lying around?" Instead of you doing all the talking, interact with them by asking questions allowing them to reflect on previous discussions you have had. This keeps an open conversation between you and your child.

You can also say, "You were kind to our visitors today; would you like to choose dessert tonight?" However, ensure that you refrain from repeating the same incentives. It might lose value over time, and they might become bored.

Avoid Restrictions

Do not restrict your child from physical movements and activities. Using this consequence method for your child's misbehavior has more negative impacts than positive ones. For example, if your child gets overly excited and runs around the house, causing a mess and being loud, you may feel frustrated and send them to their room so you can get a break.

The immediate results of this might seem favorable since you would have nothing to worry about for the next 30 minutes and save them from getting hurt. However, it would be best if you considered the long-term effect of such a punishment. Children with ADHD need lots of physical movement and exercise to exert focus. Allow them to be restless, as this helps them work more productively; they could lean against a table or lie down on their chest or back as long as it allows them to focus on the task. You might notice that your child likes to hold onto a fidget toy like a ball that helps them maintain focus for long periods when performing tasks. This is common amongst children with ADHD as it aids the process of maintaining attention.

Create a Schedule and Practice Routine

Children with ADHD need structure, and a schedule can help to support that. Reduce your child's workload and ensure the tasks are broken down according to your child's age and ability. On the other hand, do not overload them with work. There should be breaks between each daily task; it is important to help them understand the essence of structure and how it is beneficial to perform tasks.

They should know what tasks they have to carry out, how long each task will take, and how to check off the tasks that have been completed. To make this fun for your child, you can draw a chart with colorful pictures that lists the tasks and explains how to perform them in clear and simple terms. You can set a timer to ensure they stick to the stipulated time frame for each task. This keeps your child engaged and helps them to be responsible and effective around the house without giving them room for procrastination.

Remember that positive comments and accolades strengthen your child's resolve and attitude toward work. When you pay more attention to positive behaviors than negative ones, you stand a better chance of promoting behavioral changes. Constantly nagging or highlighting your child's negative behaviors can make you come off as an overbearing parent and unintentionally damage their self-esteem. To avoid that, apply a reward system that includes giving them tokens or stickers when they do a good job within the right timeframe or for following through on simple instructions. If your child is older, consider taking them to lunch or stopping at their favorite smoothie shop. Be sure to tell your child why you want to treat them, that you appreciate their behavior (be specific), and encourage them to keep up the good work.

Forgiveness

Martin Luther King once said, "We must strive to build and sustain the capacity to forgive. He who falls short of the power to forgive lacks the power to love."

Parenting is a challenging task, especially if you have a short fuse. In the heat of the moment, when your frustration and stress levels peak, your temper flares, and you impulsively make hurtful statements fueled by anger during family interactions or directly to your child. Young children and teenagers test limits; unsurprisingly, you would have difficulty managing intense feelings. However, resentment may trickle in over time.

Practicing forgiveness with your family shows how intentional you are about letting go of blame and thoughts of revenge towards those who have hurt your feelings, whether inadvertently or on purpose. Forgiveness doesn't imply that you overlook their wrongdoings or condone misbehavior; it simply means that you rid yourself of the heartache that comes with holding onto grudges and other ill feelings.

To forgive is to be compassionate and show love and mercy because, deep down inside, it is the most effective means of responding to crises in your relationship with your child and other people. Forgiveness also shapes your thoughts about people with ADHD by helping you understand the many environmental, emotional, and social factors influencing their behavior. With forgiveness, you understand in-depth that your responses and reactions can be controlled.

For example, when your child litters the house with his dirty socks, frightens the cat, or breaks your favorite photo frame because he was being hyperactive, practicing forgiveness in your mind towards yourself and your child will help you maintain control of your emotional outbursts and responses to the situation. True, it doesn't diminish or invalidate the fact that you were annoyed and disappointed in your child's actions; however, you chose to be more understanding, kind, and lenient because you know your child struggles with ADHD, and none of those actions are influenced by utter bad behavior.

In place of an angry reaction and emotional overload, forgiveness teaches you to be more logical in the process of disciplining your child. Other times, it just teaches you to let go.

It is easy for people to say you should always show compassion towards children and others without addressing how their actions initially made you feel. However, holding your head up, suppressing your negative emotions, and showing compassion is hard. It is even harder in the heat of the moment when your child has made you feel terrible; feeling immediate empathy is nearly unachievable.

Frequently, you might find yourself directing the anger elsewhere by behaving passive-aggressively towards other people in your life. You are not perfect, and no one should ever expect perfection when dealing with your emotions and restraining yourself from escalating the situation. You are not a miracle worker, either. Emotions are elastic—there are limits to how far they stretch. It takes willpower to create an open mind, practice forgiveness, and maintain consistency, even when difficult. The following tips can serve as guidelines in the process of learning to accept yourself and forgive others, especially your children:

- Reduce the expectations you have of yourself concerning parenting skills.
- Instead of constantly berating yourself when your parenting measures fail to yield desired results, practice acceptance.
- Pay extra attention to your current resources and how you manage them rather than the resources you are still missing.
- It is okay to make mistakes; acknowledge them and strive to improve next time.
- Don't self-loathe or blame yourself.

- Start small. That is, forgive yourself for little things like snapping at your child because you are running late for getting them to school and situations where they do not perform tasks within the stipulated time frame you gave them.
- When faced with a thought-provoking situation, acknowledge it and brainstorm likely solutions.
- Don't strive to be a perfectionist.
- Forgiveness is a never-ending practice; free yourself of resentment and embrace your capacity for happiness, compassion, empathy, and contentment.
- Perform a loving-kindness meditation routine.
- Adaptability and understanding are key for ourselves and our children with ADHD. Often we remember the things that do not go right. But, we also need to take stock of what does. Try to remind yourself of the good each day. If it helps, keep a notebook, even if it is just for a few weeks, to get you into the habit of recalling something good from each day. Finding the positive instead of the negative is also good for our mental health. One thing I try to do every day is to ensure that my child's day doesn't start on a negative note. Maybe we are running behind, maybe they are being loud, or maybe they didn't get their teeth brushed. I have made choices that I acknowledge which tasks did not get completed or have delayed us, but then ask how we get back on course tomorrow. I do not yell about the issue. It is unfair to your child to explode or yell at them and then send them off to school and expect them to be able to focus. Tell them you love them, have a great day, and can't wait to see them later.

SUPPORT FOR YOUR CHILD WITH ADHD

The most promising child with ADHD has a support system that is intentional and dedicated to shaping their life for a better future. Every child needs to feel supported and, most importantly, made to feel that they'll always find a safety net in their parents. You can only successfully achieve this as a parent when you fully understand what ADHD is and how you can be supportive. Unlocking the right ADHD coaching method for your child might be the key to establishing a healthy family life and mending your relationship with your child.

Many things can become difficult for a child with ADHD, and you need to recognize them. For example, many adults agree that nothing compares to getting a full night of sound sleep after an activity-filled day—you desperately yearn to lay in the comfort of your bed and relax your tense muscles in preparation for the next day. The same applies to children, especially those with ADHD who have experienced peak activity levels all day. Unfortunately, they usually have difficulty getting a good night's sleep, which harms their health.

Every child should get a certain amount of sleep according to their age. In the absence of sufficient sleep, your child's health might suffer a decline. In addition, children with ADHD who have difficulty getting enough sleep tend to become less attentive in school and at home. The lack of attentiveness can, in turn, worsen their capabilities in school, during homework, while regulating emotions, and while socializing amongst their peers. As a parent, you might create a schedule encouraging your child to turn in early at night. If the child has been diagnosed with

ADHD, however, this might be easier said than done because they tend to be over-stimulated most of the time and may have difficulty staying in bed for too long.

Other important aspects of their lives also require a solid support system. Developing and maintaining healthy eating and sleeping habits, helping them function appropriately in the home and social settings, setting expectations, and enacting positive parenting styles represent core approaches that can help a child with ADHD navigate life easier and become better versions of themselves. Remember that you do not have to be the perfect parent in showing support to your child. All you need to do is find the right balance between offering support and attention. Emotional regulation results from having a schedule, maintaining healthy eating and sleeping habits, and having strong parent modeling.

The following are actionable steps for supporting your child at home:

- Ensure that your child gets positive attention as often as possible. They should never feel neglected or different from their siblings and peers.
- Keep your child away from the TV before bedtime. There can be much overstimulation from watching a late-night animation or movie.
- Instead of seeing a movie before bedtime, try other, less stimulating activities like doing a quick puzzle or reading a bedtime story. This would also be a good time to teach your child about gratitude.

- Add a new healthy food to the meal plan every week. Your child should eat a balanced diet and drink lots of water. You might even get your child to help you choose between a few food options to reward good behavior.
- Encourage exercise. This is an integral aspect of supporting your child through ADHD, as exercise promotes a happy vibe and, at the same time, keeps them healthy. It doesn't have to be strenuous—even walking can do the trick!
- Take parent coaching classes for parents of children with ADHD to help for a smoother parenting process with your child. Family therapy is also effective and essential to your child's growth.
- Don't yell at your children. Set clear expectations in the most simplified way possible and emphasize the consequences. Yelling at every mistake can make your child feel that they can never do anything right, and you are modeling that you cannot regulate your emotions, so why should they listen to you.

4

BUILD THEM UP!

The stepping stone to a better and progressive parenting style for children who have ADHD is understanding what the disorder entails and moving on to identify effective and ineffective measures for managing it. Building up children right from their infant years into other developmental stages requires a good understanding of the positive and the negative. Children are mentally fragile and have impressionable minds, so the wrong measures can jeopardize their healthy growth. You do not want to be in the position where you make a statement in a fit of anger that stays ingrained in your child's memory and affects their sense of self. You can recognize that you are not a perfect parent, but it is essential also to remember what tools create good parenting for children with this diagnosis and what to avoid. Children with ADHD who have moments of explosive behavior will require even more care to build them up so that you can ensure that they can have a positive and happy life. They likely hate how they feel when experiencing the behavior, but they need your help to deal with it, both when they are with you and in situations when you aren't there, such as at school or with friends. Your child's ADHD is something they will have to deal with their entire life; therefore, finding the right coping methods for them early on can pave the way for their future. Finding the right methods may also require trial and error, as what works for one child with ADHD will not necessarily be the same for another child, even if they have the same ADHD symptoms.

POSITIVE REINFORCEMENT

Parenting styles differ from family to family. The family structure and environmental and social factors determine how the "average" child turns out in the future. For example, children raised by authoritarian parents experience growth under strict rules and high expectations that control rather than nurture them. On the other hand, positive reinforcement represents an alternative parenting style. In this case, you are encouraged to apply a reward system when your child does what you taught them.

For example, imagine you are walking with your child at the park, and they mistakenly bump into a stranger because they were not looking, and then say, "oh, I'm sorry." This may seem new and unexpected to you because you have constantly reminded them of being polite to people but have not witnessed them put it into action. Following this new development in your child, reinforce their positive behavior by, for example, getting them a popsicle or extending their playtime. Regardless of the reward, tell them that you witnessed this behavior and you are proud of them. Your child understands that their reward results from their polite behavior earlier at the park; therefore, they are encouraged to do it again.

This parenting style encourages children to be respectful and well-behaved without using violent discipline, threats, physical and emotional abuse, humiliation, shame, or punishment at the slightest provocation. You should adopt the positive reinforcement parenting method with your child for several reasons. First, even if this concept is new, it can still be effective. The disciplinary methods you grew up with or have seen from other parents don't have to be the ones you use. Keeping an open mind when parenting your child with ADHD is important, and positive reinforcement can work. Managing children with ADHD when school is in session can feel like a lot, but imagine that it is summer break, and you must take full responsibility when their symptoms peak. What do you do then? How do you enforce an effective positive reinforcement style without worrying that your child might slip into bad behavior again and feeling the toll it takes on your well-being? Some tips include:

- Pay extra attention to your child's environment and plan accordingly. For example, when your toddler is hungry, they are likely to throw a fit, so you can tell they need food. Also, when children are tired or overwhelmed, they tend to exhibit extreme behavioral patterns that ADHD influences. It would be best if you were prepared for moments like this by providing food for your child minutes before they are due for the meal, ensuring that their needs are met and preventing any type of explosive reaction.

- Do not hold back when giving your child well-deserved accolades for performing a task or showing good morals. Be sure to highlight the good quality that has earned them praise specifically. If they put their dishes in the dishwasher after using them, tell them, "I see you put your dishes in the dishwasher. I appreciate that. Thank you." Tell them clearly and simply what they have done right and why you are pleased with it. When you notice your child has prevented themselves from having an explosive moment, this is the time to recognize that. "Hey, I want to say thank you for not getting upset when your friend wasn't nice to you today. You let her know you were upset but did not yell or lose control. You did a good job."

- Become familiar with positive reinforcement phrases like "You have done a good job," "Well done," "Thank you," "This is wonderful," etc. Remember that over-using these terms can make your child too familiar with them and, thus, may decrease their value. Therefore, develop new phrases from time to time to keep your child's interest.

- Avoid instilling confusion in your child as to what you expect of them. Be clear with your expectations so they can fully understand what you require of them and where you draw the line. For example, if you frown on watching television during mealtime but overlook the action when your child flouts the rule once, you might send mixed signals about what you deem acceptable.

- Avoid only giving verbal cues to reinforce positive behavior in your children; use visual cues that can serve as directions to help them remain focused on the tasks you have assigned. With consistent practice, your child will understand certain visual cues and what they mean while fulfilling obligations.

TRIGGERING PHRASES TO AVOID

Every parent has the well-being of their children at heart; you always want to be positive around them and say reassuring and encouraging things. However, children with ADHD can test your limits so much that you might get out of line and make insensitive statements that could damage your child's mental and emotional growth. Some of these phrases include:

- "Don't blame your ADHD. It's not an excuse." Truly, this diagnosis is not an excuse for lagging in certain aspects of life. However, people with this disorder, especially children, have no control over it. They struggle mentally and emotionally. They often need to be efficient in assigned tasks and complete them on time. They want to be able to pay unflinching attention and focus but cannot do so successfully because the disorder creates roadblocks. ADHD affects the ability to exert self-control, and managing hyperactive and overwhelming emotions can be just as strenuous. None of these insufficiencies is their fault. It would be insensitive to rub it squarely in their face that they are to blame for being unable to function adequately like other children.

Instead of making this statement, you can replace it with, "I understand you have ADHD, and that makes things more difficult for you. I still need you to be accountable, so how can I help?" and "What would you have done differently if given a chance to make changes?"

- "Everyone can get distracted sometimes, and you aren't any different." The reality of this statement is that while everyone can experience distraction occasionally, it is not the same with children with ADHD. They are easily distracted all the time! This statement might not necessarily imply that you are trying to make your child feel bad about their disorder, and perhaps you just do not want them ever to feel alone and different; however, you are not facing the facts. You will be giving your child a false sense of relief. Children with this diagnosis tend to get easily distracted—with friends, in school, amongst family members, and in society.

They are not like other children, which is okay; there is no stigma. Instead of making this statement, tell them that everyone in the universe has situations they struggle with, and theirs is not uncommon. Assure them that they are unique but not alone.

- "You can focus on your video games, so maybe try focusing harder on other things. It shouldn't be that hard." Children with predominantly inattentive symptoms tend to only focus on things that interest them or come with a sense of urgency. With other tasks, they might need help to apply the same focus level successfully. This is how their brain functions; they have no control over it. Telling your child that they should focus on work the same way they focus on things they find fun is like saying they had a choice but have refused to do so.

- It also means you have difficulty believing your child has a problem focusing on things and that they may be selective about tasks as an avenue to be lazy. Instead of making this horrifying statement, say, "I understand doing this work can be difficult for you. How can we break the tasks down, so they are more manageable? We will build breaks into the tasks as well."

- "You don't need to tell anyone you have ADHD. They don't need to know." You might be your child's direct caregiver, but you are not the only one leaving an imprint on your child. They have friends, schoolteachers, sports coaches, and so on that will be a part of their life whether you like it or not. How do you expect your child to get other people's support and guidance if they are private about disclosing their ADHD? If you encourage your child to keep their mouth sealed about their disorder, you will inadvertently enable others to criticize and judge them harshly. Here's another hurtful instance. Say you have a full-spirited child who is overly playful at a particular moment. You may be urged to ask if they have taken their medications to quell their hyperactive behavior. This can feel awful to a child because they were probably engaging in harmless fun, and how awful they might feel if they truly did take their meds and their parents criticized their normal childish behavior.

Making this statement does not in any way protect your child. Instead, you enable them to become vulnerable to social isolation and neglect. Having this disorder isn't something you should be ashamed of. Instead, creating awareness that they have ADHD can help people understand them better and work around it. Treating your child respectfully and coming to terms with their diagnosis is necessary when dealing with it. Especially if your child exhibits explosive behavior or acts inappropriately because of their ADHD, you may feel embarrassed about it. This could cause you to react incorrectly, especially if you are in public and want to take some of the focus away from you. However, your child is likely to recall your reactions. Therefore, to help your child, you must remember how hurtful the triggering words and actions are.

MANAGING YOUR REACTIONS

Words and phrases like "stupid," "lazy," "you should be ashamed of yourself," and "I do not care" should be erased from your vocabulary when you are dealing with your children. They can trigger self-esteem issues in your children because your words emphasize their inadequacies and incompetence. For example, imagine that your child struggles to get their schoolwork done and lags academically, so you blurt out of annoyance and frustration, "I don't understand why this is so hard for you. It's easy." Your child recoils in shame as your words echo in their head repeatedly, and the criticism hits home. They might never recover from that; at every juncture where they need to improve and overcome inattention or compulsivity, your words keep reminding them of how they are incapable of doing anything successfully. This new thought process will cripple their chances of evolving even before they have begun.

No child deserves to constantly hear criticisms from their parents about how they cannot behave like other children or how they have so much to put up with —parents are the models they revere and look up to for guidance and support. Therefore, you must learn to manage your emotions when on the verge of an outburst. Instead of focusing on their wrongdoings and always paying extra attention to their flaws, focus on the positive. For example, if your child does the dishes for the first time, focus on the newly developed sense of duty and accomplishment, and praise them for it instead of emphasizing how they didn't load the dishwasher efficiently or didn't get the dishes clean enough. Praise and teach.

Sometimes, as humans, it can be exhausting to constantly hear someone nag and complain about everything we do wrong. This can be overwhelming for children with ADHD because every feeling is heightened for them. A simple hug and a "thank you" or "you have done well; I am proud of you" is all it takes to encourage your child to do better and keep progressing. Children with ADHD are already known to be more disorganized than other children, but they are exceptional at remembering impor-tant details about subjects that excite them. As a parent, you should focus more on these strengths and find measures to help them stimulate and strengthen the things they do better.

Employ the use of humor to ease the intensity coursing through your child's veins. Making a joke can unknot your child when they are sad; it brightens their mood and helps them to feel better about negative or difficult situations. Assign tasks like writing a simple list of things that make them happy or things they want to learn about to let them explore their hobbies and other subjects that excite and stimulate their interests. They are more efficient when given tasks that allow them to discuss and express their feelings about a favorite topic. Most importantly, learn to forgive yourself.

Your child can achieve healthy growth and a fun family lifestyle. However, you are an experienced adult, and it is up to you to find strategies that help build up your relationship successfully. Offer your child immeasurable love and affection, and do not hesitate to apologize when you handle situations poorly. Whether a child with ADHD becomes a functional adult lies mostly in their caregiver's hands. Do not cause lifelong consequences through the poor management of your emotions.

5

SHOWING THE WAY

E mpathy plays a significant role in any human interaction or relationship. Every person—young and old—wants to feel heard, loved, and understood. Children with ADHD in all spheres of their lives should be empathized with just as much as they need to be capable of showing empathy. This exchange can only be made possible if you have a child who understands what empathy entails and how it can greatly impact their lives and others. The question is, what does it mean to be empathetic?

EMPATHY

Empathy is understanding someone else's feelings, including their perspective. Instead of responding, you are listening to understand other people's perceptions and imagine their feelings about the situation. For example, say your teenage daughter returns from school one day and complains to you about an argument with her best friend. Based on her story, you can already tell that your daughter is to blame for the fight. So instead of faulting her, you make statements like, "I bet that made you feel sad and disappointed." With empathy, you can experience your child's mental and emotional distress and become sensitive to it, so it is easy to console them with the right words.

What every child and adult needs during an overwhelming emotional experience is a supportive, understanding, and empathetic listener. When these traits are absent, you are most likely dealing with a narcissistic child or adult. Therefore, encouraging empathy in children with ADHD is important for a healthy family relationship and for how they interact with friends and other people.

IS YOUR ADHD CHILD UNSYMPATHETIC?

Has your child shown behavioral patterns suggesting difficulty identifying other people's feelings? Or perhaps they disregard others' feelings easily and focus too much on themselves? Children with ADHD tend to act impulsively, be hyperactive, lose interest in things, and find it difficult to concentrate for long. All of these ADHD symptoms can influence their ability to empathize. How can anyone listen attentively when it is hard to maintain focus? Or how can anyone imagine and internalize another's pain and perspective when easily distracted and impulsive? Exactly—it is going to be a struggle.

Sometimes, it is not that your child is unsympathetic. Instead, they are unaware of the demeanor they are expected to assume when other people are having a bad time. Hence, they are indifferent and unsympathetic toward people. If this nature persists in your child until adulthood, they may have difficulty maintaining close relationships with friends, and having a best friend would only be a fantasy. Likewise, being cordial with siblings and parents will also be difficult, as the absence of empathy drives a wedge through families.

This does not necessarily have to be the case. Your child can develop a strong sense of empathy. Being an empathetic child is a strength. It is beneficial to them, to you as their parent, to their siblings, and to the society they become a part of. The following tips can help your child embrace empathy and live a better life:

- Demonstrate empathy toward others. Teaching empathy has much more to do with demonstrating than merely instructing. Children tend to pick up important details when acceptable behavioral patterns are modeled.
- Express compassion, kindness, and love towards your children and other people when your children are present. They'll learn quickly.
- Do not suppress your emotions with your child. Teach them to positively express their feelings verbally and respond to them how you hope they would respond if they were in your position. If they have difficulty expressing their emotions verbally, there are other tools you can use, such as pictograms or asking them to draw a picture to attempt to explain their emotions.
- Do not ignore or belittle their emotions. Every little feeling and expression should count.
- Celebrate your child's successes, no matter how small. Do not downplay their efforts.

- Teach your child to identify feelings. For example, what gives sad people away? What kind of facial expressions do they make? How can your child become sensitive around them and empathize? Teach them the negative impressions they leave when unaware of how their actions affect others. That is, create awareness.
- Teach them to bounce back from adversities and become stronger. Resilience helps to build empathy in children; therefore, they need to learn how to be good problem-solvers. This does not mean ignoring their feelings just to move past them. Instead, they need to be taught how to recognize their feelings and manage and resolve them.
- Explain to your child that there are different kinds of people in the world with varying belief systems, cultures, lifestyles, and faiths. Teach them that everyone is unique in their way and that no one should be segregated. Every individual deserves love, compassion, and empathy.
- Be patient. It is going to be more than a one-day job. You will have to exercise lots of patience to establish and sustain empathy in your child. Work together as a family.
- It is okay to seek help when you feel lost about what to do and how to handle your child with ADHD. Seek professional help or join support groups.

STAYING POSITIVE

It is becoming increasingly difficult for the average person to maintain a positive outlook on life. Everyone has hurdles they need to overcome on an almost daily basis. So many factors can test your resolve, and it is only human to respond accordingly.

Now, imagine what that feels like for people—especially children —with ADHD. As a parent, if you also have ADHD, praise you as you understand their struggles. You have to manage a home and care for children who likely have the disorder and can get out of hand. You are also on the verge of losing it, yet you must maintain positivity, peace, and order around the house. That's a god-level ability.

There are lots of methods to help you maintain positivity in the house and also simplify its impact on you as a parent:

- Put your well-being at the top of your list of priorities. An African proverb says it takes a fed, refreshed horse to help humans travel farther. The horse will only make it very far if it is sufficiently fed and refreshed. In a metaphorical sense, you are your child's horse, saddled with the responsibility to love and care for them and to see them through each stage of development and growth —with or without ADHD. Regardless of these overwhelming tasks, it would be best to learn ways to control your temper and withhold negative outbursts that could negatively influence your child. Schedule thirty minutes or an hour of your day for personal time and take a break to be alone. Meditate often and tap into nature to help you feel refreshed and enable a positive mindset.
- Work together as a family. Keeping peace and order in the home should be more than your responsibility; it can become overwhelming over time. Instead, break down tasks and split them up amongst your children and

partner. Let your children clean their rooms and pick up their toys and dirty laundry so you can create time to organize your workspace. This way, it is manageable. Your child's age should be considered, as you do not want to overwhelm them either. Set a daily schedule for what tasks should be completed and when. You can make this fun by turning it into a family game with a reward. For example, the fastest person to complete a task in a neat and organized manner could win a prize.

- Encourage family events that strengthen bonds. Bonding is an essential factor that influences healthy growth in families and helps to enhance positivity. For example, you can introduce a family bonding weekly event such as going on a nature walk, growing a garden together, or playing an interactive game where there is plenty to keep a child with ADHD focused. Also, children with ADHD may be able to focus for hours when it comes to their passions. There may be bonding activities that can be built around those pastimes that the whole family will like. For children with ADHD, family-sharing opportunities help them express themselves positively and mentally note the tasks they must commit to the following week.
- For some activities, using a timer will also let a child with ADHD know how long the activity will take. More frequent activities with shorter times attached to them can be beneficial for children who lose focus easily.
- Have fun. In everything you do as a family, have fun. Young children naturally radiate energy, and children with ADHD are over the top. You should help them

channel these energy surges into activities that benefit them. Make sure you have fun things to look forward to as a family rather than repetitive daily tasks and chores. Put something new and fun on the calendar for you and your children. These events are the sparks your family needs to keep positivity stirring in the air.

FORGIVE IGNORANCE

People can be illogical, judgmental, unreasonable, and ignorant of certain things. However, it would help if you forgave them when they hurt you as long as you understand that your ability to exercise forgiveness liberates and brings you peace to move on with life. Forgiveness does not imply that you excuse the emotional hurt from being misjudged. It simply shows that you are one step ahead. With ADHD, your child is bound to face certain challenges, like having difficulty making friends and sustaining friendships. Regardless, children must be amongst their peers and engage in social activities. This is why you need to take extra measures to ensure your child learns to explain their disorder to their friends. Moreover, with people older than they are, make it your duty to intercede on their behalf.

Say you are at a store with your child, and they ask for a toy. After you refuse this request, your child goes into a full-on meltdown and eventually even starts to grab things off the shelves and throw them. Now you have other parents staring at you and possibly judging you. They do not understand what your child is going through, and their judgment should not affect your parenting style. Even in public, you should be able to come down to your child's level and work with them to calm their nerves, just as you would at home.

Most times, people tend to judge what they do not understand properly. Therefore, it is important that the people around your child—including family, friends, and teachers—are aware of their disorder; make sure to be open about the diagnosis. This makes it easier for people to understand why your child might be slightly different from other children and to show empathy toward them.

There are ways you can enlighten friends, family, and acquaintances who are a part of your child's life about what ADHD is and how it influences certain behavioral patterns in your child. Remember that enlightenment might not necessarily guarantee your child will be understood; some people might never be able to grasp the concept of ADHD. They might even begin to question certain things and hurt your feelings or your child's; this is ignorance. You must learn to forgive such people and continue enlightening them when you can. Some tips for doing so include:

- Make a script. Every human being has different and varying confidence levels regarding verbal expression, especially with delicate matters. If you think you might have difficulty explaining ADHD correctly to people without omitting important details, you should write a script for how you want the conversation to play out. Practice and perfect the sentences to help you build enough confidence for the conversation.
- Be positive when relaying information. In the process of enlightening people, you should avoid sounding overly assertive. Instead, you should embody positivity and

communicate your gratitude for the person's presence in your child's life and for their role. This way, you have established a good foundation for them to empathize with your child when you share information about their disorder.

- Explain your child's diagnosis as specifically as you can. Be certain about your child's predominant symptoms and how they compare to neurotypical children, and state the differences. Some children with ADHD undergo behavioral treatments or medications, while others might have a combination. Therefore, whatever treatment has been administered by the pediatrician or specialist for your child's disorder, ensure that you enlighten others properly. If you have goals to help your child lead a much more fulfilling life, you can also share those. Some friends and family might be interested in helping you actualize some of these goals. Please encourage them to ask questions and provide substantial answers to them. This way, you can learn what issues your loved ones have no idea about and help them to understand.

- Show support to your child's teachers. Since your child spends most of their day within the four walls of the school and the remaining hours of the day in the house, you can be sure their teachers are just as overwhelmed by their hyperactivity as you are. Not every teacher understands the influences and impact of ADHD on children. Your child might become difficult to manage. Therefore, when your child's teacher brings to your knowledge how hard it is to keep your child reined, be ready to partner with them. Ensure that the line of communication is always open and that you are always ready to share strategies for alleviating their concern and managing your child's behavior in school.

- Maintain some distance from those who are unsupportive. Truly, to forgive is divine. Sometimes you are better off not being in contact with people who are hell-bent on failing to see the bright side of the situation. Some family members and friends may never get on board with your child's ADHD diagnosis; they may even make derogatory statements to hurt your and your child's feelings. Understand that it is important to forgive them to avoid the emotional burden, but do not keep them in close contact. ADHD is not the end of your child's life; they can thrive like every other neurotypical child. You do not need to be in contact with unsupportive people.

Showing your child ways to react appropriately in situations is the best method that you can use to help them to succeed in life. When you show them how to interact with people, it can help them understand appropriate behaviors. For some children with ADHD, especially if they have explosive behavior issues, it can require additional work and conversations to help them understand that the way they sometimes react isn't their fault. But, even when it is not their fault, it doesn't mean they can't learn coping methods to help improve things in the future. There are many different avenues that you can take to show your children the best ways to react to situations. In addition to the explanations above, talking out issues as well as role-playing scenarios can also be effective.

6

ADHD ADVOCACY

C hildren will thrive under most circumstances. However, if they are struggling, chances are there is an obstacle hindering their success despite their efforts. These obstacles must be addressed, and you can do so by advocating for your child's needs. In addition, advocacy creates greater awareness, which can help your child and others who are just as easily misunderstood due to their disorder. As ADHD presents differently in each individual and cannot be diagnosed with a simple test, it can be more trying to advocate effectively. It can be even more complicated if the child has behavioral and emotional issues. With these issues, it can be more challenging to pinpoint the underlying causes and deal with them. Since you cannot always be with your child, you need to advocate for them so that other adults can support them when they cannot independently regulate their emotions and behaviors.

ADVOCATING FOR YOUR CHILD WITH ADHD

As a parent, you can imagine your child's struggle when they must work twice as hard to succeed compared to neurotypical children. Often, even when given the same learning opportunities, children with ADHD have greater difficulty achieving the same level of success as other children. This produces a lot of mental and physical stress on children with ADHD, and older children may even suffer from occasional emotional breakdowns. Other times, they can be subjected to bullying. People who are ignorant of the disorder's impact call them clumsy, badly behaved, annoying, lousy, and other negative terms. As a result, children may carry the stigma on for most of their lives and never recover. Advocacy can help address such ignorance and eradicate the chances of lifelong implications for your child.

Advocating for your child with ADHD should be done in the home, school, doctor's office, and community. These are places your child's life revolves around and where they will come into contact with people from all walks of life with different perspectives on ADHD and other disorders.

HOW TO ADVOCATE EFFECTIVELY

Naturally, you want to give your child the best home, school, and community support. You may worry that you can only do your best within the confines of the home and a little when it comes to advocating in the community. School, however, might seem out of your jurisdiction, as teachers are equipped to do their jobs. There is a lot you can do as an effective advocate in every aspect of your child's life. The following are some measures to take into consideration during the process:

- Keep an open line of communication with your child. The effectiveness of healthy communication cannot be overstated. Children tend to excel academically, function better amongst their peers, and make healthier choices when they have a warm and healthy relationship with their parents. Direct ice-breaking questions like, "what part of school do you enjoy the most?" "What is your favorite thing to do?" and "What is your least favorite subject in school?" should be asked regularly if you aim to help your child overcome primary school challenges.
- Identify how your child's behaviors at home and in school are different. Your child spends up to six hours in school, and chances are the teacher knows how they function in this setting. Consistently, but not too frequently, contact the teacher for information and updates on your child's strengths and weaknesses. Get comfortable asking their teacher how well they function, deal with being organized, and stay focused on their assigned tasks. Inquire about their social behavior: Do they get along well with other children? Are there situations of violence? Etc. This information will help you become an effective advocate for your child.
- Get support for your child as soon as you can. Be sure to take action on significant matters that concern your child before the school organizes a parent-teacher conference. Request a comprehensive evaluation of your child's academic, cognitive, social, and emotional functioning in

the school. The teacher should give a personal perspective on your child's progress over time, as federal law requires special education services for children with ADHD and other disorders. This provides them with the same learning opportunities as their peers to fulfill their potential; the school is expected to take measures to ensure the implementation of this requirement.

- Meet the people who evaluate your child. Most schools provide a written evaluation of a child; your child's school should not be any different. Those who will evaluate your child must make decisions in that regard. The results should be discussed so you can decipher whether the basic educational objectives are being met. Request an independent one if you realize they are not being met or that certain things need to be changed or adjusted during the evaluation.

- Be sensitive to your child's moods. Being diagnosed with ADHD as a child is very challenging. Children rarely have it easy in any aspect of their lives. A large number of these children also have dyslexia and can potentially develop depression over time when they become adults. Therefore, one of the best ways to support your child is to be sensitive to their moods and emotions. Parental instincts should be trusted when concerned about your children's well-being. Do not brush aside the small voice that points out something different about your child's behavior. You can confidently say you know your child well enough because you have spent years raising them and understanding their behavioral patterns. So, when you pay extra attention to those moments when their moods falter due to a change in their environment, issues at school with a decline in grades, or disagreement with friends, you will know how to empathize and take action to help them become better.

- Become familiar with the Individual Education Plan (IEP). In order to effectively advocate for your child with ADHD, you must understand what the IEP process entails and how it can benefit them. The education plan is created by the parents, teachers, and experts on special education, amongst others. It serves the purpose of considering a child's specific needs and outlining curricula with goals that aid the child's success academically. With the plan, you can easily monitor your child's progress and assess whether your child is meeting the required practical goals and how much support you can give to simplify things.

TIPS

Most children with ADHD are constantly subjected to stigma in school environments and the community. Even though they are problematic and unfair, these stigmas still exist, and children can become victims. People tend to make judgments and say unfair things, whether to your child's face or behind your back, without any consideration for conversations with you that could enlighten them further. Research has shown that there are parents who prevent their children from associating with children who exhibit hyperactivity and impulsiveness because they find the behaviors non-conforming and do not want their children influenced negatively. These stigmas do the community a great disservice, and your child might be subjected to them at some point.

The following are practical tips that can help to prevent or lessen the implications of unfair treatment and stigmas on your child:

- Be educated on the benefits of reducing stigma. Knowledge is power. You need to gain basic knowledge to know how to impact something positively. Taking on a big role, such as being an advocate for ADHD, requires a vast knowledge base to help your child and reduce stigmas in the important areas of any child's life. Most parents of children with ADHD often complain and become overwhelmed by the intensity of their child's behavior and how they can be very difficult to manage around the house. You can easily tell from how upset they are that they have little knowledge of how ADHD works. Until they can transcend that ignorance, they might never be able to understand, let alone advocate for ADHD. Sometimes, having significant knowledge is all it takes to effect the big change you want in your child's life.
- Pursue behavioral parent training. Being a parent to children with ADHD already guarantees that you are saddled with great responsibility, including caring for the child and advocating for their disorder. One of the most effective ways to handle children with ADHD and ensure improvement is through behavioral management techniques. It is also important for teachers who are academically responsible for children within that age

range to provide behavior management techniques to help improve the lives of children with ADHD.

- Participate in the school system. The baseline for this tip is to become acquainted with the basic knowledge of what ADHD entails more than anyone else because you have to care for a child with ADHD. It is strongly recommended that you consider being a volunteer in your child's classroom, even if it is just once or twice a month. Doing so will help you understand what the teacher expects of the children and how you can reinforce the same expectations in the home. This way, you can easily strike a balance in the behavioral consistency of your child in school and at home.

- Seek help from your community. It always helps to know what professionals or organizations you can contact in the community for advice and learn the rights and policies surrounding advocacy. Every school, workplace, and community has a distinctive language for how things operate; if you need help understanding the language, you might have difficulty being an advocate. In every community you hope to advocate, ensure you know "who is who" and "what is what."

- Be observant and learn to convey expectations. Often, people's actions will not align with your expectations if you do not communicate them. If your child's school is not enlightened on ADHD or what you expect of them concerning your child, potential challenges could arise. See your child's teachers as members of your advocacy team, and work with them for your child's progress and improvement—do not work against them. Take your time observing how your child functions in the school environment to serve as a pointer to how they can be managed in the house and vice versa. Your child, despite being young, is not always innocent. Sometimes, children tend to cook up lies against their teachers because they are not allowed to have their way. You must observe keenly without prejudice and convey your expectations for every community in which you advocate.

TEACHING YOUR CHILD SELF-ADVOCACY

Self-advocacy is a skill that every child with ADHD or any other kind of disorder needs to learn. Your child will mature as they grow and reach new developmental stages. With maturity comes responsibility and, most importantly, the need to advocate for themselves. Self-advocacy increases children's potential for life-long success, and parents constantly underestimate its importance. The fact that you now understand the importance of helping your child self-advocate indicates that you are willing to help them hone it as a life skill and learn the strategies they need to succeed in every aspect of life, now and in the future. The following are invaluable pointers to kick-start the process of helping your child develop self-advocacy skills:

- Begin at an early stage. Children are very sensitive; your child might constantly be reminded that they talk too much, ask too many questions, or are not well-behaved. The reactions they get from teachers and their peers might spark negative feelings, so you need to reassure them when they are still young and impressionable. Make them understand that teachers will always respect active learners and have no problem helping all students, irrespective of their learning styles.

- Instill self-awareness. Your child should have an in-depth understanding of their strengths and deficits. Encouraging self-awareness helps your child understand what is at stake and how to improve to lead a better lifestyle. Your child should never feel alone or alienated from their peers because they have no idea how to advocate for themselves. You should help them learn how to seek help positively. Reinforce that with the use of a polite and positive attitude and advocacy can yield favorable outcomes. For practical purposes, use role-playing to perform situations that may seem uncomfortable or impossible for your child to get past. This way, they can apply the same approach in real-life situations and overcome fear and insecurity.

- Stay positive. Positivity drives most of life's successes. Provide vivid examples of people with learning differences who have made it to the top through positive self-talk and the determination to prevail. Your child should understand that learning differences have nothing to do with their intelligence or capabilities.

- Build self-esteem. To guarantee successful self-advocacy, your child needs to be free of low self-esteem and, instead, radiate confidence. It is impossible to advocate for yourself when you do not feel best. Therefore, if you have caught your child doing something right or extraordinary, do not hesitate to praise the effort they put into completing it.

- Support critical thinking. It would be best if you always created avenues for your child to develop the act of thinking critically, especially in non-confrontational situations. Help your child to develop strengths and address weaknesses so that when faced with situations in which you are not there to advocate for them, they can confidently speak for themselves.

- Make plans for the future. It is one thing to help your child live through the present; it is another to help them prepare adequately for the future. Children are constantly experiencing growth and development in every aspect of life. With ADHD, they must be prepared for real-life situations like summer school, internships, college, applying for jobs, etc. Since they will most likely be away from your direct guidance, you must prepare them for the transition.

A WELCOME BREAK

"Only by giving are you able to receive more than you already have"

— REV. JESSE JACKSON

Let's take a break.

It feels good, doesn't it? Just a moment to take a breath without taking in any new information or having to handle a situation with the kids.

You probably don't get many of these moments... Not many parents of children with ADHD do. So it's important that you *do* give yourself a break – both in terms of how much you expect of yourself, and in the practical sense. Those advocacy tips in Chapter 6 are important... remember that advocating for your child is another way to show them that they are not alone in their diagnosis.

Take a moment, too, to acknowledge the extra work you're putting in to help your child and your own journey as a parent. You don't have a lot of time, but you're here now, with this book. Don't be hard on yourself if you can't read the whole thing. Your life is full, and you're doing everything you can.

Nonetheless, if you'd like to make this break last a moment longer, you have a glorious opportunity to help out other parents of children with ADHD.

By leaving a review of this book on Amazon, you'll help other parents who are looking for this guidance to find it quickly and easily.

No matter how much you've read, sharing how it has helped you and what information you've found here will signpost to other new readers with limited time and energy where they can find the help they're looking for. You're doing an amazing job. Thank you for helping me to make sure other parents know they are too.

If you are in the UK, please scan the QR code below to leave your review.

If you are in the US, please scan the QR code below to leave your review.

7

MANAGING ADHD AT HOME

P arenting on its own is a tedious task that demands patience and a great deal of sacrifice. Given how taxing parenting already is, raising a child with ADHD requires even more effort. The normal ways and routines you need to organize in the home are different and form unique routines. The degree of adjustments you must make to give your child a secure home environment depends on the type and severity of your child's symptoms. This means you must adopt different strategies or approaches to find what works the best and gives your child a quality living experience despite their symptoms.

Managing a child with ADHD in the home setting comes with a whole lot of changes. Understandably, there are several points at which your natural strength falters. In addition, the entire process can become more frustrating to cope with than you had anticipated when dealing with some of the behaviors which result from your child's ADHD, but rest assured, there are helpful approaches you can adopt to make life easier both for you and your child.

The first step starts with accepting and understanding your child's disorder. We talked about these in previous chapters, but going over some of the points raised earlier will offer keener insights on this particular topic, especially concerning how you, as a loving parent, can recognize the symptoms and behaviors in your child and better understand their actions and how to respond.

If their disorder was not diagnosed, most people might assume a child with ADHD is lazy, stubborn, and rebellious. However, suppose the child has explosive behaviors as part of their ADHD symptoms. In that case, other people's perceptions of them can be even worse as explosive behaviors result in meltdowns and outbursts at some of the most minor things. As a result, they may resort to lashing out harshly at the child or berating them emotionally. Such an ignorant approach would destroy the child's self-esteem and damage your relationship with them because they would withdraw and feel unsafe with you.

This is why it is necessary to recognize the child's ADHD and know that this influences their behavior and actions. With this knowledge, you can learn helpful ways to modify your home environment conducive to the child's growth and regulate your emotional responses to be more accommodating. So, understanding that this disorder and its accompanying symptoms make children act in ways that are hard for parents to manage will give you one less headache to fret over.

Your child with ADHD can still learn important life lessons and get the same education as other children their age. However, this means you must develop a different, better, kinder, and softer way of parenting the child. Your job as a parent now falls under providing an environment and structures that prevent the child from hurting themselves based on their impulsiveness and help them complete expected tasks successfully, have meaningful interactions, and build relationships with others.

THE IMPORTANCE OF STRUCTURE AND ROUTINE IN MANAGING ADHD AT HOME

We know that parents contribute a large percentage to the child's development in our society. If you are now parenting a child with ADHD, you will have to modify your behavior and learn to manage your child's behavior to foster their development. You will also need to adjust the home environment, enact certain routines and systems limiting your child's destructive behavior, and encourage your child to overcome self-doubt and develop confidence and self-esteem.

Children with ADHD generally have deficits in executive function. This means they do not possess the ability to think and plan, organize, control impulses, and complete tasks. Their attention span is low, and they are prone to rash and impulsive actions and hardly focus on tasks. Having to cope with these behavioral inconsistencies from your child as a parent is stressful and tiring. However, setting up an efficient structure in the form of consistent routines and house rules will help achieve two key things—reducing the stressful moments you have to endure and shaping the behavior of your child with ADHD. You and your child get the best out of this arrangement, and it also improves your relationship with them.

The many benefits of a structured environment for your child must be considered. First, knowing what to expect brings a sense of security and safety. This is what you get from establishing routines. It helps your child feel safe, and in that cocoon of safety, the child can now develop life skills, build healthy habits, and improve their interactions and relations with those around them.

Setting up a good routine offers safety and predictability in their daily life, teaches the child to manage time better, and gives them the confidence to perform their daily tasks effectively. This creates structure, helps them be more productive and disciplined, and develops good habits.

For you as a parent, routines would help reduce the stress you have had to deal with and alleviate the accompanying anxiety. As a result, you can find time for other enjoyable activities.

Below are some of the benefits routines can have for your child:

- Allows the child to develop positive habits: This can be traced to the fact that developing a habit takes practice and repetition; the more you practice something, the longer it stays with you and becomes part of you. So, providing your child with a routine will allow them to learn positive habits.
- Improves the ability to handle tasks: Many children can structure their chores, schedules, and activities, but such a seemingly easy feat is not the same for a child with

ADHD. Handling duties and activities becomes more complex because of how the disorder impairs their ability to be organized. With a set routine, you can guide your child through the activities they should carry out until they learn to perform them independently.

- Alleviates parents' stress and exhaustion: With a routine, the family becomes more organized and has time freed up for fun and enjoyable activities. This gives parents and children a healthy opportunity to bond, play, relax, or be creative.
- Inspires a sense of responsibility in children: A routine instills a sense of responsibility in children because they know what they need to do and when to do it. Knowing their duty, chore, or activity, they set off to do it. This can be incentivized with a reward system.
- Provides external control: The symptoms of ADHD lead to problems with self-control since the child is prone to impulsive behavior and cannot plan analytically or think ahead. Setting up a routine or structure will provide your child with a structured life and help them manage their symptoms successfully.
- Reduces conflicts: Another benefit of structures is that they help parents to regulate their emotional responses to the behavior of the child, lessen the arguments, anxiety, and family stress that would have ensued, and at the same time, improve the child's behavior.
- Creates a feeling of inclusion: When there is a structure in the home, and everyone is obligated to adhere to the routine, this will reduce the chances that your child will feel left out. Having uniformity from other family

members makes the child with ADHD more willing and eager to participate in the structured arrangement.

- Establishes a blueprint for success: By establishing routines, positive reinforcements, and reward systems, the child's confidence in their abilities grows, and this lays the foundation for more remarkable success and motivates them to develop skills. These successes replace their misconceptions about themselves, such as being disorganized, forgetful, or incompetent.

TIPS TO START A HEALTHY ROUTINE FOR YOUR CHILD

Outlined below are simple measures that you can take to help your child develop a healthy routine.

- Organize your home. Your home must be organized because having too much clutter can cause many distractions. Also, it would reflect that you do not have things under control, and the child would notice and imitate this. Keeping your home organized provides order that a child can follow. Aside from decluttering spaces and keeping things in their rightful place, you can also establish rituals around meals, homework, playtime, and bedtime.
- Involve the children in planning the routine. When children are involved in planning a schedule, they are more likely to adhere to it because of the sense of responsibility and accountability it bestows them. With input from the children, you can make the routine easy to

follow, which is an effective way to help children stick to the schedule.

- Use pictures and visual cues. Children are naturally captivated by pictures. You can gain the attention and compliance of your children by using photos when making a schedule.
- Use checklists to help your child stay on task. A checklist enforces the feeling of accomplishment in children because they can easily monitor their progress and have pride in it. It also allows the children to stay focused until completing a task. Completing tasks will also give your child a natural dopamine boost. *Dopamine* is a neurotransmitter that acts as a happy booster. People with ADHD frequently need to increase their dopamine levels as they are not as high in their brains. Often small things like finishing a task can help provide the dopamine the brain needs. Breaking tasks into smaller completable tasks can therefore make the brain even happier.
- Use a timer for daily tasks. The use of timers helps curtail distractions and keep the child focused. Set timers only for a short period because too much time leaves room for your child to become distracted. Your timers can be set for five minutes to ensure your child stays immersed in the task.
- Include breaks. Because it is harder for children with ADHD to stay focused on a task over a long period, frequent breaks are essential. Break up study sessions into shorter periods and tasks into manageable pieces.
- Limit electronic distractions. Children with ADHD are easily susceptible to distractions, including electronics

like television, video games, phones, and the computer. These devices encourage impulsive behavior, and children's exposure to them should be monitored and regulated.

- Encourage regular exercise. Research has shown that physical activity burns excess energy in healthy ways and can also help a child focus their attention. Having your child exercise regularly is an effective way to reduce impulsiveness and improve concentration.

- Set clear expectations. You must talk with your child and explain how you expect them to behave. Let them understand which behaviors are acceptable and which are not.

- Stick to the schedule and routine but allow some flexibility. It would be best if you were flexible with your child. Remember that children with ADHD do not adapt to change as quickly as others, so you must exercise patience and offer room for flexibility.

- Encourage communication with your child, both verbally and through pictographs, depending on what they respond to best. There could be days when it is impossible to stick to the routine. If you can prepare your child for this in advance, it can help them. For example, if you know that your child has a medical appointment and instead of having lunch at noon, you have to have it at eleven and then prepare to leave for the appointment. You can let your child know earlier in the day that there will be a change to the typical routine so you can try to prepare them. Adaptations to your approach will likely be required depending on your child and how they adapt to time and a routine.

- By reinforcing your child's routine, you can help them learn that some days will not go as planned. Continually reinforcing this with your child can help them to learn that adapting will be necessary. You are doing your child an injustice if you only provide them with a routine that goes according to plan. Life does not work that way, and children must be able to adapt to unplanned changes. If your child has explosive behavior, changes in routines could cause outbursts or tantrums, but by continuing to work with them, you can defuse these behaviors before they occur.

Also note that when you start creating structure and a daily routine, especially if you have never had it before, the child may initially resist and protest against it. Still, it would help if you stuck with it while being patient yet firm; eventually, they will adjust and adopt the routine.

- Manage your own emotions. As a parent, you must learn to manage your emotions and keep yourself in check. This is important because you cannot help an impulsive child if you are easily aggravated. You must remain composed and controlled during an outburst if you expect your child also to pick up such healthy habits.

Thus, if you begin to feel angry or frustrated and feel like lashing out, remember that your child did not choose his disorder. Do not be harmful in your criticism or berate your child for mistakes or impulse behavior.

- Manage your child's emotions. Dealing with the emotional outbursts of children with ADHD can be very challenging. You must understand, firstly, though, that children with ADHD experience the same emotions as other children. However, their disorder makes their feelings more frequent, intense, and longer-lasting. Their ability to manage their emotions is affected by ADHD, and as a result of emotional dysregulation, their well-being, and success are equally affected. This also contributes to low self-esteem and social difficulties.
- Use tools such as diagrams with emotions on them to try and determine how your child is feeling. Emotional dysregulation is common in children with ADHD, but they will also experience normal emotions. Therefore, determining the underlying causes of your child's actions and emotions is essential. Working with your child to comprehend their emotions is a must. You need to see if the emotion results from their emotional dysregulation. It may also be actual sadness or anger caused by a situation. Your assessment can help your child to work through the situation. Especially if your child has explosive behavior, which causes them to lash out, it can be even more important to understand if a meltdown is the cause of overstimulation or frustration they cannot express or an underlying emotion that needs to be felt and worked through.

To help them overcome these challenges, you must help them practice gratitude and direct their attention to emotionally rewarding activities. These activities make them feel good, build a sense of pride, and increase self-esteem. When a child's self-esteem is improved, their interactions and relations with others also improve.

- Give praise and rewards. You must learn to praise and reward your child's efforts—especially when rules are followed. This is how you enforce positive behavior.

Children with ADHD often receive heavy criticism, which badly impacts their self-esteem. If you want to help your child learn and adopt positive behavior, you can start by offering kind words, hugs, or small prizes for good behavior or when they reach small goals. This motivates them to do more and increases their self-esteem and success rate.

It is also essential that all parents are committed to the routine and the plan that is placed to help their child succeed. If only one parent is committed, it can derail the other parent's efforts. This can apply in a family where the parents are together or apart. The most important thing is providing the best environment and support to a child so that they can thrive even though their ADHD comes with numerous challenges for both child and parent.

8

ADHD IN THE CLASSROOM

ADHD not only affects your child's ability to concentrate, remember, and pay attention, but it might also affect their ability to make and keep friends in school. All these factors can make you worried, and you might be concerned about how your children will cope in a regular school without being able to concentrate or with being constantly hyperactive all the time. Moreover, you are worried about how your child will enjoy going through school without having friends to play with. Worrying about this is valid, mainly because these are all critical factors that need to be addressed for your child to have the best learning experience.

If you send your child to school without prior preparation, then the chances of them having a successful school life will be low. This includes preparing your child for how to manage themselves in school and preparing yourself to be actively involved in your child's life by preparing the teachers and school authorities. This preparation will give your child a better quality of life in school by helping them to fit in completely.

School can be a major adjustment for any child, and that comes with numerous adaptations. For a child with ADHD, it can be even more difficult as school requires a lot of sitting and concentration that they likely do not have, especially if the subject is not something they are passionate about. If the child has explosive behaviors as part of their ADHD symptoms, it can be even more difficult as it can lead to lashing out or having a meltdown in the classroom or on the playground. Working on coping mechanisms at home are important because they can help the child wherever they are. You also need your child to be aware that you will not be with them at school but that they can still use the methods you have shown them. You also need to prepare the school for your child's attendance. There could also be days when your child does not go to school or must return home early because of a meltdown or being uncontrollable. Especially in the beginning, while your child builds a relationship with the teacher and trusts them for help when it comes to defusing a situation, they may be resistant to having anything to do with the teacher when they are having a difficult time regulating their emotions and behavior. Through trial and error, and the experiences that you and other teachers have had with your child, you can develop a plan to help your child and the school manage as best as possible. With each new school year, you should be prepared to speak with the professionals who will be with your child to try and create smooth transitions. Each school year also brings new routines for the child, which can take time to adapt.

MANAGING ADHD AT SCHOOL

Managing ADHD at school is always a cause for concern for parents who have children with this disorder. Although ADHD is a lifelong disorder, your child can still have a great school life if you manage it adequately.

To manage ADHD at school and create your best chance for success, you should do the following:

- Be consistent in your expectations. Consistency serves as a good safeguard against ADHD symptoms. Consistent rules and activities can help your child ease into daily school life. Everything in school should be concise enough for them to understand.
- Limit distractions. Children with ADHD do not perform well with distractions. They must be kept on the side of the class that is void of excessive diversions. They must be seated at the front of the class or in any area with no windows or doors, which can distract them.
- Provide frequent feedback. Every child needs feedback when learning, which is even more critical for ADHD children. If they exhibit improper behavior, appropriate feedback should be given; a reward should follow if they do what is right.
- Reward them. When you reward a child with ADHD for their good behavior or for achieving set milestones, it will encourage them to continue exhibiting that good behavior. The reward you give them should be based on the things in which your child has a deep interest.

- Give breaks. ADHD children might find it challenging to focus on learning for a lengthy period. You might catch their attention drifting to several places if it becomes too long. If you want to manage them in school and keep them focused on the task, give them breaks that will allow them to get active a little before concentrating.
- Use flexibility. If you are too rigid with a child with ADHD, you might not achieve good results. Be flexible in handling them and make some exceptions in challenging situations. You can let them hold stress balls to help them pay attention in school while pinching and squeezing.
- Avoid drowning them in schoolwork. This is counterproductive in managing the disorder. If you soak them in schoolwork, they will easily be distracted and turn towards procrastination or unhealthy outbursts of emotion. It would be best if you looked into breaking large tasks into smaller ones so they can finish quicker. If your child struggles with homework (most children with ADHD do) do not cause yourself more grief by forcing it upon your child. Find ways to be creative with it but if it becomes too much, involve the teacher to see what else can be done. The task of homework is not worth sacrificing your relationship with your child.
- Create supportive measures for them. Every child with ADHD needs support in the classroom. Having support not only includes adults but could also include fellow students. A fellow student can be an excellent support since peers tend to understand each other better. As you pair a child who has ADHD with a child who does not struggle as much, it will help them to be less distracted

and also remember pending tasks. These benefits can also lead to the blooming of a new friendship.

- In creating a plan for your child with the teacher, also be prepared to discuss appropriate discipline for your child. Oftentimes teachers will take away recess if the child misbehaves, but recess is the one time each day when a child can get their energy and wiggles out. Other disciplines should be proposed to ensure that the discipline/punishment is appropriate and can be tied to the child's behavior. Recess should never be taken away for a child with ADHD (unless there are safety issues). Instead of teaching the child how to cope with their behavior, this would actually be making their day worse and potentially causing more disruption during the day by not allowing them to get their energy out. Taking away school trips or rewards in the classroom can also be a detriment for the child. Feeling singled out or different from their classmates can lead to resentment and escalate bad behaviors. Adaptations are always required on both sides to create the best teaching environment for the child and the other students. However, how the situation will affect the child should always be a main concern for everyone involved.

SPEAKING TO THE SCHOOL ABOUT YOUR CHILD'S BEHAVIOR

ADHD problems might not manifest in your child's behavior until they begin school. However, once they start school, you must be prepared to work alongside the school to manage their disorder so their potential can be maximized.

While your child is at school, you will not be with them the majority of the time. So, informing the school about your child's disorder is imperative. If you do not tell them, they will not know and will not give your child the support required to manage the disorder. The following sections discuss how you can ensure your child's school understands their needs.

Especially if your child has explosive behaviors as part of their ADHD symptoms, you need to explain to your child's teacher(s) what that means and how it affects your child. The key to defusing the behaviors is to ensure that everyone is prepared for what could happen. As a parent, you may have keywords or actions that you do to help your child through their explosive behaviors. Sharing these with the teacher(s) is necessary, so your child can get the support they need even when you are not present.

I have a personal experience that I want to share with you so that you know how important this communication is. My son started at a new school, and I did not inform the teachers of the techniques we use when he is upset. He did not want to get out of the car that day for school while his dad was dropping him off. They pulled out of the drop off line, and my son began hitting his dad.

His dad got out of the car, and my son followed. Some teachers saw what was happening and came over. My son was really upset and walked off. He started walking in the grass, and the school could not get him to come back. He was not walking somewhere unsafe, but they felt they needed help. A school officer was there, so he came over to help. My husband called me, and I drove to the school. I had to explain to the school that I had been teaching him to remove himself from a situation if it became overwhelming. He was trying to do that, but without knowing that information, they felt he was being unsafe. After talking to my son for a few minutes, I was able to get him to agree to go with the counselor to calm down and talk about what happened. When I asked him why he would not go with the teachers before I got there, he did not want his classmates to see how upset he was. When I talked to him, I suggested meeting with the counselor to calm down before he went to his classroom. Sharing these techniques with the school would have prevented the situation from getting out of hand.

Be Enlightened

If you are unfamiliar with the laws protecting your child, how are you supposed to advocate to the school to understand what your child needs? Do your research and find out what works for your child. There are three main things for you to know that will help you give your child the best experience:

- Your child's rights.
- The support available in your child's school.
- How to prepare the school for your child's resumption.

Your Child's Rights

A behavioral plan should be created with the input of any child with ADHD. The teachers, parents, and the child should collaborate on this plan and determine the types of behavior that are unacceptable in a classroom and those that are helpful. There should be agreed-upon consequences so there are no surprises for the child or the parent. Staying in communication with the teacher is vital. Good reports are just as powerful as the ones that are not so positive.

You may be unaware that government policies protect children with disabilities at school. These laws can be found in the Individuals with Disabilities Act (IDEA) of 1975 and the Rehabilitation Act of 1973, section 504. They require that schools provide services to support the learning experience of children with disabilities. Check out my upcoming book that provides parents with clear explanation of an IEP and 504, what rights you have, what rights your child has and how to ensure you get the most of plans.

There are two plans that the government offers to the parents of children living with disabilities. These plans help the parents express the needs of the child to the school:

- Individualized education plan
- 504 plan

Individualized Education Plan (IEP)

As the name suggests, an IEP is tailored to a child's individual needs. This plan allows your child to learn alone or in smaller groups. This plan is ideal for children with different learning needs and varying learning expectations. It is also beneficial for a child that finds it hard to regulate their emotions most of the time.

This plan is very clear about the needs of the child. In addition, this plan details the child's needs to the school. However, detailing the plan to the school is not enough for a child needing special care, the plan explains the services the school will be rendering to the child. The plan also describes how the child's progress will be measured and allows the school and parents to keep track.

Having a solid IEP in place can help alleviate specific behavioral issues. If there is appropriate support, this could help your child feel less frustrated and even perform better and reduce outbursts.

504 Plan

This plan is tailored for children who have a disability but can keep up with the regular curriculum in a regular class. In addition, this option is for people whose children have little control over their emotions and impulses. Although the plan is for children that will learn with other children in the class, it still caters to their particular needs.

The document covers the needs of the child and all the necessary steps the school must take to support them. Remember, your child will be learning the same thing as their classmates; the difference is how your child is treated regarding the school activities. Common ways the school might bend the typical activities for your child include the following:

- Take verbal tests instead of written ones. As your child deals with ADHD, it might become hard for them to focus on written tests and lose focus every few minutes. Due to this, they will be more likely to focus when listening than reading. When they take oral tests, it will be easier to call their attention back when they are beginning to lose focus and latch onto irrelevant things. This program will allow them to take oral tests to ensure they are on track and do not fail because of their hyperactivity or inability to focus.

- Typically students with ADHD struggle to both listen and write, so having one less task to do so that they can focus on the lesson being taught is helpful. Therefore, if the teacher can provide worksheets that have already been completed, the student will have one less thing to need to try to concentrate on. This can significantly improve their chances of succeeding. I have seen this to be of great help when both of my children are in class and preparing for a test. As the teacher is reviewing and preparing for the test, most children would fill in the blanks. This suggestion is the teacher provides them the sheet that already has the answers completed so your child can focus on what the teacher is saying.

- Get audio textbooks instead of written ones. In most schools, textbooks are readily available to all the students, but only in exceptional cases will a student get a text in audio format. This plan takes care of this, as it informs the school about the child's need for audio textbooks for optimized learning. These audio textbooks help the child to enjoy reading. Since they would enjoy studying because they can hear rather than read, it will prevent boredom which causes a lack of focus.

- Take tests in a room with less stimulation. Since your child will be learning in a typical classroom setup, many distractions will occur. A typical classroom has charts, drawings, colors, sounds, many other students, and usually windows. Anything can cause your child to lose focus in class. It could be the color of a classmate's backpack, the type of shoe the teacher wore, the trees blowing outside, or even a chart hanging up nearby that can cause distractions. These distractions can hinder your child's success at being able to focus on classwork or tests. Your child might have impressive knowledge of test content but immediately get distracted and struggle to focus on what they were doing. When children get frustrated and are not able to focus and are up against a time limit, this could increase the chances of the child getting upset and into a situation where they become emotional.

This plan eliminates this problem. It prepares the school for your child's needs on tests, explaining how hyperactive and easily distracted they might be. This helps the school prepare a classroom where your child can take tests. Since they know your child's needs, they will ensure that the room is plain without so many distractions in sight so that your child can comfortably take their test.

- Some children experience time blindness, so giving them more time will be ineffective. However, breaking the test or schoolwork into smaller pieces and allowing for breaks in between might be the answer. The breaks might be the necessary measure for keeping the child on task while they need to work. This does not mean they might not still lose focus but reminding them that there is another ten minutes before a break might help to bring them back to the task.

- This plan covers this need, as you do not need to be worried about your child spacing out or needing more time to finish tests or exams. This plan will let the school know that your child cannot simultaneously complete these tests and exams with other children, even if kept in a separate room. They will also understand that your child needs enough time to finish things properly. This plan will let the schools guide your child at their own pace.

The Support Available in Your Child's School

The support available in schools varies and depends on the school. Apart from knowing your child's rights and relating them to the school, you must know the specific services your child's school provides for students like your child. Ask the principal of your child's school about the services available to your child. Take your questions seriously. Ask them what services they have to make your child comfortable with being at school and what will give your child the best chances of being successful. Ask them how they can help your child become socially inclined without disrupting school life.

Some schools teach small groups of children basic social skills by letting this small group of three to seven students intermingle until they get used to each other. The school psychologist or therapist often leads the groups. These groups will enlighten your child on how to behave in social situations and how to talk with their peers. In addition, it teaches the child basic conversational skills.

HOW TO PREPARE THE SCHOOL FOR YOUR CHILD'S ATTENDANCE

It is not enough to have a plan and know the school's services; you must understand how to prepare the school for your child's attendance. It is easy when dealing with an old school because you do not need to go above and beyond in preparation. However, if it is a new school, you have to get the school acquainted with your child and vice versa before your child's attendance. If you do not do that, everything will seem strange to your child when they go to school, and the school might find it hard to help your child keep up with other students. Therefore, to prepare the school for your child's presence, you must contact the school and tell them your concerns.

Explain to them how your child learns so they can assign your child to a teacher that matches their ability. You can also arrange with the school to keep your child in a class more suitable for their learning abilities. For example, some classes can be noisy and too overstimulating for your child, so before school starts, you can get the chance to pick the class that you feel is more suitable for your child.

In addition to preparing the school for your child's arrival, it is necessary to prepare your child with ADHD for the upcoming school year, whether it is in a new school or a different classroom. By preparing your child in advance, you can help work on any anxieties or stresses they might feel about the routine changes. Adequate preparedness can help smooth the transition as it can greatly reduce the likelihood of your child experiencing explosive behaviors such as meltdowns. Talking about the new school or classroom and using pictograms or photos to initiate the conversation and discuss the changes can be effective techniques for helping your child get ready for the new school year. After school breaks, such as longer holidays like Christmas, you should also be preparing your child for their return a few days in advance.

Before school begins, your child can meet the essential people in the school that they will see every day and prepare your child to interact with them. It also helps that there are familiar faces your child will see once school resumes. Some people you might arrange for your child to introduce themselves to include your child's teachers, the nurse, the psychologist or guidance counselor, the speech therapist (if the school has one), and the principal.

The people your child needs to see before school begins depends on how often these people will be around your child. If these people will not be around your child often, then there is no need for your child to meet them. Instead, the reason your child is meeting them is to ensure that there is a comfortable atmosphere when your child sees them at the beginning of school.

If you are worried your child might have trouble connecting with other students, you can set up a playdate. This playdate can consist of two other children in your child's peer group. During this playdate, your child can get to know these children and even become friends with them. Even though they will have a playdate, ensure they are supervised so you can let your child rest when they are overly emotional.

Meeting with people is one part of school preparation; the other is letting your child get acquainted with the environment. It is not enough to know people at school. If your child does not know their way around the school, it might be detrimental to their experience. So, you can choose a person that will spend lots of time with your child in school to accompany you and your child around the school. It might be the school's nurse or therapist. Whatever you choose, the person should accompany you to places your child needs to go. This will give your child a sense of familiarity at the beginning of the school year.

HOW TEACHERS CAN HELP

Teachers play a significant role in your child's ability to fit in with a class. If your child's teachers know what they are dealing with, it will be easy for them to help your child. Unfortunately, with ADHD, your child will also find it difficult to explain themselves to the teacher, making it quite difficult for the teacher to know what is wrong. Since ADHD symptoms differ from person to person, it would be better for you to elaborate on your child's symptoms so the teacher can use appropriate methods to ensure they are successful. The ways you can talk to the teachers to get them to help are explained below.

Schedule an Appointment with the Teacher

You might think it is easy to breeze into the school and have a quick unannounced talk with the teacher, but it is not. If you choose to talk to the teacher after school, the school might be in rush hour, so your conversation would have several distractions and would not be very beneficial. If you meet up with the teacher before school begins, it might be similar to the previous option. The teacher might be rushing to get back to class, and you might also be time conscious because of work. It is also important to respect the teacher's time as they may be unavailable and have a previous commitment.

What is the use of two people attempting a meaningful discussion if their minds are elsewhere? A conversation where both minds are unsettled is pointless. For a delicate discussion about your child's education, you and the teacher must be fully attentive to avoid missing important details. Therefore, make an appointment with the teacher and choose an appropriate time that you would be free to discuss. The length of time does not matter because as little as twenty minutes is enough to discuss the important details.

If there are no distractions, then a little time is enough to let the teacher understand the details. You can set the appointment before resuming school or during school; the selected time does not matter. All that matters is that you set an appointment to review the details thoroughly.

Explain the Meaning of ADHD

Although the teacher is well educated, they might not know what ADHD truly means. There is no doubt that they might have heard about ADHD, but there is a possibility that they do not know a lot about it. Sometimes people tend to have more misconceptions about a disorder than facts. Due to this, the teacher might only have a vague understanding of ADHD.

This is not out of the ordinary; many believe that ADHD is a mental health disorder that can be cured. While discussing with the teacher, you are gradually becoming a guide that will help them understand the disorder. Although some teachers might have had students with ADHD under their care, not many truly understand the intricacies involved, especially as each child is different. You are most aware of your child's ADHD symptoms and behaviors. Your knowledge can be a powerful resource to the teacher. Make sure you respect the teacher and do not assume they know nothing about ADHD but do not assume they know everything. Provide education in regard to ADHD for how it relates to your child.

Explain the ADHD Symptoms in Relation to Your Child

Explaining how ADHD most affects your child to their teacher is a significant step toward helping them understand and take care of your child. However, it is not enough to tell them about it; you must elaborate on your child's ADHD. Only when you discuss ADHD with your child's teacher will it no longer seem like a lecture. Telling your child's teacher about ADHD is explanatory but, at the same time, vague because many symptoms of ADHD vary from person to person. The fact that your child has emotional outbursts because of their disorder does not mean every other child managing that disorder suffers the same. The symptoms of ADHD in each child are different, so if your explanation is vague, the teacher might be looking to help with the wrong aspects of your child's behavior.

Be specific about the symptoms that your child experiences. For example, if your child experiences daydreaming, you can explain it to the teacher. As the teacher learns about your child's symptoms, they become aware of what to look for when in the classroom. Through the symptoms, they begin to observe your child better to ensure that your child achieves great academic excellence. Talk about everything you know about your child's disorder, as leaving out any detail will not be helpful. If your child has negative coping mechanisms like lying or irrational outbursts of emotions, it will be better to explain that to the teacher. The more information provided to the teacher, the better because it will help the teacher be prepared should the behaviors occur in the classroom. Sharing your methods for dealing with the situation can also help. Perhaps you have certain words that you say to your child to help them calm down after a meltdown. You could use a fidget toy or stress ball to help them pay attention or refocus them when they need to listen. Simple actions that will not disrupt the rest of the class but work to keep your child on task can benefit everyone involved in the care of your child.

Tell the Teacher About Your Child's Current Plan

Telling your child's teacher about the type of plan your child is on is crucial. Even though the teacher knows about the symptoms, a good understanding of your child's plan will help the teacher take the proper steps to ensure a good learning atmosphere for them. It is best not to be vague about your child's plan. Saying your child is on an IEP or 504 plan is not enough information for the teacher to know what has been discussed and agreed to.

To better understand the topic, bring a printed copy of the plan so they can understand the intricacies and how they can adapt their teaching plan or style to meet your child's standards. Remember to explain to the teacher that these requirements do not mean your child should be excluded from the school curriculum. Instead, explain that you want your child to meet school expectations; these are the only requirements that will improve their learning and help them reach their highest potential.

Communicating with your child's teachers is necessary beyond their ability to complete schoolwork. It would help if you spoke with them about what can trigger certain behaviors in your child. They are at the school for a full day, including recess, lunch hour, and physical education classes. All of these things can have triggers for your child. Making your teacher fully aware of your child's ADHD symptoms and behaviors is necessary so the school can help your children. For example, the lunchroom may trigger your child because it is too noisy. Maybe the noise causes your child to be anxious and become overwhelmed, which could lead to a meltdown or a tantrum. Let the teacher and lunch hour supervisors know this so they can try to help your child. Wearing a set of earplugs can help your child in this situation, and the teacher/staff at the school can remind your child to use them if they are struggling. Often solutions for helping a child deal with their emotional regulation can be simple as long as everyone is prepared for the possible outcomes and has some ideas of solutions they can use to deal with the situation.

Talk About the Strategies You Have Used With The Child

The talk with your child's teacher can be considered complete if you talk about the strategies you have used in the past. Also, whether the strategies worked or not is not important. The main thing is communication so that the right strategies can be used. It will be best for you to tell the teacher every strategy you might have tried. That way, the teacher will have an insight into your struggles and a glimpse of what they should or should not try. If your child experiences explosive behavior, the coping mechanisms you have used to defuse these situations must also be shared. Perhaps what works for you is providing the child with a specific tool, such as a stress ball, to help them calm down. It could be singing them a song or a key phrase that you use to help empower them. Every detail shared, whether it be little or big, is beneficial. No detail is insignificant when communicating with your child's teacher about your child's ADHD, so do not forget to share all the failed strategies. The details you share are beneficial if it concerns your child's behavior and how it relates to their education.

Be Open to Hearing the Teacher's Opinion

You are conversing with your child's teacher rather than instructing them. Doing all the talking will make you feel like you are instructing the teacher. So, how about you ask for the teacher's thoughts on what you said? If you do all the talking, you may never know the wealth of knowledge the teacher has or the areas they need help understanding. Ask them what ideas they have about dealing with your child's behavior. Some teachers have worked with children who have behavioral issues, so they might have first-hand experience that you will find helpful.

Due to asking their opinions, you might find out something about behavioral management you did not know. They might offer management skills that work for other children. Their suggestions might intrigue you and might be what your child needs. You see how well they understand these things as you let them talk. Hearing the teacher's opinions will put the teacher's mind at ease, as well as yours, after understanding that they are on the same page as you and willing to go out of their way to help your child succeed.

Show Interest in Partnering with the Teacher

Your child's teacher will be happier to work with you if they realize that you are willing to partner with them or help them manage your child's school affairs. Asking them how you can help indicates that you trust them to do a good job, but you are also interested in making their job easier. In addition, every teacher who sees a parent willing to help their child succeed at school will be happy.

So, this will be good news for both parties—you and the teacher. You could always show your interest in wanting to help out by keeping in touch with the teacher. It would help if you chose a platform where it will be easy for both parties to talk, including emails, text messages, or any other messaging platform you agree on. As you regularly talk to the teacher, you will be informed regularly about your child's behavior, and rarely will things get out of hand before you notice.

HOW TO WORK ALONGSIDE THE TEACHERS

Working alongside teachers is necessary for a parent with a child managing any disorder. It is easy to work with teachers, but you might offend the teacher and make them shut down with a wrong move. Remember now that you and the teacher are on one team and working towards a goal together. You must think of what approach you will take with the teacher.

- Talk carefully. If you are not tactful while speaking, you might say something that offends the teacher or puts them on the defensive. This is why choosing your words wisely is imperative, especially when you need help getting answers or the help you plan to get. Please do not say you are blaming the teacher or insinuating that they are not doing their job. Instead of asking them why something is wrong, rephrase your question as you are concerned and willing to help. When you do this, the teacher will not always be guarded around you.
- Do not be defensive. There will be times when issues about your child will be brought up. There are times your child might cause a stir in school. You know how your child can behave; therefore, even if these reports come to you and seem like something your child is incapable of, you should listen attentively.

Do not lash out or be unnecessarily defensive. Instead, only discuss the way forward and steps to avoid such actions from your child. Commend the teachers for their efforts in curbing your child's excesses. When you do this, the teacher will strive to help your child perform at their best, knowing that you support them.

- Keep the teacher informed. As much as you regularly keep in touch with the teacher, asking about your child's performance in school, it would help if you kept the teacher informed. The information passing back and forth between you and the teacher is the key to optimal breakthroughs. Sometimes, situations at home that may be considered normal or unimportant can affect a child more than we know.

Change is constant; therefore, you must understand how to manage the change. In this case, managing change involves communication. Tell the teacher about the change in ADHD medications, if any. If there is a death in the family or a separation/divorce, also inform the teacher because these changes can affect the child's behavior. Informing the teacher will make them prepared to handle any situation arising.

- Work on shared goals. When you and the teacher meet one-on-one, you should encourage working on shared goals. Your goal is to effectively manage your child's disorder; however, managing it alone in school is ineffective. Working on shared goals will help you and the teacher monitor your child's progress and work together to encourage the development and ultimate management of ADHD.
- Take parent-teacher meetings seriously. Parent-teacher meetings usually are brief, so taking them seriously is

essential. Attend every one because they are necessary to learn more about your child's progress in school. Also, ensure you are prepared because you must be organized to remember what you might have been eager to ask. Before you go, you must list all the questions that need to be answered on paper, so you remember them. Remember to organize report cards, teacher's notes, and every other school item of great importance.

- Volunteer. Volunteering is imperative if you are trying to work side-by-side with the teacher and your child. You can pitch in as a chaperone if the school is going on a trip. Doing this will give you a glimpse into your child's behavior in school. It will also make the teacher see how immersed you are in the school affairs of your child. In most cases, your child might be happy to see you there even though they do not interact with you much.

- Appreciate the teacher. Never underestimate the importance of appreciation. Appreciation can make a person continue what they do because they are happy that their efforts were acknowledged. Similarly, if you appreciate the teacher, they will be more comfortable doing more for your child. Do not appreciate them just because you read that here; appreciate them from your heart because you believe they have done a great job. If a teacher goes a mile or two to understand your child, they deserve to be thanked. There are different ways you can appreciate them. Sometimes, a small thank you note on their table might make them smile. A gift can be great too. The appreciation depends on what you can do and afford.

9

NAVIGATING SOCIAL SKILLS

S ocial skills play an important part in our lives as humans. Social skills encompass all the skills from verbal (speed of speech, volume, and tone of speech) to non-verbal (facial expression, body language, and eye contact), enabling us to interact and communicate with others. Unfortunately, due to executive dysfunction, children with ADHD might find it hard to use these social skills and act inappropriately in social interaction.

Some inappropriate behaviors that will put off their peers when interacting with them include:

- missing social cues
- being inattentive and missing several pieces of information
- being easily distracted by sounds
- Having difficulty listening to others for long periods
- frequently interrupting while conversing with others

- talking fast or too much
- being highly focused on one topic
- having disordered thoughts
- sharing thoughts in a disordered manner
- initiating conversations at inappropriate times
- displaying aggression or lack of emotional control
- lacking boundaries and being unaware of others' personal space

Your child might engage in inattentive, hyperactive, and impulsive behaviors that drive other children away. Your child might miss social cues necessary to make a friend; even when they make one, they might be too distracted by little things and miss important information shared by their friend. This behavior offends adults as well as children. If a person does not listen and you keep repeating one thing over and over again, it makes you feel like they are not interested in being your friend. In many cases, the other child will back out from initiating a friendship.

They might also find it hard to listen to their friends for long periods, which can put their friends off. If they have a friend who listens to them rant and talks uncoordinatedly, it is normal for the friend to expect the same thing from them. If the friend expects them to listen and they do not, they might appear rude or insensitive. Since conversation is a two-way street, people find it disrespectful for a person to be the only one talking without letting them say their views. No one will remain friends with a person that is constantly interrupting them. Having disordered thoughts is one thing, but voicing those thoughts is another and genuinely a put-off.

Children with ADHD, especially if they display explosive behaviors, might also be triggered to have a meltdown or show some aggression, like hitting in a social situation that is not going their way. Sometimes simple things like the other child doing something different in a game that the child is used to playing with someone else might be enough to make their explosive behaviors appear. Being overwhelmed can be another reason that the child may show these behaviors. On the playground, for example, a lot can happen with the activity that your child and their friend are doing and what the other children are doing. Your child might be on the swings with their friend and looking over at the soccer field, the slide, monkey bars, etc. Working with your child to prepare them for social situations and all the feelings that can come from their condition is important. This behavior can be frightening for the child they are trying to befriend, and it will also be difficult for your child. It can be helpful to have a conversation with the parent of the child your child is trying to befriend to explain some of the behaviors to the new friend. That way, a plan can be implemented to benefit everyone. The solution might be for the friend to seek out the assistance of an adult in order to help manage behaviors.

Respecting personal space is one of the keys to maintaining friendships. However, if your child does not understand personal space and keeps invading others' space at school, it might be hard for them to have friends. Initiating conversations at the wrong times, even when they have been told not to, is another negative social skill that might affect their ability to make friends. However, the scariest of the negative social skills is the display of aggression and lack of emotional control. If your child lacks emotional control, other children might not want to come close for fear of being poorly treated.

The above factors represent various reasons your child might struggle to make friends or maintain long-lasting friendships. However, do not worry; there are tips for helping your child socialize and have a successful social life.

Also, try these methods for short time frames and with small groups, at least initially. Children with ADHD, especially if they are prone to explosive behaviors, can easily become overwhelmed, and this can create an undesirable situation. It will all depend on the child and how noises and situations affect them when it comes to what they can handle. For some children with ADHD, being in a social situation can be difficult since their executive dysfunction might cause them to hear every little sound around them, which can be overwhelming. The right place and people are essential to your child's social interactions. If possible, try to get your child to explain how they felt once you are home so that you can adapt social situations in the future to their specific needs.

TIPS TO HELP YOUR CHILD SOCIALIZE BETTER

- Provide immediate feedback about miscues and inappropriate behaviors. ADHD might make your child lack self-awareness; hence, they might not know when they are doing inappropriate things around their peers. Help your children learn the importance of being social, such as greeting their friends when they meet them in public, or saying please and thank you when they ask for a toy or sporting equipment at recess. Some behaviors can be off-putting to others. However, you can work to improve these situations through role play, pictograms, and conversations with your children. Positively reinforcing good behavior can also help. When possible, reinforce the behaviors right away. Also, be sure to be clear in letting your child know what behaviors you are proud of so they know what to strive for. For example, instead of just saying a good job, you might say good job sharing the ball when you play. Ensuring connection is vital in helping your child achieve their full potential in all life situations.
- Focus on strengthening the areas that your child struggles with the most. The fact that your child has ADHD does not mean they will have problems with all areas of their life. They might have issues with emotional control but understand personal space. The areas a child with ADHD will need help with depends on the child. Since you know your child and the possible areas that

might be a problem, focus on them rather than general issues.

- Playdates are important. Playdates are important when trying to develop your child's social skills. Since children with ADHD will thrive better in smaller gatherings than in larger ones, a playdate of ten children might be counterproductive. Instead, it will be preferred if the playdate consists of at most four children. This will help your child to socialize effectively without social anxiety.
- Reward them accordingly. If your child displays appropriate behaviors during a playdate or uses new social skills successfully, reward them immediately. This encourages them to keep up that good behavior. You can reward them for making a new friend unassisted and reward them when they have successful playdates.
- Communicate with your child often. Communication reveals so much that we might not have guessed. Many children with ADHD face bullying and other types of adversity in school. Even while facing these situations, they might not tell anyone or say they forgot when you find out. Many children like this are the bully's target, so if you do not talk to your child, you might not know the underlying cause of your child's disorder.
- Prepare your child for social interactions. Preparations are always important for a child with ADHD. You have to ease them into a routine before they can get used to it. It would be best to create real-life scenarios at home that mimic what they might encounter eventually. When you do this, teach them how to respond by asking them what they think about certain situations. Guide them where

they need guidance. You could also watch movies with your child and ask them what they think about some characters. You should also prepare your child for playdates, so they do not do and say the wrong things. You can teach them how to manage conflict that might arise during the playdates so that they will control their emotions when it happens.

- Encourage your child to take notes. Since children with ADHD might forget many details because of their attention span, encourage them to take notes on their friends' names and other important facts, they think they might forget. This will help them remember these details when they interact with their friends.

- Teach your child about boundaries. Boundaries are an important part of our lives. If you teach your child about boundaries by speaking to them when you notice that they overstepped, you can help them understand how important it is to respect others' personal space.

- Be prepared to take time outs from social interaction. Even at a playdate, a child can become overwhelmed even if, just minutes before, it seemed like they were having fun. Calling a break when your child appears to be getting distracted or suggesting that the children switch to a quieter activity if you sense your child is becoming overstimulated can be helpful. You may also want to set time limits for activities with friends. Even a thirty-minute to an hour playdate might be plenty for your child to handle, especially in the beginning. Especially if your child displays explosive behaviors, you want to keep things from reaching that point. Through work with your child, you will hopefully be able to help them learn when to identify that they need a break. The more you communicate with your child and work with them on finding solutions to their behaviors, the better their chances for positive interactions with others.

- Sign your child up for team sports. Although individual sports can benefit children with ADHD, team sports can also be great. If they play these sports, they might learn teamwork, improving their social skills. For some children, team sports might be out of the question. For example, if your child with ADHD is triggered to have explosive behavior when the whistle goes off or there is too much cheering from the crowd, it might not be the best option. Some children are too distracted by a lot of activity to succeed in a larger group setting, such as on a soccer team. Exploring other options, such as playing badminton, might be an option, as there are fewer people to interact with. Plenty of studies show that activities such as horseback riding can be extremely therapeutic for children with ADHD. Your child's teammate does not necessarily have to be a person. They can make friends with animals which can help to boost their confidence levels too. Also, children with ADHD are often known to hyperfocus on their interests. Therefore finding activities that interest them could be the key to having them interact in a group setting. For example, if your child loves art, drawing classes might be a good option for them. There has been lots of research about the benefits of art therapy too.

- Praise them for good behavior. Children with ADHD deal with many emotional problems. Due to their social challenges, they might also have reduced self-esteem. If you praise them when you see them exhibit good behaviors, you will boost their self-esteem and make them strive to manage their symptoms better.

SOCIAL SKILLS GROUP

Social skills group is a group that enhances the social life of children and adolescents that are enrolled. Since children with ADHD find it difficult to fit in with their peers, they might need extra training to learn how to act appropriately in social situations and become capable of handling conversations, friendships, and conflicts.

How They Work

This group handles social life's nonverbal and verbal aspects and merges them to help the child become socially comfortable interacting with their peers. These groups teach the child how to communicate verbally with other people. It ensures the child understands appropriate and inappropriate things to say to people in various situations. It also teaches the child about nonverbal communication, like how to interpret body language and facial expressions. Interpreting body language and facial expressions will help the child understand when they are doing things at inappropriate times or creeping into someone's personal space and the person is upset.

How to Create One

Professionals create a social skills group based not on diagnostic history but on the child's social skills. Although it is created based on the child's social skills, it is also age appropriate. A social skills group cannot consist of a seven-year-old child and another thirteen; it does not work that way. Group leaders are flexible in their group creation to ensure their training impacts the children. These professionals use different means like modeling, role-playing, and teaching. Training is practiced over a long period until the child has a grip on it.

10

MEDICATING

It is sometimes a struggle to choose between medications and other therapies. As a parent, this decision might make you stall for several months before taking the next step. Delaying before deciding to use medication to control your child's ADHD is not bad. It is essential to consult your health professional to know if your child should begin using medication. Their advice is also crucial in understanding the suitable times for starting these medications. Sharing all information about your child's behaviors is necessary when choosing the right option with your child's healthcare provider. You may want to keep a log of their behaviors to share with your doctor. The right medications or treatments could depend on how often certain things happen. For example, there is a difference if your child has daily, weekly, or monthly explosive behaviors. If a situation happens infrequently, medication might not be needed for that specific ADHD symptom.

Keeping track of how a medication affects a child after receiving it is also important so the medical professional can determine if the child has the right medication for their specific situation. You should also frequently ask others with your child for feedback. For example, their teacher can let you know if behaviors in the classroom have changed.

ADHD MEDICATIONS

The medications used in treating ADHD are divided into two branches according to their effect on the central nervous system. The branches are:

- stimulant medications
- non-stimulant medication

Stimulant Medications

Stimulant medications are popularly prescribed for ADHD by medical personnel. Their action is to increase the amount of dopamine (known as the happy hormone) and the amount of norepinephrine in the central nervous system. The action of these medications calms the central nervous system and reduces hypersensitivity. This will provide your child with calmness and proper concentration. Discussed below are some examples of stimulant medications.

- Amphetamine-based stimulants: These stimulants are made from Amphetamine, the most popular type of stimulant. Some examples of these stimulants are:

- Adderall
- Dextrostat
- Dexedrine

- Dextromethamphetamine stimulants: The most popular type of this stimulant is Desoxyn.
- Dexmethylphenidate stimulants: The most common type of this stimulant prescribed for ADHD is Focalin.
- Methylphenidate stimulants: These stimulants are derivatives of methylphenidate, and examples of this class of stimulants are:

- Concerta
- Daytrana
- Metadate
- Ritalin

Non-Stimulant Medications

This option is used when there is no significant improvement after administering stimulant medications. These medications are also used when stimulant medications have substantial, lasting side effects.

There is no exact knowledge about the actions of most ADHD non-stimulant medications in the central nervous system. However, four non-stimulant medications are indicated as medications that stimulate the release of norepinephrine in the nervous system to bring calmness and concentration to the user.

- Strattera (an Atomoxetine derivative)
- Pamelor (antidepressant-like nortriptyline)
- Intuniv (guanfacine)
- Kapvay (clonidine)

ALTERNATIVE MEDICATIONS

The medications used to manage ADHD in children are not limited to stimulants and non-stimulants; your physician can prescribe other medications depending on your child's disorder and the most suitable option available. The two classes of medications used in place of stimulants and non-stimulants are:

- Antidepressants
- Anti-hypertensives

UPSIDES OF ADHD MEDICATIONS

Although you might consider the side effects when using medication for ADHD, there are significant benefits your child will reap that you cannot ignore. These benefits span all types of ADHD medication. They include:

- reduction of hyperactivity
- increase of motivation
- increase in productivity
- reduction of procrastination
- increase in attention span
- the manageable pace of thoughts
- decrease of impulsivity

- improvement in school performance
- promotion of a better social life
- increase in the ability to focus for more extended periods

THE DOWNSIDES OF ADHD MEDICATIONS

Many people are skeptical about using medications to treat ADHD because of the potential side effects that might follow. Of course, every drug has its side effects, but side effects are drug dependent. Still, some common side effects might occur while using stimulants and non-stimulants to control your child's ADHD. Outlined below are some common side effects:

- headache
- insomnia
- upset stomach
- nervousness
- irritability
- loss of weight
- dry mouth

The common side effects can be present in stimulants and non-stimulants. These side effects may not need a trip to the doctor every day and can be easy to deal with. However, severe side effects might need urgent attention, although they rarely occur. The serious side effects also depend on the class of the drug used.

Severe side effects that may accompany the use of stimulants are:

- auditory or visual hallucinations (hearing or seeing things that are not real)
- blood pressure increase
- allergic reaction
- suicidal actions back up the contemplation of suicide that may or may not

Severe side effects that may accompany the use of non-stimulants are:

- seizures
- suicidal actions back up the contemplation of suicide that may or may not

Understanding that these side effects do not occur in typical cases is imperative. It is rare for the side effects of stimulants and non-stimulants to reach this level of severity.

SHOULD YOU MEDICATE?

Before reading this, you might have been aware that side effects could follow the use of these medications. After reading about these side effects, you might wonder if it is a good idea to start or continue using medication. Unfortunately, several decisions plague parents' minds when deciding whether to use medications as therapy for their children with ADHD.

Some parents fear these medications will make their children behave like mindless zombies. You might feel the medication will stunt the child's true personality but is that the case? With medication, a child might not be as active as they used to be, but that does not mean they have lost their personality. This new development means the child is aware of the appropriate actions instead of mindlessly being hyperactive.

You might also worry about your child becoming dependent on the medication. Your child having to use their medication does not mean they are automatically addicted. Instead, the medicine is like a pillar they can fall back on to make them feel better. It is very similar to the way we drink water. It is a feedback mechanism where we experience thirst and take water to quench it. This analogy is similar to a child that has ADHD using their medications. They are not addicted. They need it to have a better quality of life.

Another concern might be why medication is an option while there are other therapeutic ways to manage ADHD. The reason why medication might be advised to you is plausible. Not every situation can be handled using a natural approach. For example, if you want to align your teeth to have the perfect dentition, you might decide to wait it out and hope your teeth straighten naturally. But how many times have you seen that work? Even children in middle school must wear braces to straighten their teeth out rather than wait for nature to take its course.

Braces are unnatural, but they serve their purpose perfectly well. This is similar to taking ADHD medications. You can choose natural therapy, but if your child's hyperactivity continues, the doctor might ask you to take medication. To manage the disorder medicine can make a substantial difference in managing ADHD. Even the natural therapies that you might be more inclined to are not perfect and might not give you the effect you are looking for.

Another thought that might plague your mind when considering the suitability of medication is believing that you might have failed as a parent. If you have this thought, it would be wise to discard it from your mind before you start feeling like it is true. Giving your child medications for ADHD does not mean you are lazy or have failed as a parent. Contrary to what you might think, you are helping your child become the best version of themselves. Do not think you are doing it to relieve yourself of dealing with your child's ADHD because you know deep down that you want your child to live a healthy and happy life.

Think of medication like you are helping your child eliminate the burden of not being able to concentrate. Instead of guilt-tripping yourself, pat yourself on the back because you are trying your best to ensure your child has a better quality of life.

The thought of beginning medication alone might be over-whelming. Sometimes, when faced with challenges, we might want to back out of what seems like an arduous task. You might be thinking of all the trips you must take to the doctor's office. You might also wonder about the numerous tests your child will need to undergo and the medications they will need to try to choose the most suitable one. In a world where every parent is busy and trying to create a favorable environment for their children, frequent trips to the doctor to run countless tests might not seem like a great idea.

If you are a parent that has tried other therapies to manage your child's ADHD, you might be wary of introducing medications into the treatment. You might think, "If this has worked so far, why do I still need to use medications while treating my child?" It is imperative to remember that as a person ages, their needs also grow. If you compare how you were when you were little and how you are now, you will notice that your needs are more significant and different. For example, consider changes in your appetite; a small bowl of cereal when you were little might not fill you at thirty. This is the same with the growth of a child. The child's needs at five would differ from their needs at twelve. As they grow, their needs grow too.

Remember, ADHD is a lifelong disorder, so sufficient treatment in previous years might not be enough in later years. If natural therapy was adequate in treating a child of seven, you might need to do it alongside medication by the time they are fourteen. Naturally, the older they get, the more responsibilities they will have and the more executive functions they need. Although your child survived only on natural therapy in grade school, they might need to add medication in high school when they have calculus and arithmetic to concentrate on. Adding medication simply helps your child focus so they can identify their strengths and weaknesses. It is never too late or too early to begin medica-tion; if prescribed, be assured that it will improve the quality of your child's life.

Whether you choose to medicate or not is in your hands. It is not mandatory to use natural means, just as it is not compulsory to use medications to manage ADHD. No textbooks or rules say that if you do not medicate your child, they will not have a good quality of life. Diving into medication the minute your child is diagnosed with ADHD is unnecessary. If you decide to begin medicating your child immediately, you must weigh your options and reasons for medicating above other options. You must determine if you are choosing medication from the start to improve executive function or reduce excessive hyperactivity, which can cause emotional instability and impulsive actions.

Weighing your options will let you know the most suitable for your child. For example, suppose you choose not to start medicating from the onset of the diagnosis but have consistently found relief from other approaches. In that case, you might eventually need to use the medication and the non-medication options you already use. Regardless of which option you choose to manage your child's ADHD, you might need to complement it with others. Using the two options will lead your child to a more relaxed state. Although they are both valid, you must discuss the best option for your child with your physician.

ADHD THERAPY

Therapy for this diagnosis refers to the other methods (sans medication) that can be combated without medication. Again, discussing with your doctor whether this will be a better option for you is crucial. The methods of therapy include:

- psychotherapy
- social training skills
- parental and teacher training skills
- support groups

Psychotherapy

Psychotherapy is the use of psychological means in treating ADHD. Psychotherapy will help your child monitor behavior patterns and choose to act correctly. Typically, psychotherapy is done in two phases:

- behavior therapy
- cognitive behavioral therapy (CBT)

Behavior Therapy

In behavior therapy, the psychologist guides the parent and child on scrutinizing the child's behaviors. The use of scrutiny will help identify the details of behaviors that require change. A positive feedback mechanism will change the child's behavior gradually. The positive feedback mechanism depends on the suggestion of the psychologist. For example, the psychologist might recommend a reward following a positive behavior from your child.

Cognitive Behavioral Therapy

This type of therapy aims to rectify adverse thinking patterns that are often associated with this disorder. One significant negative thinking pattern is perfection. If they do not perceive a thing done by someone with ADHD to be perfect, they might lose motivation. As motivation is lost, the next step is to ignore the task or procrastinate. Instead of doing this, cognitive behavioral therapy will teach them to change this mindset of perfection or nothing.

Social Training Skills

Sometimes, people with ADHD have limited social skills because of their inability to focus. This social training will help to suppress bouts of energy that might seem impossible to control previously. As a result, they will experience a healthier social life at school and home as they learn to control some of these behaviors.

Parental and Teacher Training Skills

As a parent, there are skills that you need to manage a child with ADHD. Parental skills give you insight into what you are dealing with and a thorough understanding of managing the disorder. With these skills, you will handle each aspect with ease. Teachers also need these skills to manage the child's ADHD symptoms. The following skills and therapeutic measures will give your child the quality of life they deserve.

- Reward system: The reward system is an important strategy for managing your child. You have to know what your child loves, which can serve as a reward. Also, you must monitor your child's behavior to note when they have good behavior at home or school. For every excellent behavior they exhibit, it is imperative to reward them with their favorite thing (could be snacks or toys). You cannot carry out this system alone, so you might need the teacher's help. The teacher could monitor your child's behavior in school and give you daily feedback about the positive and negative behaviors your child exhibits. Then, depending on their behavior, you can decide whether to reward them for the day.

- Healthy meals: Believe it or not, healthy meals play a vital role in managing many health disorders. Your child's disorder can quickly improve or take a downhill turn depending on their diet. A healthy meal is a balanced diet with each nutrient your child needs. Never neglect your child's nutritional needs because it could worsen things. A study showed a lower level of omega-3 fatty acids in children with ADHD. The interaction between ADHD and Omega-3 fatty acids is not clear. Still, you can mix up your child's diet with fruits, whole grains, vegetables, and fish (which could be a source of omega -3 fatty acids for your child) or other proteins. There is little research on the appropriate meals for ADHD children, but if you have any concerns, you could talk to your health provider. Dopamine is also extremely important for your child. In someone with an ADHD deficiency, the level of this neurotransmitter in their brain is lower than in someone who does not have the condition. There are ways to increase your child's dopamine levels to help them feel better. Some foods have the ability to help your child's brain release this dopamine, such as apples, eggs, leafy green vegetables, and watermelon.
- Stress management: Stress management is critical because stress can be a trigger of ADHD. There are different ways to manage stress appropriately for your child.
- Setting a strict and healthy sleep routine: Never underestimate the power of a healthy sleep routine.

Children with many disorders manage their symptoms better when they can truly rest while they sleep. Sleep reduces restlessness and lack of focus. Many children with ADHD find it hard to sleep. If you set a healthy sleep schedule in which your child sleeps at the same time every day and consistently perform a bedtime routine, you can also reduce symptoms. You can have a bedtime routine of bathing, putting on their pajamas, reading a book, then making the room sleep conducive (dark, calm, relaxed, and soothing).

- Exercise: This is an important factor necessary for every child. Give your child time to play and run around with other children, but with supervision to ensure they do not get too stimulated. Exercise is essential for their physical and mental health.

- Meditation and mindfulness: Meditation and mindfulness will train your child's focus and sharpen their awareness. Meditation might also combat their lack of self-control. The benefits of meditation can significantly reduce the symptoms of ADHD.

- Music therapy: Listening to your favorite music can calm your nerves and brain and help you focus more. Music therapy does not require your child to play an instrument or sing. You can play your child's favorite music to calm their nerves and help them immerse themselves in a task.

- Art therapy: Like music therapy, coloring, drawing, or painting, doing crafts can be calming for children with ADHD. They do not have artistic talents for these activities to help them. The simple act of sitting down to work on them can have calming effects.

- Spending time with your child: No therapies are as effective as quality time. As you spend time with your child, you allow them to loosen up and express their feelings to you. You can do something fun during this time to keep your child engaged. While spending time with them, remember to praise them when you notice positive behavior changes.
- Join support groups: You need support groups to meet other parents like you. Managing your ADHD child can be a long road, and it often feels lonely and exhausting when you have not met other parents going through the same thing. When you join these support groups, you gain a sense of belonging and new ideas to help you manage your child's disorder.

11

SUPPORT RESOURCES FOR PARENTS

A s a parent, living with a child with ADHD can be overwhelming, and sometimes it can feel like there is no way forward, but rest assured, there are several ways you can take control of the situation. You are not alone in this journey; others have gone through what you are going through and are facing what you have to deal with. Numerous resources have been made available to help you navigate your way through this journey. You are not alone in your quest to give your child the best care and attention possible so that they can be happy and successful. Other parents are going through the same things, and they can help you learn about all aspects of your child's ADHD, such as inattentiveness and explosive behaviors. However, you must remember that your child is unique, and what works for one family might not be what works for yours. Similar symptoms of ADHD do not mean that the same action plan will work for your child.

BEST ADHD PODCASTS

Parenting a child with ADHD can keep your hands full all the time and make you wonder if you can ever fully understand your child's struggles. Your busy schedule might hinder you from reading books or doing adequate research, but there is always a solution. One solution is listening to podcasts. You can do this anytime without worrying about it interfering with your busy schedule; while on the go, you can just tune in, and you are good. Via podcasts, you can listen to experts who have substantial knowledge about what you are experiencing and are willing to walk you through this journey. Podcasts are one effective mechanism that can guide you on the right path. Below are several podcasts that focus on different aspects of ADHD.

- Parenting ADHD: This podcast is hosted by Penny Williams, a mother who was prompted to learn more about ADHD when her son was diagnosed. Her topics cover everything a parent needs to know about understanding their children, and her personal experience also makes her discussion relatable.
- Distracted: Podcaster Mark Patey was in fifth grade when he was diagnosed with ADHD. His diagnosis was not a hindrance to him having a bright future, as he went on to become a successful businessman. His show serves as an eye-opener to what it means to live with ADHD.
- ADHD Essentials: This gives the parents blueprints for assisting their child with activities such as homework. Guests on the show range from parents to mental health experts and professionals.

- Adulting With ADHD: After her diagnosis, Sarah Snyder launched this podcast to shed more light on how ADHD affects women, especially regarding hormones. This podcast features women who discuss how they dealt with ADHD during various phases, such as pregnancy and menopause.
- Faster Than Normal: This show shares the accomplishments of people with ADHD. Successful individuals who have become well-known talk about their struggles and how they made a name for themselves despite their diagnosis. The host, Peter Shankman, sees his ADHD as a gift and is set on making others see the positive side of living with this disorder.
- ADHD reWired: This podcast consists of interviews with professionals in this field and individuals living with ADHD. The discussion is made relatable, and strategies are also disseminated. The host, Eric Tivers, addresses his journey living with ADHD and how he maneuvered his way through life.
- I Have ADHD: The podcaster is an ADHD life coach who has devoted time to assisting people diagnosed with ADHD. She educates them on managing their time effectively and wields their skills. The show also answers questions born out of curiosity and provides guidance on how to live a successful life. She uses her experience to enlighten listeners on the diagnosis and how to live with it.
- ADHD Experts: This podcast from ADDitude has experts with concrete knowledge about ADHD answering

questions and passing on information about the medical disorder.

- Hacking Your ADHD: The host, William Curb, advises his listeners on how to deal with the dilemmas of ADHD. His advice comes from his personal experience and information from guests he has on the show.

Listening to the right podcast goes a long way in helping you understand your child better because you have a broader awareness of the challenges they are going through. In addition, hearing from people who understand the situation encourages you to move forward.

BEST ADHD APPS

People diagnosed with ADHD often find it difficult to remember certain things and handle complex activities, which is where ADHD apps come in. The major focus of these apps is to boost the productivity level of the user. ADHD apps can never replace professional health personnel, but they help get chores done. The apps do not remove the symptoms but make you productive and organized. The advancement in technology has had a major role to play in creating an even ground for individuals diagnosed with ADHD, in the sense that it helps them to dig deep into themselves and bring forth their potential. Several apps have been created to this effect and can be customized to suit your needs. The following list includes some of the best apps:

- RescueTime: This app helps an individual manage time effectively. It keeps track of your activities, allows you to set goals, and tells you how much time you spend on each activity. RescueTime ensures users do not waste time doing unproductive activities by setting limitations. It also has a special feature that measures the user's improvement.

- Dragon: This is an incredible app for taking voice dictation. Rather than typing out your thoughts, all the user has to say aloud is recorded and transcribed into text.
- Headspace: This app encourages meditation and helps to relax the mind. It helps an individual stay calm and focused through guided breathing exercises.
- Trello: This is an app that helps you manage your to-do list. It enables you to organize tasks according to your style. Trello also encourages teamwork by providing the means to collaborate on projects.
- SimpleMind Mind Mapping: This app enables the user to create a map of one's thoughts and ideas. The user can also upload voice recordings, documents, and other media to back up information, allowing the user to follow their train of thought.

FACEBOOK SUPPORT GROUPS

Much time is devoted to caring for an individual with ADHD, which can hinder physical contact with people with similar experiences. A support group is a community of individuals confronting a common issue and coming together to share what they are going through. It is a safe haven for people to express their sincere emotions about their experiences and learn from the experience of others. ADHD support groups can be via conference calls, in-person meetings, or online forums. Their meetings can either be regular or occasional. An online support group is a great avenue to meet with individuals far and wide who are dealing with ADHD or have loved ones with this diagnosis.

There are numerous support groups on various social media platforms that can provide comfort for you as you tread this path. A social media platform such as Facebook boasts various groups where individuals diagnosed with ADHD or relatives with this medical disorder can share their stories and seek advice. Facebook can be used for several reasons, including obtaining more knowledge about a particular subject matter. There are a ton of educational groups on Facebook that can give you a substantial amount of information and also support you in this journey. Some of these groups are:

- ADDitude ADHD Support Group.
- Parenting a Child with ADHD
- ADHD Diagnosed in Adulthood
- ADHD Meds Question & Support Group
- Unlocking ADHD Support Community
- My Child Has ADHD Support Group

You stand to gain many benefits by joining a Facebook support group as a parent taking care of a child diagnosed with ADHD. The advantages of joining a Facebook support group include the following:

- gaining more information about understanding your child
- creating an avenue for you to share your experience and learn from the experience of others
- getting advice
- being well-informed of the latest studies on how to help your child overcome certain difficulties
- achieving a sense of belonging and avoiding loneliness
- getting exposed to fresh strategies
- engaging in personal growth and development
- developing a feeling of being helpful

TIPS FOR SELF-CARE

The word self-care can be translated to mean caring for yourself. It entails doing things that will keep you healthy in all aspects of your life, physically or spiritually. Tending to a child diagnosed with ADHD can leave you with little to no time to look after yourself and the family. It might occasionally seem like a lot to juggle, leaving you out of touch with things happening around you. Therefore, it also becomes fundamental for you to pay close attention to your well-being because it influences the core of the family. So how do you care for yourself while caring for your child? The following is a list of tips that will point you in the right direction and help you focus on cultivating a healthy lifestyle amidst the fatigue you are experiencing:

- Open communication: Never think that you are alone. Communicate openly, especially with your spouse. Communication is vital in maintaining your well-being, especially mentally. Keeping your feelings and struggles bottled up will eventually take a toll on you. As parents, you need to learn to assist one another and work as a team. Set aside time to discuss what you are going through and what systems can be implemented. Doing this will help you find yourself when you think you cannot go on.

- Daily evaluation: There will be days when it seems like you have gotten to the end of the road and you cannot go further and days when you feel discouraged. Such time is when you focus on the positive aspects of your day rather than dwelling on the negative aspects. At the end of each day, critically consider how to improve what has been done so far. If possible, write it down to remind you of your achievements and what remains to be done. This act will keep you moving forward and help you focus on the positives.

- Realistic expectations: Set feasible goals for both you and those around you. Do not entertain certain expectations merely because they might improve your child's growth and learning. Instead, everything should be done based on your child's pace of understanding. To do this, you need to discern their level of progress, as this will help you generate practical expectations. You set goals for your child as you set them for yourself. Do not try to be a hero and do everything at once, all by yourself. Accept all the help you can get since you can only care for your child when you are in the right frame of mind.

- Positive self-talk: Parenting a child with ADHD can be overwhelming sometimes, making it difficult to maintain a positive attitude. Just as it is crucial to instill good manners in your children by setting an example as a parent, you should also exercise positive self-talk. This is one of the most important parts of self-care. Our thoughts have a way of influencing our actions, so it is paramount that we choose our words and thoughts carefully. We find it difficult to compliment ourselves even when we deserve it, and we are always quick to criticize. Even if something seems like a small win compared to what we envisioned, we should still learn to appreciate it. When you practice positive self-talk, you are relieved from stress, and your outlook on the day is altered positively. Do not be hard on yourself; speak positively and appreciate what you do. Be mindful of how you speak to yourself, and do not be in a hurry to critique yourself. Compliment yourself from time to time after reflecting on your accomplishments. Daily affirmations can also have a positive effect on your life. They have helped me so much that I created an audiobook for mothers called 'Take a Breath, Mamas.' You can find the book on Audible under Carmen Lyons.

- Time to rest: You might wonder where you will get the time to rest despite being so busy trying to make everything work. There is always time for anything when you consciously try to create time. Spend quality time getting ample sleep. Take a break and get yourself involved in things that interest you. Taking a break does not necessarily mean you have to sleep; you can take a walk or practice yoga. Meditation is a good form of rest, as it helps you find your inner calm. Having your "me" time is vital. You are only helpful to others when you are at your peak level of performance, and this will not be possible if you are strained.

- Professional help: Figuring out a working pattern for you, your child, and the family can be overwhelming, and it is not a journey that should be embarked on independently. Seek professional counsel, as this will equip you with the right insight on what to do and what not to do. Talk to experts who are knowledgeable in this field and can guide you through the necessary steps. One suggestion is to reach out and find a parenting coach. This person should be available to you and can help you create a unique parenting plan that fits your life and your family's needs while also prioritizing your needs.

- Regular exercise: It might seem impossible to find time to exercise, but it is a great stress reliever. It also has a way of making you happy as a result of the endorphins it releases. Remember, you can only care for others effectively when you are best. Exercise does not have to be strenuous— it can be as easy as walking in the park or around the house.

- Fun activities: The definition of fun differs for everyone, but the goal is the same—relaxation. Carve out time to do something you truly love that relaxes you. It can be as simple as picking up a book to read. Only make sure that you do something you relish.

- Quality time with friends and family: Enjoy their company and have solace in companionship despite your busy schedule.

Focusing on yourself does not make you selfish; it will help you maintain a happy home. Seizing time to look after yourself helps you relieve the pressure of your daily activities and reset. One of the advantages of self-care is that it helps you refine your attention and increase your energy level.

CONCLUSION

You are a parent. You have tried everything possible to help your child understand and control their emotions, but they will not listen. You are tired of the fighting, yelling, destructive behavior, and disrespect, and you just want to escape the mess. But remember, your problems will follow you wherever you go. The guilt of not being able to help your child is the worst feeling in the world. The good thing is that help is abundant for those who seek it.

Being diagnosed with ADHD does not hinder your child from being successful or leading an exemplary life. However, as a parent, you must help yourself and your child by keeping your emotions in check. Emotions can claw into your decisions and affect your actions, so you must make time for yourself to unwind.

Work towards bringing out the best in your child. Your support, intentionality, and dedication will shape your child's future and guarantee a good life. Refrain from speaking negatively to your child. Instead, you should build up their confidence with positive words. Avoid using triggering words or phrases that threaten their self-esteem. Your child's success lies in your hands.

The importance of empathy in relationships cannot be overemphasized. We all desire to be loved; the same is true for your child. Treat your child's feelings with the utmost respect, and never disregard how they feel. View your child positively and be determined to see them achieve tremendous accomplishments. ADHD may cause your child to seem detached and lacking in remorse or empathy. However, the truth is that they might be oblivious to the proper ways to conduct themselves in various situations.

This is where you come in as a guide. Children with ADHD often face emotional breakdowns because they have to put in twice the effort other children make to succeed at basic skills. In addition, they are often misunderstood by those ignorant of their medical disorder. As parents who care for individuals diagnosed with ADHD, you must rise and support your child in all situations. This goes a long way to prevent your child from carrying a life-long stigma that will affect their future. Communicate openly with your child and work together on building self-esteem.

The debate between using medications or alternative therapies for your child can be an intense conflict; nevertheless, it is still subject to the advice of a professional health practitioner. In treating ADHD, stimulant and non-stimulant medicines can be used depending on the child's level of improvement. Using medication as a form of treatment has its benefits and drawbacks, but this does not imply that it should not be used. On the contrary, medicine and therapy will be needed in the long run when treating ADHD. Aside from medications, other methods can be employed, such as psychotherapy, social skills training, parental and teacher training, support groups, etc.

Structure is key to maintaining organization and focus when tending to your child. Creating a daily routine for your child enhances the child's concentration level, which, in turn, yields success. It may take months before the routine can be done without hiccups, so stay vigilant and change what is necessary, but only a little at a time. You should not leave your child to figure things out alone; rather, you should stand as a guide and instructor. As parents, ensure that the structure you have put in place in your home is conducive to your child's development.

With consistent support, proper strategies, and conscious effort, it is possible for a child with ADHD to have a normal school life. First, you must inform the proper authorities of your child's disorder; the rest is as easy as possible. ADHD should not be seen as a hindrance to academic excellence, as it can be managed in a school environment. Promote social activities for your child, give them ways to deflect peer pressure, and help them develop their social skills. The principal element to achieving this is to establish communication. Do not use ADHD as an excuse to seclude your child.

As parents who have to cater to the needs of children with ADHD, you must realize you are not alone in this journey. You do not have to do it all on your own, and several aids have been made available to guide you and provide the knowledge you need to care for your child adequately. You can use resources like podcasts that focus on dealing with ADHD and apps that direct you on what to do next while also paying attention to your child's improvement. In everything you do, remember that others are going through what you are experiencing and understand how you feel. Support groups help you relate with others, which is one of the vital resources you need to maintain your mental and emotional stability.

As a final observation, you must understand the significance of being open to knowledge. Aspire to know more than you already know. Pay close attention to your child's needs, and in the process, do not lose sight of your goal to help your child live a happy, fulfilled, and successful life.

Read this book's chapters, apply them confidently, and see the change yourself. This book explains how you must evaluate your strategies and address your child's issues. Make notes, set reminders, and consistently practice strategies to forge confidence in yourself and your child. Some strategies may work, and some may not. But do not get disheartened. Remember—where there is a will, there is a way!

You have no excuse not to raise an extraordinary child. All the resources you need are here, so do not hesitate to take action! In a few easy steps, find the key to peaceful parenting. Stay determined and optimistic, and you will get through this!

WANT TO HELP OTHERS?

You're doing a remarkable thing, and everything you've learned here will make your journey that little bit easier. Now you have the perfect opportunity to give that chance to other parents!

Simply by leaving your honest opinion of this book on Amazon, you'll show new readers where they can find the guidance they're looking for – no matter how little time they have. Don't have an Amazon account? Please consider leaving a review in Goodreads and sharing in other Facebook Groups to help parents know this is a resource they can't pass up.

Thank you for your support. The parenting journey can feel terribly isolating at times… but when we share information, we see that none of us is really alone.

If you are in the UK, please scan the QR code below to leave your review.

If you are in the US, please scan the QR code below to leave your review.

REFERENCES

Bertin, M. (2022, April 6) *Calm starts at home: How to teach emotional regulation skills.* Additude. https://www.additudemag.com/emotional-regulation-skills-adhd-children/

Carlson, G. (2022, February 9). *A new diagnosis for explosive behavior: The pros and cons of disruptive mood dysregulation disorder.* Child Mind Institute. https://childmind.org/article/a-new-diagnosis-for-explosive-behavior/#:~:text=The%20fact%20is%2C%20you%20get,%2C%20hypersexuality%2C%20and%20disordered%20thinking

Dodson, W. (2022, August 10) *When angry kids lash out: How to defuse explosive reactions.* Additude. https://www.additudemag.com/angry-kids-explosive-emotional-dysregulation-adhd/#:~:text=Create%20a%20Diversion,regain%20a%20sense%20of%20control

Hallowel, E. (2022, April 9). *To master anger, first understand it.* Additude. https://www.additudemag.com/your-add-life-13/

Miller, C. (2022, August 3). How to help children calm down. Child Mind Institute. https://childmind.org/article/how-to-help-children-calm-down/?fbclid=IwAR1vgvR0oPuJyBkM752dVDkxaRdO0a3iAfhySZH_6LlsAZB-m16NwV1tWPM4#

Schuck, P. (2022, March 31). *Why your child's ADHD outbursts are so explosive—and isolating.* Additude. https://www.google.com/amp/s/www.additudemag.com/outbursts-in-adhd-children/amp/

THE SPECIAL EDUCATION PLAYBOOK

THE ULTIMATE GUIDE TO EMPOWER PARENTS IN THE 504/IEP PROCESS TO UNLOCK YOUR CHILD'S UNIQUE LEARNING PROFILE

Follow me on Amazon to see my collection of publications!

Click here to Follow Me **Rose Lyons Author Page**

INTRODUCTION

"Courage does not always roar. Sometimes courage is the little voice at the end of the day that says I'll try again tomorrow."

— MARY ANNE RADMACHER

As a mother raising two children with ADHD, I know the concerns and worries that might keep you up at night. Both of my children were relatively young when they first got diagnosed. I was quick to cover miles of research and learn all that I could understand more about the condition my kids would be living with. I needed to know the system, laws, and regulations governing the education of students with disabilities inside out to ensure that my children received the education and support they were entitled to.

Furthermore, I have tried out numerous strategies to help my children engage with their daily life to the best of their abilities, and it has been rewarding to see them do better with each passing day. Through my efforts to ensure my children's educational needs were being met, it occurred to me that it was the lack of school support, not the disability itself, that was a contributor to academic failure. Your child deserves to live a happy, healthy, and fulfilling life. They have a right to quality education, and you have the right to advocate for your child's special needs.

I've been where you are right now. Navigating the nuances of special education advocacy raises many concerns and questions. I'll address some of your concerns for your child's future in this book. You will learn how your child can be eligible for special needs services in their education and what those services look like. One of my main aims is to elaborate on the special education laws and policies your child can benefit from. The 504 Plan and the IEP (Individualized Education Plan) are some terms you will hear frequently, but you may not quite know what they mean. We will clear up their meanings and see how they work in your child's favor.

Speaking from experience, raising a child with a disability comes with constant worry about the future. I wanted my children to have the best education possible, to be able to build stable relationships, to find a job that is morally and financially uplifting, and to enjoy the same kind of independence that people experience without disabilities. "Will my children be able to take care of themselves? Will they be able to make friends? Will they do well in school?" These are just some questions I would ask myself, panic-stricken.

After years of researching and advocating for my children's special needs myself, the answer I have learned is that, indeed, every child can have a bright, fruitful future. All children can learn and have so much potential to achieve all their goals and aspirations. Of course, taking proactive measures to ensure your child's availability of support and resources comes with challenges, but it is worth it. As parents and guardians, it is up to us to pave the way for our kids to follow their ambitions as best we can.

Seeing how our society lacks in supporting your child can be disheartening. Not to mention, setting out to challenge the system to remove barriers and shape a more inclusive environment can be daunting, at the very least. I know I felt scared, alone, and lonely when other parents or teachers alienated my children at school. I have observed how children with disabilities encounter stigma and discrimination due to negative perceptions about disability held by some teachers or other students at school. It comes from the viewpoint that certain ways of appearance, behavior, and functioning must be accepted. I did not want my kids to feel like there was something "wrong" with them, that they needed "fixing," or that they were less capable of participating in the same activities as other kids.

I have met parents who felt overwhelmed by the constant special care and attention they had to provide for their children. It is common for parents caring for a child with far more severe and complex disabilities to feel physically and emotionally exhausted. It pains me more to see parents who feel hopeless or lost in caring for their children with disabilities. Parents can feel this way due to a severe lack of knowledge and access to the vital resources and services for children with disabilities. So many new parents may not know where to start when finding the right support for their child. Even when they know what is missing, requesting a board of professionals for your child's needs is still scary. It can even be intimidating to speak up with your child's teachers. I, too, felt powerless at the start of my journey until I came across compassionate professionals who could offer me advice and guidance.

Through the experiences of my fair share of struggles, I was inspired to write the books from a caretaker's perspective centered on understanding ADHD. Additionally, I focused on writing about tools for building resilience and self-confidence for a child with ADHD. My work mainly targets parents looking for ways to nurture and support their children with disabilities. I have been researching a range of disabilities and mental health conditions, including ADHD, for the last 15 years. With all the information I have accumulated, I realized that I want to spread my knowledge to those around me and raise awareness for children and adults with special needs through my writing.

I have curated in this book a universe of my knowledge and experience to provide insight into effective strategies and processes that can be used to practice advocating for your child in the educational setting. More importantly, I want to put down everything I wish someone had told me before I had to learn the hard way. In addition to touching upon the basics, I hope to walk you through navigating the nuances of the special education system. A broader understanding of special education can help to make well-informed decisions to better advocate for your child's educational needs and rights. Once you have learned what actions to take, you can also uplift your child's learning experience and accomplish the best outcomes to polish their future.

After years of navigating the school system, I was able to attain individual IEPs (Individualized Education Programs) for my children who have ADHD. It is worth noting that while I may specifically talk about IEPs (worry not, I will explain more in due time), the principles, logic, and research I discuss in this book can be applied to any education system. My objective is for you to have all the basic tools and knowledge you can use to advocate for your child's education needs, regardless of where you are and what laws or education system you have in place.

Through sharing experiences and advice, we can learn from each other and go on in life to work together as well. Hence, I've written this book in hopes of guiding and inspiring other parents who are raising a child with a disability to bring about positive change in their lives as well as in our communities. As the saying goes, "The more, the merrier." So, come along. Here's to building a brighter future.

1

YOU ARE YOUR CHILD'S CHAMPION

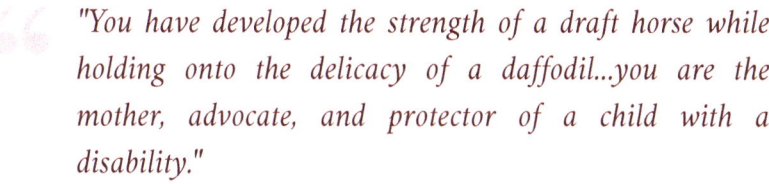

"You have developed the strength of a draft horse while holding onto the delicacy of a daffodil...you are the mother, advocate, and protector of a child with a disability."

— LORI BORGMAN

WHAT IS AN ADVOCATE?

Advocates make room for people in communities whose voices would otherwise be left unheard. Without advocates, we would not have a lot of ways to give support to the people that need it the most. Advocacy brings attention to critical issues. It challenges the conventional way of running things and calls for changes that can be made to empower others. By advocating for your child and special needs, you choose courage, which is no small feat. People are often unaware of the problems that students with disabilities can face in school. Your efforts can help shed light on this matter and help your child have the opportunity to live up to their potential in school.

To plead your case, support a cause, or argue for change is the act of advocating. As a parent, you will be the primary moral support for your child when you choose to speak up on their behalf to improve the status quo. You may hire a professional, i.e., a special education advocate, to help you with the legal approaches, but of all the people that can be there for your child, you are their best ally and advocate.

Special education advocates help you understand your available services, interpret your child's screening and test results, identify your child's learning challenges, and assist you while approaching the school boards to plan an IEP tailored to your child's special needs.

Why does your child need you to be their advocate?

No one sees your child's dreams, aspirations, strengths, and weaknesses better than you do. More importantly, you can model self-advocacy, a strong and crucial skill, for your child. Watching you speak up for their rights, your child will be able to subconsciously understand and learn the importance of expressing one's needs and opinions. Without you, your child cannot attain the best of the services and accommodations available from special education services. Parents are the key substrates as well as catalysts in the process of decision-making for the child's educational needs.

As the default bearer of your child's complete medical and academic history and the knowledge of their desires and preferences, you are the sole member of the IEP team for your child that can truly lead. While the institution your child attends will be known to them for a few years, you will be known to your child their entire life. As a result, you are more likely to have your child's best interests at heart and work more intently to meet their needs than anyone else.

Moreover, the system allows you the power to make decisions that favor your child's education. Use your power wisely. In doing so, allow yourself to feel empowered by the work you choose to do in advocacy. You are integral to your child's well-being by being involved in their education process.

Kids at school don't have more than a few minutes of their teacher's full attention daily. However, you can spend longer periods with your child and walk them through their learning activities and other areas where they may face difficulties. No one else can pay closer attention to your child and understand them how you can.

As a parent of a child with a disability, you are already your child's most significant and capable advocate. For instance, in the educational setting, you may have spoken to a teacher, the school principal, a counselor, or an administrator, on behalf of your child.

Learn all you can about your child's disability

First and foremost, it is crucial to learn all you can about special education and your child's disability. Gather facts and information regarding your child's diagnosis, medical history, and educational history. After you are well-acquainted with what your child's disabilities are and what they would benefit from, you may approach the school board or district to discuss what is needed for your child.

You can join online forums or support groups for parents of children with disabilities. Start by asking lots of questions and listening carefully to the answers you get. Engaging with others in the same boat as you and building a social network will support you on your journey in advocacy.

Become knowledgeable about special education law

The next most important step is to become knowledgeable about special education law. A system of laws for your state and policies and regulations looks after special education. These laws elaborate on the following:

- The rights and protections of parents concerning participation in their children's education
- Eligibility of students for the available special services

Legally, parents have the responsibility and every right to advocate for their children with disabilities. In addition, the federal special education law known as 'The Individuals with

Disabilities Education Act (IDEA)' requires the participation of parents.

You will be learning the rules of a game you are about to play, except the rules, in this case, are your legal rights. Chapter 2 covers the basic laws regarding special education in greater depth.

Your role as a parent is vital to the IEP process. Therefore, being well-versed in the district and federal laws that govern special education in your state is important. Unfortunately, many school administrations don't follow the rules, and some may be unaware. That is why you have to step up and be prepared.

Become a master planner

Remember to consider your child's future as you plan their education. It is easy to get wrapped up in the present. Often, the present is all that most parents will focus on, which does not get one very far. This is not to say that you must micromanage and control every aspect of your child's life down to the t.

You can achieve your long-term goals and objectives more effectively once you master the art of organizing and planning. I advise organizing files of educational records, contact information, and meeting notes.

You can save report cards, worksheets, artwork, or any proof of your child's academic performance, to help record a pattern of their progress. Unfortunately, dealing with the special education system comes with abundant paperwork. Therefore, you will need to devise a document managing system that's easy to access.

In special education, you will attend multiple meetings with IEP team members. Consider all the information that needs to be presented to the team to help them make the right decisions for your child's education. It will help you and the special education team to have copies of your child's file that includes accurate and up-to-date information regarding their disability, educational history, and all the meeting agendas.

Think long-term

While gathering all the information you need to prepare your child's file, you will gain a clearer view of the bigger picture. You will start to see where you stand and what your child may be struggling with in school.

Once you understand the present situation, you must ask yourself questions to build a vision for your child's future. Listen to your child and gain awareness of lived experiences of people who struggle with disabilities. What do you hope to help your child with in school? What are your long-term goals?

What can improve the special education system? First, judge your child's limitations in school, and create a vision of what support you want for your child at school.

As a parent, you will see the most value in your child's positive traits. You must make the right call and devise long-term plans for your child's security. You have the right to suggest improvements for the learning environment in school so that children with disabilities can adapt as easily as students without disabilities.

Be a problem-solver, not a problem-maker

At times, your arguments may be overlooked, or you might feel like you are not getting enough engagement from the administration while trying to convey your message. Remember to keep a cool head at all times. While assertiveness and persistence are important, aggression and anger will not work in your favor. Instead, emphasize healthy relations with everyone on the team. A key element in advocacy is patience. There is no promise of a silver bullet or an overnight solution for your child's special needs in education. So, trust the process.

In the advocacy world, you learn to ask questions and listen carefully to the answer you get. You will gain a stronger grip on using "Who, What, Why, When, Where, and How" questions. You will be able to solidify your communication skills and learn to identify communication gaps when they arise. Granted, there are numerous flaws in the education system. However, as an advocate, you are meant to develop strategies for improvement and communicate effectively rather than look for people to blame.

Get to know your childcare provider or teacher

Once you have learned the importance of having a solution-oriented mindset, you will find it easier to work with other care providers and the authorities concerned with your child's education for the best outcomes. So, first, work with your child's teacher or care provider to understand the complexities of the education system and solve problems together. Then, to get your child an appropriate education, you want to see how the educators' and caregivers' sides work as well. As I said before, it is like learning the rules of a game.

Stay in touch with your child's teacher. Provide them with information regarding your child's disability, strengths and weaknesses, and any factors affecting their learning and development. As a parent, you are in the ideal position to observe your child's learning styles and convey them to the teacher. This way, the teacher or care provider can be well-informed and support your child as needed. By getting to know your child's teacher, you can gather information about the learning environment at school and offer suggestions and strategies for improvement. In addition, it will be helpful to have insight into the approaches used by the teacher and see how well they may be working for your child.

Special education teachers and childcare providers are usually highly qualified and won't tell you all about their advanced degrees, so it is up to you to ask. You can nurture a healthy bond with your child's teacher and other professional care providers by acknowledging their efforts and appreciating their hard work.

Communicate with teachers and other professionals in education consistently and in writing, and hang on to these connections so that you can refer back to them as needed.

WHAT IS THE IMPORTANCE OF 'PARENT PARTICIPATION' IN SPECIAL EDUCATION?

Parents are a part of the IEP Team of their child and any other group that makes decisions relevant to their child's educational placement.

As a participant in special education, you will be engaging with the school personnel on three levels: individual, system, and policy. While your part in the IEP team is important, you may feel like the team members see you as less informed about the decision-making process, especially if you disagree with how things are run. Don't let these thoughts hinder you, and don't let school faculty intimidate you. Instead, let's examine how involvement can make a difference in your child's life.

Parents bring a valuable element to decision-making in their child's education: familiarity. They have an in-depth understanding of their child's physical, emotional, and social development. They are aware of all the ups and downs their child has encountered. Parents are the only special education team members who have been and will be actively involved throughout their child's education and career. You can judge and offer insight into whether the current techniques and instructions are helping your child learn and whether the strategies used are supportive or counterproductive. Your input into the policies, programs, or practices that affect the services for children in special education is highly influential.

Parental participation opens the door to better outcomes for children. It involves them in the system that will serve their child. As an active team member that decides your child's educational placement, you can ensure that your child's due legal rights are being fulfilled, i.e., children with disabilities have a legal right to Free Appropriate Public Education (FAPE). For example, suppose you feel the school or district fails to provide an appropriate education. In that case, you can intervene and request a due process hearing with the special education team members to convey your concerns. By choosing to work with special education, you will also be able to build a better network of support to help you with concerns.

Other benefits of parent involvement for your child include better attendance and participation in class, better grades, and a more positive attitude towards school in general. In the long run, children with involved parents are more likely to excel in their classroom activities and studies, graduate on time and pursue higher education. In addition, knowing what is happening at school allows you to be a stronger advocate for your child.

Examples of basic parent participation can include

- participating in parent-teacher meetings,
- attending school activities,
- volunteering in classrooms,
- maintaining communication with your child's teacher at school,
- coaching your child,
- helping with homework, and
- simply talking to your child about their day at school.

Every effort counts as it conveys a valuable, impactful message to your child: "You are important to me."

TIPS TO HELP YOU ADVOCATE FOR YOUR CHILD AT SCHOOL

During this process, remember that you are not alone. You will find many people who agree with you and join your cause. You might even help other parents seeking support for their child with a disability. However, to succeed, keep clear-cut goals and realistic expectations in mind.

- **Be okay with speaking up**

As I have mentioned before and will continue to explain throughout this book, the law is on your side. You have the right to speak on your child's behalf to ensure they receive appropriate education from their school. Many parents underestimate their importance to the IEP team and other school personnel when deciding on their child's education. They feel intimidated or uncomfortable speaking with educators as if they might be over-stepping or over-efficient. Remember that you are a critical part of the decision-making team for students with disabilities. You are a voice for your child.

- **Jot down your thoughts**

This applies to every step you take while seeking educational resources and services for your child. Ponder about the way things are run and write down your sentiments. Parents who wish to advocate for their child have a say in how the learning environment at school can be improved or how the IEP team can provide better services. Write down your thoughts ahead of time so you can bring them up in meetings as needed.

- **Speak to someone you can count on**

It can be a friend, partner or spouse, counselor, teacher, or parent going through the same process as you. If you could use an outsider's perspective or a second opinion, you can share your thoughts and experience with someone you trust. It will help you feel more confident about your decisions and the next steps you would like to take. You might even be able to brainstorm ideas with the person you choose to open up to. Talking to someone also lessens the weight of the stressful or emotional experience you might be facing. Initially, I lacked motivation because I was afraid of being alone. My friends and family were often there to remind me that I was on the right track by looking out for my kids. I was pleased to learn that I wasn't alone; I met many parents along the way whose goals and objectives aligned with mine.

- **Don't be afraid to show emotion — but be respectful**

One's passion for a cause drives advocacy. While it is important to stand your ground and assert your side of the argument, it is better to always remain calm and collected and communicate politely. My advice is to listen closely at all times and gauge the responses you get. Be respectful and polite, even in difficult people or situations. It is easy to get overwhelmed, especially when you are just trying to do your best to raise a child with special needs, but it is important to remember that every problem has a solution. The faculty at school is there to help you, not antagonize you.

- **Keep going**

Advocating for your child is not possible in one go. But you will likely need to keep doing it. You must keep asking the school for updates, progress reports, and time slots for meetings or discussions. School staff often appreciate parents who show up and participate in their child's education. Being an active, involved parent can significantly improve the education of your child with special needs. Your efforts won't go in vain, I promise.

WHAT TO KEEP IN MIND AS YOU ADVOCATE FOR YOUR CHILD

Only you know your child best

You are the best person to be by your child's side through thick and thin. You know your child's likes and dislikes, positive qualities, potential, what makes them happy, what upsets them, and most importantly, what they need. Other people in the education system may try to tell you what they think your child needs, but you will know whose say aligns closest with what is appropriate for your child – and it will usually be yours.

The staff members, teachers, and professionals want to help your child

Often, the people working in special education are there by choice. They genuinely do want to help and accommodate you as much as they have the liberty to do so. Remember to work with them, not antagonize them – you can put those momma bear claws away.

Focus on your child's positive traits

Schools often highlight where the students lack or what they struggle with. In meetings with teachers or school staff, you will be presented with reports focusing on the negatives or the areas where your child is lagging. Weaknesses and shortcomings are important to highlight to be corrected or made improvements. However, things can appear gloomy if "areas of improvement" and weaknesses are all the information you are being presented with. It is important to keep your child's strengths in mind and pair them with their weaknesses. For instance, your child may struggle with spelling correctly, but they can draw and color in pictures on their own.

Communicate openly with your child's teachers and care providers

Communication is key! If things are not going well at school, speaking up and expressing your concerns is important. Ask questions and engage with your child's teachers to get the clearest idea of what is happening.

Your child is unique

Embrace your child's uniqueness and celebrate it. Whatever sets your child apart from the other kids is a part of his or her beauty. Accept your child just how they are, and teach them self-acceptance and self-love. Have faith in your child and use your love for them to push yourself in advocating for them.

Advocating can be difficult

Setbacks or drastic changes can make it difficult to stay optimistic and have hope while advocating for your child. Most days, you will struggle a lot while figuring out how the system works or how to get your word across to someone. You will struggle because your child will struggle, and it pains you to see that. From signing trails of paper to chasing and tracking down officials or teachers for meetings or phone calls, advocating is hard work and a tough fight to win. A lot of swimming will be upstream, but by being mentally prepared, you have it in you to accomplish anything.

Look out for yourself

Burnout – can be deadly. If you are not looking after your basic needs and carving out time for yourself, you will fall short unexpectedly. Stress has drastic effects on the body and mind. Nothing is worth the cost to your health and well-being. There were times when I lost myself completely. I would forget to eat some days. I was running on caffeine and skipping sleep, only getting 4 hours of sleep, per night, for weeks. It was not okay.

Looking back, I wish I'd taken time to look after myself. You are not weak or less competent for taking breaks when necessary. You will do a better job at being a parent and advocating for your child if you ensure you are in good health. Being a parent of a child with special needs, remember you have needs too.

This chapter discussed the importance of advocating for your child and how you can do it. Let's now turn our attention to the legal framework surrounding special education. Understanding the laws and regulations that govern the provision of special education can be a crucial tool in advocating for your child and ensuring that they receive the services and support they need to thrive in this world.

2

THE LAW IS ON YOUR SIDE

S pecial education laws serve as a crucial safeguard for the
rights of students with disabilities and their families. They
are designed to be both supportive and protective, working to
make sure that all students with disabilities have the opportunity
to receive an appropriate education that meets their unique
needs.

They also give parents the legal tools and resources to advocate
for their children and hold schools accountable. Children with
disabilities that hinder their learning cannot be overlooked in
public schools because federal law has made it mandatory for
their needs to be looked after.

With that said, the law is on your side.

WHAT IS SPECIAL EDUCATION?

Special education refers to supportive learning environments with services tailored to meet the needs of kids with disabilities. The "one size fits all" approach does not apply to special education. Instead, special education offers learning environments, and teaching approaches, adapted to support students with disabilities.

At a glance, the objective of special education is to level the playing field and have educational goals appropriate for students of different ages. Students with special needs can be considered 'differently-abled,' meaning while they can learn, their delayed emotional, physical, mental, or social development places them behind their peers. Hence, special education teachers are responsible for instructing and facilitating each student individually with lesson plans that fit their needs.

In Canada, the USA, and the UK, students with disabilities or special needs can qualify for what is known as an "Individualized Education Program (IEP)." An IEP is designed to meet the individual child's learning needs. It includes the support the school will provide and ways of measuring the student's progress in learning.

Students with special needs face challenges that interfere with their learning, requiring more support than conventionally available in traditional classrooms.

Students in special education are engaged using different styles according to their learning abilities. For instance, most children with disabilities are visual learners who understand better through pictures than through plain speech. This approach uses alternative learning styles to make classroom activities and instructions more personalized and simpler.

In special education classrooms, teachers are trained to engage students using instructional methods and techniques to guide them better, which reduces the psychological, physical, or academic challenge of the material being taught. Teachers in special education also focus on implementing an individual child-centered approach. This approach can enhance learning and ensure that each child's learning capacity is sufficiently engaged while their physical and emotional needs are being looked after.

WHY IS SPECIAL EDUCATION IMPORTANT AND NECESSARY?

The current education system that's conventionally available may not be up to the standards required to accommodate the unique requirements of children with disabilities.

Does this mean that a large fraction of the population around the world might be missing out on a vital education?

Children with disabilities also deserve to become valuable members of society when they grow up. As grown-ups with the means of providing, it is our duty to look out for our children with unique needs and work to get them the support they need. Schools can support special needs students through the environment (the school system and classroom) and other learning aids (modifications). Some of the most important roles in a child's development are parents and teachers. After the parents, teachers have some of the most influence on a child's development.

Special education can allow equal opportunities for people with disabilities. Children with disabilities may face difficulties or even be limited in regular classrooms. For instance, students that are hard of hearing or live with deafness won't truly benefit from the conventional method of teaching that is common in regular classrooms where the teacher speaks to the class. Special education programs ensure that each child with special needs is accommodated with the appropriate learning aids and taught with methods suitable for their understanding.

Another important objective of special education is to provide students with adequate opportunities, to develop their abilities and an environment that supports their learning and quality of life. Special education grants students with disabilities a chance to be accepted, grow, contribute to their society and be surrounded by individuals with the same struggles. Hence, they know that they are not alone. This can be possible if schools and government institutions that provide free appropriate education cooperate. Children with special needs are capable of grand achievements. However, they need our help, understanding, and plenty of compassion.

INDIVIDUALS WITH DISABILITIES EDUCATION ACT (IDEA) (2004)

One of the most important laws that protect your child's right to special education services is the Individuals with Disabilities Education Act (IDEA).

What is the idea behind IDEA?

Time for a new term – FAPE (Free Appropriate Public Education). The educational rights of children with disabilities in the US come under the legal term "FAPE." It constitutes several services and supports offered in special education, e.g., trained educators, speech therapy, psychological and academic counseling, and speech therapy. In addition to providing these services, children with disabilities are to be educated in the same classrooms as their non-disabled peers, as best as possible, in what is known as the Least Restrictive Environment (LRE).

Public schools are responsible for seeking out and identifying children with special needs and getting them evaluated. This process of searching and evaluation is carried out to provide special education and other supportive resources for children with disabilities. This service, mandated by federal law, applies to individuals from birth to age 21. It is easy enough to pick up on a child's differences from their peers in school by mere observation, but how do schools look for children with disabilities? Schools and state governments may take steps to reach out by running media campaigns or posting notices in public spots. In addition, healthcare providers, doctors, and other clinicians may receive notices or information.

The Child Find Mandate and FAPE make up IDEA as the federal law that provides guidelines for special education programs.

What is the history and purpose of IDEA?

In 1973, Congress passed Section 504 of the Rehabilitation Act, safeguarding the disabled against discrimination. It allowed programs that received federal funding to include people with disabilities. Before the introduction of IDEA, states would place children with disabilities in separate classrooms or schools away from their peers. As a result, education for children with disabilities was poor, underfunded, and overlooked.

In 2004, IDEA was reauthorized, and some changes were made to the law, such as:

1. Student progress: Schools were required by the law to show proof of progress being made by students with disabilities and to make sure that IEPs mirror grade-level standards.
2. Parental involvement: The law emphasized parental involvement in the child's IEP process. For instance, it required schools to issue a written notice if any changes were to be made to a child's IEP.
3. Qualified teachers: It was required by law for special education teachers to have completed a bachelor's degree or attained certification in special education.
4. Discipline: Circumstances were defined under which students with disabilities may receive disciplinary action while taking disabilities into account.

Why does any of this matter?

IDEA guards the legal rights of every child with a disability to a free, appropriate public education at no cost to their family. If a parent believes their child is not receiving a free, appropriate education, they have the right to file a complaint or request a due process hearing. With the help of this process, you can sort out the matters legally, resolve disputes with the school district team, and enforce your child's right to a FAPE. I mean this when I tell you the law is on your side. You can use this to your advantage.

The 6 Principles of IDEA

Let's look at what your child has a right to based on the IDEA.

There are six principles based on IDEA:

FAPE:

By federal law, students in special education are entitled to a "free, appropriate public education" (FAPE).

What exactly is an "appropriate" education?

Based on a court case dating back to 1982, the definition of FAPE states that school districts must provide an educational program that is "reasonably calculated to enable the child to receive **some** educational benefits," which includes instructions tailored for each student and other services or learning aids. It is worth noting that an "appropriate" education may not necessarily mean an ideal or the "best possible" education. It does not mean an education that "maximizes the child's educational potential," either. While the IDEA allows many benefits for your child that would otherwise not be there, it is not a perfect law.

As of late, it was decided in courts that the "appropriateness" indicates that students in special education should have ease in accessing the general education curriculum, to meet the same level of challenge established for all children according to the grade-level standards.

IDEA requires that students with disabilities be granted accommodations and modifications that increase their chance of achieving standard grade-level performance. Under IDEA, schools should provide a child with college- and career readiness tools. An education that does not provide the right social and academic tools for a child to build with does not come under FAPE.

Appropriate evaluation

Students with disabilities must be evaluated in all aspects related to their disability. This can help ensure the student is placed in special education correctly, their progress is assessed regularly, and additional support is provided.

Individualized Education Program (IEP)

Each student with a disability is entitled to an IEP, the map that draws out their educational program. An IEP is designed with special attention to the child's unique educational needs, determined by teachers, parents, and other professionals, who are qualified to suggest the appropriate measures to be taken during studies. It is a written document that uses the student's evaluation information to meet their educational requirements. It includes information about the student's current educational performance, goals and milestone objectives, services and support, and details of instances where the student cannot participate in general education classrooms.

Least Restrictive Environment (LRE)

Students with disabilities are placed in the same classroom and educated alongside their non-disabled peers as much as possible, to the maximum extent that's appropriate. The IDEA insists that students with disabilities have placement in a general education setting or the Least Restrictive Environment (LRE) possible. LRE is a legal term that incorporates the idea of inclusion.

Parent participation

IDEA is dedicated to parent participation in the child's placement decisions. Under this provision, the local school boards and educational agencies must ensure that the parents of a child with a disability are included in the groups that make decisions regarding the child's placement, IEP and LRE.

In addition, parents have the right to be notified of their child's planned evaluations, have access to the evaluation and planning resources, and involvement in all the meetings relevant to their child's educational placement. Therefore, the IDEA supports your right to participate equally in the IEP process. Similarly, parents have the right to give consent or refuse further evaluation of their child.

Procedural safeguards

The procedural safeguards established by the IDEA aim to help parents and students enforce their rights. The purposes of this principle are to give parents access to the information regarding their child's placement and planning and to have procedures put in place to resolve disagreements, if any, between parents and schools regarding the child's placement.

Under this principle, parents can review their child's educational records, be notified of meetings preceding the child's evaluation or placement, and be granted an Independent Educational Evaluation (IEE) at these meetings. In addition, in case of disagreements or violation of IDEA codes, the parent's right to request a due process hearing with the state education agencies or beyond is safeguarded.

What is the caveat in the rights IDEA grants your child?

The IDEA grants children with disabilities the right to a FAPE, the right to an IEP, and to attain education in the least restrictive environment possible. These are all important rights, but this law does not promise a hundred-percent efficiency; it is not a perfect system. Here are some caveats to the rights IDEA does allow:

1. To be eligible for special education services, the child's disability must be severe enough to significantly impact their learning. The child must meet the eligibility prerequisites set in IDEA to receive special education services.
2. Parents must stay up-to-date with their child's progress and advocate for their child's rights. This would mean having to work with the school consistently.

3. Many schools may be underfunded or have limited resources to provide all the services a child with disabilities may need.

The specific criteria that qualify a child for special education services may vary by country or region. However, right off the bat, I can let you know that your child's eligibility for special education depends on two factors:

- The child has a documented disability
- This disability significantly affects the child's educational performance.

Not every child with different learning abilities is eligible for special education. This means that, by law, the IEP team has the leeway to decide if a child qualifies for special education services. Read more about eligibility in Chapter 6.

It is possible that the team may not qualify the child for special education services or recognize a specific learning disability if the differences between ability and achievement are primarily due to:

- A visual, hearing, or motor impairment
- Intellectual disabilities
- Mood disturbances
- Cultural or socioeconomic differences

WHAT IS SECTION 504?

To protect the rights of individuals with disabilities, a federal law was enacted in 1973. This helped reduce the discrimination that individuals with disabilities would have to face in different aspects of life, such as education and employment.

Section 504 was established to support the rights of individuals with disabilities to education. It strictly prohibits discrimination against individuals with disabilities in public programs that receive federal funding. This law has ensured that schools provide equal access to educational opportunities and experiences for students with disabilities, no matter how severely their learning is impacted. It stands for features of both equality and equity. To be specific, 34 C.F.R.§104 states:

"No otherwise qualified individual with a disability in the United States... shall, solely by reason of her or his disability, be excluded from participation in, be denied the benefits of, or be subjected to discrimination under any program or activity receiving Federal financial assistance."

Section 504 defines a person with a disability as someone with a history of physical or mental impairment that currently creates limitations in their daily life. It also requires that the person with a disability must have a record of an impairment, such as a medical history, and be considered to have such an impairment. In addition, they should be evaluated and have a confirmed impairment or disability or a diagnosis from a qualified professional.

The differences between IDEA and Section 504

Section 504 has a broader definition of disability than IDEA's, allowing children with disabilities to be eligible for special education support and services. However, it is similar to IDEA in that it eliminates obstacles that prevent students with disabilities from receiving FAPE. The most prominent difference between the two would be that Section 504 is a civil rights law that rules out discrimination based on disability in programs or activities funded by the government, e.g., public libraries, universities, and colleges. At the same time, the IDEA is an education law that allows students with disabilities to be eligible for educational benefits through an IEP and funds local educational agencies to help them provide special education services. Civil rights are individual rights guaranteed and protected by the US Constitution and additional laws enacted by Congress. For instance, the Americans with Disabilities Act of 1990 is a civil rights law that protects against unlawful discrimination.

The primary concern with eligibility for special education is whether an individual's impairment can be acknowledged under the law. Under IDEA, a student is eligible for special education services provided they have one or more of the 13 disabilities that IDEA has recognized and enlisted. In addition, under Section 504, a student is considered to have a disability if they have a physical or mental impairment that significantly restricts participation in major life activities and functioning, such as walking, seeing, hearing, speaking, breathing, learning, or taking care of oneself.

Regarding each law's benefits, a Section 504 Plan also provides the same services that suit a child's special needs as IDEA. Still, it does not necessarily require academic improvement during its run.

The procedural safeguards that protect the rights of students with disabilities and their parents are provided by both Section 504 and IDEA. However, it can be argued that fewer procedural safeguards are offered to children and parents under Section 504 than IDEA.

In conclusion, Section 504 can guarantee access to appropriate education for a child with a disability. At the same time, IDEA aims to guarantee the academic progress and overall success of a child with a disability.

Now that we have explored special education's legalities, the next chapter focuses on two key tools often used to support students with disabilities: 504 plans and Individualized Education Programs (IEPs).

*Definitions of special education terms compiled using www. dredf.org

Glossary	
Accommodation	A change in curriculum or instruction that does not substantially modify the requirements of the class or alter the content standards or benchmarks.
Assessment	Any systematic method of obtaining information from tests and other sources; used to draw inferences about characteristics of people, objects, or programs. An initial evaluation (or periodic re-evaluation) to determine whether a child is a child with a disability and to determine the educational needs of this child.
Due Process	In general, a course of legal proceedings according to rules and principles established for enforcement and protection of private rights. Essential components of due process are "notice" and "a meaningful opportunity to be heard."
Due Process Hearing	The formal, legal procedure guaranteed by federal law to resolve disputes relating to the education of IDEA-eligible children with disabilities to ensure that each receives a free and appropriate public education (FAPE) tailored to his/her unique needs.
Free Appropriate Public Education (FAPE)	Special education and related services are provided to students with disabilities at public expense and under public supervision and direction at no cost to the student's parents.
Inclusion [or] Inclusive Education	A belief that every student is entitled to an instructional program that meets his or her individual needs and learning characteristics; a commitment to build and maintain an assured sense of belonging for all students, regardless of strengths or challenges.

3

THE 504 PLAN AND THE IEP

W hat is the 411 on the 504 and the IEP? If you have a child with special educational needs, you may have heard these terms thrown around quite a bit, but perhaps you are unsure what they mean or how they differ. This chapter has you covered. We will demystify these often-confusing acronyms and give you the lowdown on how 504 plans and IEPs work, how they differ, and how they can help ensure that your child has the support they need to succeed school.

WHAT IS A 504 PLAN?

A 504 plan helps make the changes needed at school so that your child can learn with fewer obstacles. It is a legal document drawn up under Section 504 of the Rehabilitation Act of 1973. It summarizes accommodations and services that a student with a disability or a learning challenge can access.

A 504 plan is not to be confused with special education, which is specialized instruction for children that need more than what standard teaching offers. A 504 plan is about ensuring that a classroom fits your child's learning style. It benefits students with disabilities who do not necessarily need or qualify for special education. These plans can help children with disabilities do as well as their peers in class and be able to participate fully during learning. The goal is to break down barriers, make classrooms more accessible, and make sure that no student with a disability is cast out from partaking in protected programs (programs that receive federal funding).

The changes you can make at school using a 504 plan to support your child's learning are known as *accommodations*, which are discussed in more detail in Chapter 8. An accommodation does not alter a classroom's standard prerequisites or the content being taught. It is simply a minor change in instructions to help support a child's learning. Rather than changing what your child learns, the 504 plan changes how your child can learn.

On the other hand, the following are some misconceptions I'd like to discuss regarding the 504 plan:

Myth 1: A 504 plan only grants accommodation, not services

The U.S. Department of Education includes school services in 504 plans. These services can include study skills classes, tutoring, and speech therapy.

Myth 2: A 504 plan is not as effective as an IEP

Regardless of what program is being opted for, a good plan meets a child's needs. For example, a child whose learning abilities are not impaired to a severe extent may only need accommodations through a 504 plan. However, a student with severe learning challenges might need special education through an IEP.

Myth 3: A 504 plan is the same thing as an IEP

Both programs help children improve in school, but different laws support them and work differently. For example, a 504 plan increases a child's access to learning at school. However, an IEP focuses on special education services, which are more elaborate than 504 plans.

Myth 4: Students in Advanced Placement can't get 504 accommodations

That is not true. Multiple young students with 504 plan to take advanced or AP classes. A child with a 504 plan in an advanced placement classroom has the same rights as anywhere else in school – the right to equal access to learning.

Myth 6: Colleges offer 504 plans

There are no IEPs or 504 plans in colleges. Therefore, even if students qualify for college accommodations, they will not be provided based on a 504 plan.

What is included in a 504 plan?

A 504 plan is drawn up depending on a student's individual needs, which can vary, and their strengths. 504 plans can also vary as each school district creates plans, which might not even involve input from parents. In a 504 plan, you work with the school to specify accommodations that will improve your child's learning experience and access to general education. However, some components may commonly include:

1. An overview of the student's disability or learning challenges, how their ability to learn, and accessibility to education is affected.
2. A section or outline of specific accommodations to be provided to the student.
3. Goals and objectives for the child, such as improving their ability to focus, reducing stress and anxiety, and improving math, and comprehension, skills, are also enlisted in the plan.
4. Evaluation and reviewing procedures
5. Duration of the plan

Common mistakes to avoid in a 504 plan

Since 504 plans are relatively less restricting than IEPs, parents can easily slip or miss a key step in the process. Here are some mistakes you should avoid making:

Number 1: Not fully knowing what is achievable with a 504 plan

If you consult the school for help, they may skip over some helpful details of what a 504 plan can include. They may not elaborate on the accommodations and support services that can be provided. Have a thorough understanding of what is possible with a 504 plan before negotiating its term with the school. Use your knowledge to ask relevant questions and request more specific options that can be a part of your child's 504 plan.

Number 2: Not being proactive

Unlike with IEPs, the law does not guarantee parents the right to attend 504 plan meetings. Since quite a few schools are happy to include parents, you can ask to attend the meetings yourself. Don't expect an invitation. You must show concern for your child's needs, so let the school know you would like to participate in your child's 504 plan meetings.

Number 3: Being compliant with the school's standard 504 plan for all students with a disability

Some school districts have a preset 504 plan for all students with a certain disability that they will present to parents. Schools may try to persuade you to take on the standard plan by saying, "It has helped everyone who's struggled the same as your child." Use the standard plan you are presented with to get an idea, but remember that your child's plan must be customized to meet individual needs, not generalized needs.

Number 4: Assuming that the school is sticking to your child's 504 plan

Once your child's 504 plan is in place, it is important to remain proactive and keep track of what is happening. This can be done by regularly talking to your child about their day at school and keeping a check on their homework and grades.

Number 5: Not requesting thorough annual reviews and updates of the 504 plan

The 504 plan committee must hold up its responsibilities and revise your child's 504 plan annually. It is up to you to push the committee for a careful review of the plan. As the school year progresses, academic loads increase, and the learning content becomes increasingly challenging. Increasing difficulty levels can pose newer challenges, so you will ideally want your child's 504 plan to update regularly. An update in the 504 plan can include documentation of changing needs, changes in the accommodations and modifications being provided, and other support resources.

Tips for developing an effective 504 plan

As an advocate, you can shape the school's decisions regarding developing your child's 504 plan. Here are a few tips to help make the right decisions for your child's 504 plan:

Number 1: Make sure the plan meets your child's individual needs

As mentioned, many schools create standard 504 plans for all students who share a certain disability or the same learning differences, such as dyslexia. While it seems efficient, it is not foolproof. Choosing a standard 504 plan can result in a plan that does not suit your child. Kids with the same condition still have their differences. For instance, a child with ADHD who struggles with attention deficiency will require a different learning environment than another child who struggles with hyperactivity and lacks impulse control.

Number 2: Be specific about the services you are requesting for your child

Vague mentions of accommodations, services, or teaching strategies in the plan are not useful nor insightful for educators or service providers. Instead, be more specific and elaborate on the details of what you are requesting. For example, if you have mentioned that your child needs assistive technology as a learning aid in class, explain what kind of technology it is, when and where your child should use it, and explain the purpose of it.

Number 3: Include teacher and faculty names in the plan

Enlist the school staff, counselor, school nurse, or teachers responsible for looking after your child's accommodations, in the plan, along with their contact information. The head of the planning committee or plan coordinator should also be specified. Keep a copy of this list readily available so you know whom to talk to any time you need to address something regarding the plan.

Number 4: Check in with your child and their teachers regularly

Talk to your child and their teachers to check whether the plan is giving positive outcomes; is your child's focus improving in class? Is your child able to learn more effectively with assistive technology?

Number 5: Revise and update the 504 plan once every year

Your child's 504 plan should be reviewed by the school year to help make sure that the plan is meeting your child's needs in class. In revisiting the plan, the child's current learning obstacles and areas of improvement are specified. Any additional services and help that might be needed are also specified as the academic challenges increase in complexity.

Now that we are well-versed with the 504 plan let's talk about the Individualized Education Program (IEP).

INDIVIDUALIZED EDUCATION PROGRAM (IEP)

An IEP is a personalized plan or program for a child with a disability in school that can be acquired by a student with a disability in public education from pre-kindergarten till 12th grade.

I reiterate that the law is on your side because special education law, or IDEA, backs up IEPs and, as a result, supports the programs and resources that your child could benefit from. With an IEP, families, students, and schools are legally protected. So, parents can be involved in the implemented decisions that affect their child's education. In addition, students with disabilities have the right to a quality education that an IEP can help provide. The IEP sets achievable learning goals for a child and specifies the services and learning support the school district will provide the child with.

Who do I go to?

So, we have covered the basics of an IEP and how it is meant to help your child. But how exactly do you get an IEP? The process of getting an IEP starts with the school's administration. You can start by submitting a written application or request for special education services. The request is followed up by the child being evaluated by the school district. The evaluation will include input from you, your child's doctor, counselor, and teachers.

An alternative to the IEP is a 504 plan.

Sometimes, a school may find that a child is not eligible to receive special education services in the form of an IEP. However, this is not a dead-end. For instance, many parents request a 504 plan if their child does not qualify for an IEP. Similar to an IEP, a 504 plan provides accommodations and learning support to enhance your child's access to learning.

The IEP process is well in place if the school finds your child eligible for an IEP. As discussed previously, the IDEA gives you the right to oversee and participate in every step of your child's IEP process. Therefore, you should be automatically integrated as your child's IEP team member.

Misconceptions about IEPs

The legal definition of an IEP can seem pretty straightforward, but the details can be confusing. Below, I have discussed some of the most common misconceptions I know of:

Number 1: Every child who struggles in school is guaranteed an IEP

Your child must be eligible for special education services under IDEA, which requires meeting two criteria.

Firstly, they must have a legitimate diagnosis of a disability covered by IDEA from a qualified health professional. IDEA covers 13 categories of disability, including "specific learning disabilities."

Secondly, The school has to see if the student needs special education services to progress in school after all. Note that it is essential to meet *both* criteria.

Number 2: The school will guarantee that the IEP is implemented

The school has to provide the services and learning accommodations for your child, as agreed upon in the IEP. However, there is no guarantee that the school teachers and staff are implementing every decision outlined in the IEP. As most humans do, they may overlook certain details or simply forget about some of the IEP's components. Your role as a parent in the IEP process is pivotal in this context. Part of your job is ensuring your child gets all the services and accommodations as promised in the IEP. Make it a routine habit to check your child's schoolwork, progress reports, and how they generally feel about school.

Number 3: An IEP continues to support your child beyond high school

The IEP is terminated once the student graduates high school. Special education does not apply beyond the school years till college or work but doesn't worry. One of the major components the IEP has to look after is the transition plan, which is given particular emphasis towards the end of a student's high school career.

Number 4: Having an IEP automatically places your child in a special education classroom

Children with IEPs must be placed in the *least restrictive environment* (LRE), over the course of their education, in public schooling. Your child would receive learning support and accommodations in the general education classroom whenever possible. Any time spent in a "resource room" or a separate class for students with special needs will be mentioned in the IEP.

The differences between an IEP and a 504 plan

An IEP charts the special education experience at school for your child. Meanwhile, a 504 plan aims at removing barriers and increasing access for students with disabilities, allowing them to participate in public education the same as their non-disabled peers.

Different laws cover each program. Revisit the section on "The differences between IDEA and Section 504". An IEP is covered by the IDEA – a special education law for children with disabilities. A Section 504 plan is covered by a civil rights law, i.e., Section 504 of the Rehabilitation Act of 1973, which prevents discrimination against individuals with disabilities in government-funded programs such as public school education.

There are also differences in eligibility criteria, as listed below:

It is relatively easier to qualify for a 504 plan than an IEP. The requirements for a 504 plan are as follows:

1. A child has *any* disability.
2. The disability must interfere with the child's learning ability in a general education classroom.

An Independent Educational Evaluation (IEE) is private testing, the cost of which is covered by the public school, that sees if a child needs special education. It is usually requested when families disagree with a school evaluation, and it must be done by outside experts who don't work for the school system. For a Section 504 plan, however, families cannot request IEEs.

In devising an IEP, there are strict requirements regarding the team members participating. Meanwhile, there is a lesser restriction on who gets to play a part in making a 504 plan. A 504 plan is designed by a team of individuals familiar with the child, like yourself, who understand the evaluation data and options available for special services. This can include

- The child's parent or guardian
- General and special education teachers
- The school principal

Regarding costs and funding, an IEP and a 504 plan provide students with the appropriate services at no charge. However, states receive extra funding for students with IEPs. On the other hand, states do not receive any extra funds while providing for students with 504 plans because the IDEA simply does not serve students with 504 plans.

Common mistakes to avoid during the IEP process

Prior knowledge of these common mistakes can help you prevent future problems that could undo your progress, negatively affect your child and cost you a lot of time and money. At IEP meetings, you have to keep two things in mind:

- Obtain appropriate special education services for your child
- Build and maintain positive, healthy professional relationships with the school staff

Number 1: Not making a long-term plan for your child's education

Worrying too much about the present can make you skip over the importance of having a plan. Many parents don't consider the future until it is too late. The plan should cover aspects that could affect your child's future skills and knowledge, such as academic, behavioral, social, and emotional development goals.

Number 2: Not understanding your child's unique learning needs

Your child's disability creates learning differences. These differences require alternative, more elaborate approaches and teaching strategies that can engage children with disabilities and their learning capacities effectively. When you attend IEP meetings, present a well-researched, thorough understanding of your child's learning challenges and strong points.

Number 3: Letting the school make decisions for your child

Don't take a backseat in the IEP planning process. Lots of parents assume that they simply are not knowledgeable or of competent authority to participate fully in the IEP process. That is parallel to having low expectations from the school, which can let the school authorities get away with providing subpar services. Remember that you are a fully competent and valuable IEP team member. It is up to you to determine whether your child's needs are being met.

Number 4: Losing control of your emotions

Do not paint the IEP meeting rooms with your feelings of shock, anger, or disappointment during disputes or disagreements. There will be points where you feel let down by the system. I don't blame you. It also upset me when I felt like no one else felt the weight of my concerns. However, lashing out can cause you to lose the authority's trust, which is difficult to regain.

Number 5: Not documenting meetings and conversations in writing

If it wasn't written down, it did not happen.

How can you show proof when the school is not providing the agreed-upon services? If it holds even an ounce of importance, it must be documented in a letter, journal, or daily log. Simply state the facts, not opinions, in writing; these notes will be part of your child's file.

While this chapter has focused on IEPs and 504 plans, it is important to note that the principles discussed can be applied in any education system. However, I recommend you research comparable programs in your location to effectively advocate for your child's education needs. The pre-referral process is the first step to getting a 504 plan or IEP. In the next chapter, we will look at the stages of the IEP pre-referral process and provide some tips to help you prepare for this important evaluation and decision-making process.

Did You Know?

Did you know that private schools are not obligated to provide special education or related services to students with disabilities?

Students with disabilities who attend private schools can receive special education services through a different service plan, known as an Individualized Service Plan (ISP). An ISP specifies the special education services that a student will receive, but it is not the same as an IEP. An IEP is a legally bound document specifically for students with disabilities who attend public school. ISPs are not bound by any legal rules and regulations, and they are not required to meet the same formal development and review processes as IEPs do.

4

GETTING STARTED

T o quote Neil Armstrong, "That's one small step for man, one giant leap for mankind." As any journey of a thousand miles begins with a single step, this chapter is the first step into the journey of the pre-referral process in the IEP.

The process may seem daunting. It is hard not to have setbacks initially because starting is a learning opportunity, and you learn best through your mistakes.

The pre-referral process involves gathering information about your child's needs, abilities, and challenges and using this information to make informed decisions about their education. It is like a detective story, but instead of solving a crime, you are solving the mystery of how to best support your child's education.

And who does not love a good mystery?

Some students may have learning differences or delays in development that require special education services and support. These students have needs that may initially be recognized by their teachers, school counselor, or parents, especially if they show a pattern of underperformance or learning discrepancies in their academic, behavioral, social, and/or physical skills and abilities compared to their classmates. Such needs call for academic and behavioral support for the student. Therefore, the teacher, school counselor, or administrator will typically call the student's parents or guardians in for a meeting to shed light on acknowledging their unique needs. In addition, the student's work, test grades, and teacher's observations are commonly shared with the parents during the meeting. This sets the tone to explore the following questions in the meeting:

- Has the student always struggled in school, or is the issue recent? Ideally, the parents can fill the teachers in with any insight into the child's needs and learning capacity.
- Is the student struggling constantly? All students have a hard time at multiple points in school and exhibit problems in learning. Whatever bout of struggle, concern, or area of weakness is exhibited by the student, the teacher should document it.
- Is the matter in question or concern regarding the student appropriate for children of this age?

The student's issues at school can be addressed with a plan of action or utilization of classroom and teaching strategies agreed upon by both parents and teachers. The teacher should continue collecting work samples from the student and document any changes or signs of progress the student shows in the classroom. Meanwhile, the child's parents or guardians are kept in the loop and well-informed of the student's progress. It seems simple classroom alterations are not a sufficient intervention for helping the child improve. In that case, the teacher can inform the parents or guardians of a pre-referral process.

WHAT IS A PRE-REFERRAL?

The pre-referral process is like a formal intervention conducted to improve the student's performance in the general education classroom before considering the special education process. The intervention is carried out by a problem-solving team (the Student Intervention Team/Child Study Team/Student Success Team/Teacher Support Team) that works with teachers to help them choose and implement effective teaching interventions for students facing academic and/or behavioral difficulties.

The team will work with the student's general education teacher and become well-versed in their learning strengths and needs. It will also evaluate their progress as new strategies are implemented to help them thrive in the general education classroom. Mere academic or behavioral challenges do not directly warrant special education services. However, in many cases, appropriate accommodations and teaching strategies can be implemented to help students overcome their struggles and do well in the general education classroom. Like every other process, the pre-referral process has clear-cut stages, which it progresses with.

WHAT ARE THE STAGES OF THE PRE-REFERRAL PROCESS, AND WHAT DO THEY INCLUDE?

Stage 1: Initial concern regarding a student's progress

The initial concern about the student's performance or school behavior can be expressed informally or formally by a teacher, parent, or school faculty member. For example, after gaining consent from the parents, a teacher can fill out a form to refer a student to the pre-referral team.

The initial stage can involve a lot of mind-mapping, team discussion, and sharing of insight between teachers, parents, or caregivers regarding the child's academic performance or behaviors, such as what the underlying causes may be or whether the issue can be helped at home or in class.

Here are some examples of initial concerns that a teacher may address to the parents, particularly if they seem to be interfering with the child's school life:

- Moodiness or behavior problems, e.g., acting out in class, talking back at teachers, picking fights with other children
- The student was recently hospitalized or suffered from a major injury, e.g., broken leg or arm, concussion
- Lack of motivation or inattentive behavior
- Increasingly low grades
- Difficulty grasping basic concepts and comprehending instructions in class

- Major life changes or stressors, e.g., the loss of a loved one

Stage 2: Information gathering

The following information is important to collect for this process:

- Classroom instructional methods, teaching strategies, and resources that have been tried and tested previously
- Assessments of the student's skill level
- The student's background knowledge and skill sets
- Goals and expectations for behavior and academic performance at school and home
- Classroom behavior management strategies
- Attendance records
- Classroom observations or teacher's anecdotal notes

Stage 3: Information sharing and team discussion

After the relevant information has been compiled, we can begin sharing it and discussing it among team members. During this stage, the team will meet to review the information collected to date and sift through ideas and different kinds of interventions that may help the student.

Usually, the pre-referral team will begin by discussing the student's strengths, motivating factors, interests, and the skills that they have mastered. Acknowledging the student's abilities, and strong points, helps the group remain focused on potential solutions rather than solely focusing on the student's short-comings.

Here's an overview of the standard team members of a common pre-referral team and their roles:

Parents

- Share information about the student's strengths and learning needs, home life, previous experiences in school, and learning
- Take the teacher's advice on implementing strategies and learning exercises at home to support the student

General education teacher

- Usually, the first to identify a student exhibiting issues
- Implements suggested classroom interventions and provided feedback to the parents
- A collaborative effort with other school staff members and teachers who provide small-group activities for classroom assistance

School administrator

- Supports the organizational integrity of the teams, e.g., planning, decision-making, resources

School psychologist

- Carries out observations of the student's performance and interactions in small-group activities, academic diagnostic assessments, behavioral or cognitive screenings

Optional Team Members

Special education teacher

Helps the general education teacher develop well-informed and suitable teaching plans for individualized instruction in the general education classroom

ESL teacher

- For students who speak English as a second language
- Determines the language needs of the student

School counselor

- Involved in reviewing the student's records with the team
- Supports the classroom teacher and staff to make plans that target the learning and behavioral needs of the student

Healthcare workers or health professional

- May be asked to identify the severity of any sensory issues or health challenges and whether they are the cause of, or contributing to, the student's learning difficulties
- May provide health-related advice

Stage 4: Discussion of possible strategies

Once all the information is laid out and the team has agreed upon the primary goals and objectives, the fourth stage of the pre-referral process can unroll. After brainstorming, the team members can select strategies to meet the student's learning needs.

When strategies are being considered, the team may find that answering a set of questions, such as the following, will help complete the meeting's agenda:

- Why do we think this plan will help the student improve?
- How can we measure the student's performance?
- Have we set achievable *and* measurable goals?
- What data collection methods can we use to track the student's progress?
- How long should the intervention plan be implemented?
- When should the team meet again to reassess the plan's effectiveness?
- Does the new strategy require any special training for the teacher?

- Does the teacher need assistance in implementing the new strategy?

Stage 5: Implementation and monitoring of strategies

The new teaching plan and intervention strategies are implemented during this stage, and the student's progress is monitored. The classroom teacher upholds both implementing and monitoring responsibilities, but the team can always offer support as needed. In addition, the data and information collected during this stage will help the team determine whether the new plan is effective.

Stage 6: Evaluation and decision making

Finally, the pre-referral team meets to review the data and observations collected to see whether the student has progressed. The question reflected at this final stage is whether the student has shown adequate improvement in the classroom. If the answer is yes, the teacher will continue the intervention methods. If not, the team decides whether the intervention strategy needs more time or should be modified. At this point, the team can also decide if the student should be referred for special education services.

The pre-referral process can last for any amount of time. Although if, at any point during the evaluation stage, the team suspects that the student may have a disability, they are required to formally initiate the referral process for special education services. Whether the student qualifies for disability will be determined under the IDEA and Section 504 of the Rehabilitation Act of 1973.

PREPARATION TIPS

While you are waiting for the evaluation and decision of the intervention assistance team, during the pre-referral process, there are several things that you can do as a parent to be better prepared.

Start by considering the observations you have made about your child. For example, how long was it till your child took their first steps or spoke for the first time? Were there any delays in developmental areas, such as fine motor skills and language? Have there been any incidents of hyperactivity or inappropriate behavior? Consult with your child's healthcare provider about any health issues that could cause delays in developmental milestones. A developmental delay is a disability that can affect more than one aspect of a child's development. In contrast, a learning disability is a delay that impacts only one aspect of academic learning.

You can also approach your child's teachers and ask them for their observations and ask questions, such as:

"How is my child doing socially?"

"Is my child paying attention in class regularly?"

"Does my child complete his/her work on time?"

A step you can and should take while preparing beforehand is to request your child's school records. Is this really that important?

Yes! As your child's champion, advocate, and parent/guardian, you should be aware of the contents of your child's school records as schools use them to make educational decisions. If, in any case, the information is inaccurate, not up-to-date, inconsistent, or missing, it can cause unwanted delays in the process and incorrect decisions that will affect your child's eligibility for special education. Therefore, you need to know how to gain access to, interpret, and correct information in your child's school records. You should also be ready to use them effectively in school meetings as you go forth with the IEP process. So, what is included in these records?

First, the cumulative file is usually in the principal's possession. It contains the student's profile, identification data, records of academic achievement, teacher reports, and result cards. Second, we have a confidential file that includes medical records, summary reports from evaluation teams or independent evaluators, your child's IEP, and any correspondence between you and school staff. Third, the compliance file holds reports of eligibility meetings, correspondence between the parents and school faculty, and other similar documentation. Last, the discipline file, which not all schools hold, includes counts of disciplinary actions taken by the school authority and notices of suspension or expulsion from school.

You obviously can't just grab and run from the school's records office. So, let's see what steps we can take to obtain copies of your child's school records.

Step 1: Contact the school district

Ask about the laws and procedures that cover which student records are kept by schools and for how long.

Step 2: Ask your school what you have to do to see your child's school records

Usually, you can fill out a form of request or write a letter to the school principal or special education director to gain access to your child's records. Remember, if it is a written document, make a copy of it and store it in your child's master file.

Here's a sample letter to help you write yours.

Date

Your Name

Your Street Address

City, State, Zip Code

Contact details (your email address and phone number)

Name of the Person to Whom You Are Writing

Title

Street Address

City, State, Zip Code

Re: Name of child, Name of school, Purpose of application (Requesting for student's records)

Dear (Person's Name),

I am writing this letter to schedule a time I can come to review my child's

Complete records. My son/daughter, (child's name), is in Grade (___) at (Name of school), in

(teacher's name) class. I would also like copies of these records.

Please let me know the time and place I can come in to view the records. I would appreciate it

if I could receive these records by (choose a date at least one or two weeks from the date on the

letter). You can reach me at (Your phone number here).

I would highly appreciate your cooperation.

Sincerely,

Your name

Signature

Step 3: Send the letter

Send the letter to the school district's director of special education along with extra copies to your child's school principal and the special education teacher.

Step 4: Obtain proof of the letter's delivery

You can send the letter by email, send a hard copy with tracking, or hand-deliver it. Whichever way you go for, pick one that lets you verify that the letter has reached its address. Alternatively, you can phone the office to confirm whether the letter was received.

Step 5: Make multiple copies

When you get to see your child's records, make copies to add to your child's binder. You may be charged for copying fees separately.

BUILD-A-BINDER

A binder will be a useful and portable folder for holding the different documents related to your child's growth and development over the school years. Here's how you can build a records binder with some important sections. While you can find multiple printables for IEP checklists online, I have taken the liberty to create a checklist myself, which I have shared below:

Items	When to update	Date Updated
Communications		
Contacts	Once a year/with each new member joining the team	
Communication log	After every meeting, call, or other correspondence with the school	
Letters and emails	With every entry (Filed after noting down in the communication log)	
Evaluations		
Request/referral for evaluation (with consent to evaluate)	Every 3 years, or with each entry	
School evaluations	Every 3 years	
Private evaluations	Every time	
IEP		
Copy of parent's rights	Annually	
IEP	Annually or as often as changes are made	
504 plan (if your child has one)	Annually or as often as changes are made	
Written notices and meeting notes	Annually or as often as needed	

Report Cards		
Report cards/ performance reports	As often as they come in from the school	
Sample work		
Samples of schoolwork	Once a month or whenever you see signs of noteworthy progress or concern	
Standardized tests	With each result	
Behavior		
School disciplinary guidelines	With each new copy	
Intervention plans	Annually or with each update	
Disciplinary notices	Whenever your child receives one	

The checklist holds details about the contents of each of the tabbed sections in the binder. In addition, each section of the binder holds its importance, as discussed below.

Communications: This section will include the school contact list, i.e., the phone number and email of each member of the IEP team, a communication log, and copies of letters and emails to and from the school. As mentioned before, it is important to have proof of any exchanges that have taken place between you and any team member regarding the IEP to maintain a proper time-line of communication.

Evaluations: With every copy of an evaluation request or referral, attach the dated copy of your consent form. All evaluations, whether held by the school or privately, should be included in this section.

IEP: Keep a copy of the vision or the list of goals and objectives for your child's education career on the front page of the IEP.

Report card/Progress notes: Note concerns or signs of progress on sticky notes and attach them to the reports you get on your child's grades and performance from school.

Sample work: Samples of assignments or homework work as examples of your child's abilities and progress.

Behavior: Attach a copy of the school's disciplinary guidelines, any disciplinary notice from the school or teacher's notes, and the updated intervention plan.

For clearer guidance and professional help with navigating the nuances of this process, you may consider hiring a special education consultant independently. A special education consultant can walk you through the services that are available for your child, help with interpreting evaluation reports, and work alongside you with the school to develop IEPs. You can get advice on the right services, programs, and accommodations that cater to your child's educational needs. Writing requests and drafting complaints to schools is another service the consultant will be able to provide. You will have someone to help you prepare for IEP and 504 meetings efficiently and accompany you to offer advice throughout. Most of all, you can know your case's strength before meetings. This is someone who could make a lot of difference in the future of your child's education. It would only be fair to take your time when considering the expertise of potential consultants before you hire one. Here are some questions to ask when you are interviewing different consultants:

- What degrees and certifications do you hold?
- Have you shared any written work or articles regarding special education needs?
- How much experience do you have working with parents?
- What outcomes do you usually achieve in the special education committee meetings you participate in?
- What services can you assist with?
- What mode of communication do you prefer?
- Are you available for phone calls or queries after hours?
- How soon can you respond to emails?
- How do you decide what a child needs in school?
- What factors do you consider when it comes to placement options?

Let's move on to the next step: the actual referral and evaluation for an IEP. This stage involves formally requesting an IEP evaluation and working with the school to assess the student's needs and determine their eligibility for special education services.

In the next chapter, we will take a closer look at the referral and evaluation process, including what to expect and how to prepare and your rights and responsibilities as a parent during this process.

5

REFERRAL AND EVALUATION

A re you starting to feel a little overwhelmed? That's perfectly normal. But don't worry; I'm here to help guide you through this sometimes-complicated process.

The referral and evaluation steps are an important part of the IEP process, as they help to determine whether your child is eligible for special education services and, if so, what those services should look like. We will give you the lowdown on what to expect during these steps, provide some tips for preparing, and explain your rights and responsibilities as a parent.

WHAT IS AN IEP REFERRAL?

This is the starting point for determining if a child qualifies for an IEP. If the child struggles at school despite interventions and accommodations, they can be referred for a special education evaluation. A referral is a request made in writing for an evaluation. No evaluation will go through without the parent's written consent. The request is forwarded to a Child Study Team that determines whether the child should be evaluated further. A referral looks into concerns regarding the child and whether they might be due to a disability.

What kind of information should one include in a referral? The referral should include the following:

- reasons why the child needs learning support,
- the problems that they are facing in school,
- a brief discussion of the child's strengths and needs,
- a description of your child's learning challenges and the interventions that have been attempted
- and information regarding the child's previous diagnosis and evaluations (if any)

Once your referral has been approved, your child can undergo evaluation.

Here's a sample letter to help you write your draft:

Your Name

Your Street Address

City, State, Zip Code

Contact details (your email address and phone number)

Today's Date

Name of the Person to Whom You Are Writing

Title

Street Address

City, State, Zip Code

Re: Referral for (child's name)'s evaluation

Dear XYZ

I, parent/guardian of (your child's name) who is currently a student at (school name) in the (___) grade, would like to place a request for a referral of assessment for special education services, as required by 5 C.C.R. Sec. 3021(a).

I am concerned about my child's progress in school, and I think he/she may be eligible for special education services. I would like to request that he/she be given a complete assessment by the school district, followed by an IEP meeting. As a part of the assessment process, I also ask that my child be assessed under Section 504 of the Rehabilitation Act of 1973 to determine whether he/she can be qualified as "disabled" and to see what accommodations can be received.

I look forward to hearing from you. If you have any questions or concerns, please feel free to contact me at (your number here). Your cooperation and assistance would be highly appreciated.

Sincerely,

(Yourname)

WHAT IS AN IEP EVALUATION?

An IEP evaluation is a process that determines whether a child with a disability is eligible for special education services. It investigates different aspects of the child's disability, and the result includes detailed descriptions of their educational performance and special education needs. The IEP evaluation team includes professionals from multiple disciplines, including the child's parents, general education teacher, and health specialists. The evaluation review may cover the following:

- Results of standardized tests
- Observations
- Review of academic history and performance
- Review of medical history
- Review of behavior and psychological assessments

Evaluation rights and benefits

Here are the legal rights you should know of before you get your child evaluated:

1. The right to request an evaluation
2. The right to receive written notice from the school
3. The right to consent (Schools cannot evaluate without your consent).
4. The right to a thorough or prompt evaluation (IDEA requires that the school conduct the child's evaluation within 60 days, but different state laws can have different time frames).

5. The right to be a member of the team
6. The right to special education services
7. The right to be free of discrimination
8. The right to plead decisions
9. The right to an independent education evaluation (IEE)
10. The right to request a reevaluation

Many parents feel reluctant or unsure about getting their child evaluated because it seems strange to feel like something may be wrong with their child. They worry that their child might get discriminated against due to their differences or that their child would get labeled and treated differently. However, an evaluation holds numerous benefits for the child, including lesser difficulties at school.

You, and the school's teachers, can understand what your child struggles with, including the strengths of their academic, cognitive, and social skills. Testing not only lets you see what your child is struggling with but also what their strongest points are. This information can help you use your child's strengths to promote their learning. An evaluation can check for special education eligibility, and if your child is eligible, the evaluation results can be used to design an IEP. Furthermore, the evaluation results will be a relief for both you and the child. Your stress and uncertainty can subside when you learn that there is support for your child to have as they grow. Additionally, many children feel better when they can understand their challenges with help from their parents and the evaluator. It can help them feel more confident in their abilities and gain a sense of self-acceptance.

What happens during an IEP evaluation?

- **Creating an evaluation plan**

An evaluation plan covers all areas of concern, including academic, behavioral, cognitive, and social-emotional skills and abilities. First, the team meets to review the referral and then decide what tests the student needs. The review is followed by a framework that outlines the testing agreed upon.

- **Consent to do the evaluation**

Parents and guardians of children must provide the school with written informed consent before initiating the evaluation. Before consent, you can ask questions and get all the necessary information. For example, you may ask questions such as:

- "What is the purpose of each test mentioned in the plan?"
- "What factors will be observed?"
- "Who will be evaluating my child?"

- **Having the evaluation**

Depending on the school's policies, you will be informed beforehand whether you can be present during your child's testing. Usually, the evaluation will take place at the child's school or a professional's office. At least two professionals have to be there to evaluate and observe the child.

Who are the evaluators?

The evaluators have training and qualifications in the areas of development they are testing, such as speech or mathematical skills. They'll know what is expected of children of different ages.

- **Going over the results**

Each evaluator writes feedback on the assigned parts to test in a report. The report includes scores and summaries of observations; some may even give recommendations for what kind of help the student might benefit from. Finally, the evaluation team meets with the IEP team (including you) in an eligibility meeting, where parents determine whether their child is eligible for special education services.

You have the right to view the evaluation results at least three business days before the eligibility meeting. If you don't receive a timely copy of the results, contact the IEP coordinator.

Types of evaluations

The right evaluations can provide information pointing everyone in the right direction. While planning evaluations with the team, the following are some types of evaluations you might come across:

Assistive Technology (AT) Evaluation

In this evaluation, a student's environment and daily tasks are observed to determine whether they could benefit from assistive technology while learning. The factors considered include the student's need for computer access, communication skills, motor skills, mobility, and recreation. In addition, an AT evaluation can help find a device that could help the student with specific tasks that are relatively more demanding.

Audiological Evaluation

An audiological evaluation consists of various hearing tests, a balance test, and a physical exam. It assesses the type and severity of a student's hearing loss to create a management plan. Following the plan set in place, audiological evaluations are conducted regularly to monitor the student's hearing loss.

Auditory Processing Evaluation

This evaluation assesses a student's central auditory processing skills. It is usually recommended when a child exhibits behaviors that suggest difficulty understanding auditory information. These skills include retaining and recalling information orally, processing spoken language, and comprehending speech in an environment with additional noises.

It can determine the student's strengths and weaknesses in auditory processing and functioning. In addition to any evaluation, the results generally include recommendations for useful interventions that benefit parents, students, and teachers.

Functional Behavioral Assessment (FBA)

An FBA is conducted as a series of observations that identify inappropriate student behaviors and possible triggers and suggest consequences or interventions address the behaviors. It is usually required before developing a Behavior Intervention Plan, which includes behavioral support and services to manage and correct a student's problematic behaviors while pinpointing the causes or triggers of those behaviors. In addition, an FBA may be considered when a student's behavior interferes with their or peers' learning. On the other hand, an FBA is mandatory when a student is suspended from school for the behavior resulting from their disability.

Neuropsychological Evaluation

This set of standardized procedures assesses the student's cognitive and behavioral functioning. A neuropsychological evaluation that examines a student's IQ, attention, memory, language, fine motor skills, academic abilities, and social-emotional functioning. It can help distinguish any problems with cognitive functioning, behavior, emotions, and intellectual abilities.

This evaluation may be recommended when a neurological impairment may be suspected, such as after a head injury or if there is a history of epilepsy, ADHD, fetal alcohol syndrome, or trauma during birth.

Occupational Therapy (OT) Evaluation

An OT evaluation assesses a child's sensory processing and fine, gross, oral, and visual motor skills. It is meant to identify sensory or motor deficits that might impact a child's ability to look after their needs, do schoolwork, or participate in playtime and recommend interventions or treatment. The goals for the evaluation include developing the child's sensory and motor skills. Work may include:

- Working on skills such as sequential planning.
- Copying words and letters.
- Using scissors.
- Increasing the child's tolerance for different textures of clothes or food.

This kind of evaluation typically follows concerns about a child's fine motor or sensory skills when diagnosed with autism.

Physical Therapy (PT) Evaluation

This evaluation assesses a child's motor abilities, including gross motor skills, such as their range of motion, coordination, muscle strength and tonicity, gait, and motor control. It is recommended when a child has difficulties with mobility that interfere with movements in their daily activities. Often, children who undergo this evaluation have a medical diagnosis that compromises their muscle strength and functioning, such as spina bifida, cerebral palsy, neuromuscular disorders, and autoimmune diseases.

Psycho-Educational Evaluation

This evaluation combines the sets of tests that assess psychological and academic abilities. Academic testing measures the student's reading, math, writing, and listening skills. The results of this evaluation identify anomalies between the child's cognition and their current academic abilities. For instance, if a child shows average cognition but tests below average in academics, this may be a positive sign of a learning disability. This is typically part of a child's initial special education evaluation and is reconducted at least every three years to keep track of their academic progress.

Psychological (Cognitive) Evaluation

This tests an individual's intelligence, specifically their ability to use reasoning and language and process and retain information. Some common tests include the Wechsler

Intelligence Scale for Children (WISC-4), the Wechsler Preschool and Primary Scale of

Intelligence (WPPSI), and the Stanford Binet Intelligence Scales. The aspects of social-emotional functioning are assessed using screening tools such as the Thematic Apperception Test (TAT) or a common scale such as the Behavior Assessment System for Children (BASC-2).

Psychiatric Evaluation

This is an important one. Some children may exhibit concerning signs, such as hyperactivity, aggression, sexual behavior, self-harm behavior, anxiety, depression, mood swings, or odd thoughts and feelings.

It determines whether a child has a mental health condition and follows up an assessment with recommendations for the child's benefit. A psychiatric evaluation assesses the child for potential emotional, behavioral, or developmental disorders by weighing any symptoms the child might have, their medical and family history, and their behavior. It involves interviews, behavior scales, and screening tests for social-emotional functioning.

Social History

During social history, a meeting is led by the school social worker, who explains the special education process, revises the due process rights, and considers consent from the parents to evaluate the child. After obtaining consent, the social worker proceeds with an in-depth inquiry regarding the child's medical history, educational history, development, and family background. Finally, the parent's concerns are considered, completing the social history.

A meeting with the school social worker gives parents a vital opportunity to gain all the information they need to make an informed decision before consenting to their child's special education process. It also helps bring awareness to the school about the child's disability. Social history is the first evaluation once a child is officially referred for special education services. Any additional type of evaluation follows only after the parent has consented to the social worker.

Speech and Language Evaluation

Language and speech are *the* modes of communication. Therefore, students' abilities to express their thoughts and emotions, exchange information, listen, and communicate are firm building blocks in their learning.

This measures the child's communication abilities, i.e., vocabulary, articulation, fluency, and understanding of instructions. Some common speech and language assessments include

- The Preschool Language Scale (PLS-4),
- Clinical Evaluation of Language Fundamentals (CELF-4)
- Peabody Picture Vocabulary Test (PPVT-3).

A speech and language evaluation is recommended when difficulties are noticed in the student's communication ability. One of the special education services that a student, who struggles with communication or comprehension, would benefit from largely is speech therapy.

Vocational Assessment

A vocational assessment will include the following:

- An interview.
- A survey of hobbies or interests.
- A review of the student's records.

It can be significant in helping develop plans for the student's future education, particularly for an IEP (One of the components of an IEP is the transition plan. A transition plan concerns long-term goals for the child's future studies and employment. It comes into effect when the student turns 15 years old). In addition, a vocational assessment can help decide on programs that could help enhance the student's vocational interests. Therefore, a Level I vocational assessment is required for all special education students when they are 12 years of age.

PREPARATION

Deciding and giving consent

As the parent or legal guardian of your child, you must provide written consent before any testing can be conducted. Therefore, it is important to carefully review the evaluation plan and ask questions before consenting. Here are some questions you can ask before agreeing to the evaluation plan:

- How do you know these are the right tests to assess my child for a disability?
- What is the purpose of each test?
- How is the test going to be conducted (written or oral)?
- What times will the observations be conducted?
- What are the qualifications of the evaluators?

How can you prepare for the IEP evaluation?

You have been in a tough spot for a while now. You are sometimes confused and clueless, but you have made it this far. You have learned and worked hard to fix things in place for your child's classroom achievement – you are headed the right way. Keep going, my friend. It is time to prepare for the next big thing: the evaluation IEP meeting. You can bring anyone you deem helpful, i.e., an expert on special education, to the meeting, but notify the school team in advance. Before an IEP meeting, you should have the following information ready and organized:

- Records of your concern(s), such as poor scores on tests, work samples, external assessments or reports, or parent-teacher conference feedback notes
- If your child struggles with behavioral and social-emotional difficulties, have the relevant documentation regarding teacher notes, the Behavior Intervention Plan

(if there is one), and results from a Functional Behavior Assessment (FBA).

- Early interventions or noted concerns from the child's history at school
- Complete medical history, i.e., medications, allergies, diagnoses
- Results from any additional evaluations you may have received privately, e.g., psychiatric evaluations, OT evaluations, or psychological assessments.

Help your child understand the purpose and process of the evaluation. Let them know they don't need to study for the evaluation and reassure them to keep their stress levels at bay. The tests in an evaluation are not like regular tests. They mostly involve doing basic activities like solving puzzles and naming pictures. Your child might be called out of their classroom to participate in some evaluations. Let them know who the evaluator is and what activities they'd like to do. It is important to talk about different steps and aspects of evaluations with the child so they are not surprised or confused.

Here's something you can say: "You are a very smart kid, and this is going to help you learn more easily. You might have to learn and do stuff a little differently from your friends, but that does not mean you are not as smart as them. Don't worry about other kids noticing any of that. Even if they do, it is okay. You can just tell them the help you are getting is like needing glasses to read. It is just a bunch of tests and it is going to help us help you do better in school in the best ways possible."

UNDERSTANDING THE RESULTS

The evaluation process culminates in the production of a written report. The report should also include scores and a summary of the information gathered during the evaluation process.

But what do the test scores mean for your child?

Take the report as an educational diagnosis that will help formulate an IEP. The final evaluation report is a culmination of the results of multiple assessments, often written in a language you might not be familiar with from the start.

Regarding measurement, we generally begin from zero and go up to higher numbers. However, aptitude measurements in the psychological and educational ability tests *start* from the middle and measure out to either end of the normal distribution curve.

The normal distribution curve, or the bell curve, is a tool that visualizes where the evaluated student stands compared to a given population that has been assessed the same. It is based on the assumption that the ability or skill being measured is distributed in a regular pattern in the population, where most of the scores fall in the middle (that's why the curve is larger in the middle). A few scores fall at either end of the curve (low and high ends). Most students fall in the middle, i.e., score average, while some students score higher than average, and others score below average. The curve assumes that the numbers of individuals scoring either higher or lower than average are equal in an interval.

This curve compares an individual child's scores with their peers' or between their scores and those of children of different ages or grade levels. Evaluators will report the scores as standard scores and percentile ranks.

The *standard score* assumes that most students assessed would score 100 on average (the middle of the curve). Therefore, most scores below or above average will fall within one standard deviation (15 units) on either side of the average/standard score.

This means that many students (68%) would score between 85-115 on a Standard Score measure. The difference of one standard deviation (SD) is still average. However, two standard deviations (30 units) in either direction, i.e., above or below the standard score, is considered statistically significant because there's a lesser chance of error. With a standard score comes the *standard error*, which means there is extra room in the test scores to account for mistakes in the evaluation.

For example, a child with a score of 100 on a performance test scores in the 50th percentile rank, which is the average. A percentile is based on the standard deviation curve and indicates the child's position relative to the national average. If a student scores in the 50th percentile, out of 100 students, they would perform better than 49 students, which places them in the middle. If a student scores in the 25th percentile, they scored more than 24 students out of the 100 tested, placing them at the lower end of the curve.

Here is an example of an interpretation of evaluation results: Adam obtained a standard score of 85 (-1 SD), ranking at the 16th percentile and classified as low average. This means that

Adam's score, although still considered average, is at the lower end of the average range. On the other hand, he scored greater than or equal to 16 percent of the kids his age in the population considered, e.g., his classmates or school peers.

What should you do when you disagree with the evaluation?

It is okay to be worried or skeptical that the evaluation wasn't thorough or accurate. Here's what you can do if you disagree with the school's evaluation results:

- Revisit the written notice form you received regarding the evaluation, ensure all the evaluations listed were performed, and check that you have an evaluation report for everyone
- Ask the evaluator(s) to explain the test's detail, scope, and limitations
- State your concerns and disagreements with the results to the evaluation team in a written letter. You can also share your ideas for services or learning support
- If you have results from additional testing, share them with the school

The following action steps can also be taken to resolve this situation:

- Request an Independent Education Evaluation
- Request additional testing be performed
- Request a re-do or revision of the evaluation results
- Request an IEP mediation and initiate a due process

Phew, ready to move on to the next stage of the IEP process? It is time to talk about eligibility. No, we're not talking about whether you are eligible to win a free trip to the Bahamas (unfortunately). Instead, we're discussing determining whether your child is eligible for special education services. This is such a crucial step in the IEP process, as it determines whether your child will be able to receive the support and accommodations they need to succeed in school. So hang on tight; it is about to get real!

A WELCOME BREAK

"All kids need is a little help, a little hope, and someone who believes in them"

— MAGIC JOHNSON

Let's take a break.

It feels good, doesn't it? Just a moment to take a breath without taking in any new information or having to handle a situation with the kids.

As a busy parent striving to secure the education your child deserves, it's important to take a moment to acknowledge your hard work and dedication. You may not have much time, but you're here with this book, and that's a huge accomplishment.

Take a moment, too, to acknowledge the extra work you're putting in to help your child and your own journey as a parent. You don't have a lot of time, but you're here now, with this book. Don't be hard on yourself if you can't read the whole thing. Your life is full, and you're doing everything you can to arm yourself as an advocate for your child.

If you'd like to extend this moment of respite, consider leaving a review of this book on Amazon. By sharing your experience and the information you've found helpful, you'll help other parents find the guidance they need quickly and easily.

By leaving a review of this book on Amazon, you'll help other parents who are looking for this guidance to find it quickly and easily.

This book is now a resource in your parenting toolbox that you can refer back to at any time, so don't worry if you can't finish it all at once. Your review will make a significant impact on the lives of other parents and their children. Thank you for your support in empowering families to navigate the special education system.

If you are in the UK, please scan the QR code to leave your review.

If you are in the US, please scan the QR code to leave your review.

6

ELIGIBILITY 101

E ligibility determination meetings for IEPs can be a significant source of stress for families. It is normal to have strong emotions and concerns about your child's education and prospects, especially when so much is riding on the outcome of the evaluation. Will the results show that your child is eligible for special education services? After all, the main topic of discussion at the results meeting is eligibility determination. Who decides the child's eligibility, and how is it made? These are all valid questions that can contribute to anxiety during the process. This chapter will provide tips and insights to help you feel more prepared and less anxious during the eligibility determination meeting. After all, knowledge is power!

GOALS OF THE ELIGIBILITY MEETING

The meeting scheduled by the school post-evaluation will involve reviewing the evaluation results and considering other sources of information regarding the child, such as input from parents and teachers, the child's physical condition, social background, and adaptive behavior. Therefore, the school shouldn't delay scheduling the meeting, and the parents should be given written notice that proposes an agreeable time and place for the meeting. The eligibility meeting will involve the following:

- The parent and caregivers: Although the meetings can take place without you, it is ideal that you take an active role in all the IEP meetings
- Your child's general education teacher: If your child is homeschooled or does not have an assigned teacher, any general education teacher, who teaches children of the same age, can attend.
- A special education teacher: Special education teachers are well-trained in teaching different kinds of learners and well-versed in learning difficulties. They can partner with general education teachers to lay down the learning and thinking differences presented in evaluation reports and assess eligibility accordingly. They also have valuable experience to share.
- School administrator: An administrator who knows general and special education will also have the power to approve and implement decisions that take place during the meeting
- The child's evaluator(s): Often, the evaluator who assessed your child may be unable to attend the meeting, in which case another professional evaluator must fill in. They must be qualified to interpret the test results.

With the meeting revolving around whether your child is eligible, or not, for special education services, the following requirements should be noted for eligibility:

- Your child must have a disability or condition that fits into one of the 13 categories of disabilities defined by IDEA (discussed next in detail)
- The disability has to negatively impact or have an "adverse effect" on their educational performance

13 CATEGORIES OF DISABILITY COVERED UNDER IDEA

Although the IDEA has outlined the 13 categories of disabilities, it does not elaborate on all the issues accompanying each one.

1. Autism Spectrum Disorder

Autism is a neurodevelopmental disorder that typically impairs an individual's ability to verbally and nonverbally communicate and interact with others. It is characterized by restricted interests and repetitive behaviors, which can hinder educational, cognitive, social, and functional development. Autism can make learning and adapt to different environments difficult because there is resistance to change in daily routines and an unpredictable response to different sensory experiences.

It is worth noting that a child cannot be identified as having autism if their performance is "adversely affected," mainly due to an emotional disturbance.

2. Deaf-Blindness

Simultaneous hearing and visual impairments can hinder communication. Most developmental and educational needs are unmet in a mainstream general education setting, or special education programs are solely dedicated to children with either blindness or deafness.

3. Deafness

Deafness is a hearing impairment severe enough to significantly weaken the ability to process linguistic information through hearing (with or without a hearing aid).

4. Emotional Disturbance

This condition manifests in thoughts and behaviors that adversely affect a child's educational performance over a prolonged period. Various mental health disorders can fall under this category, including panic disorder, schizophrenia, bipolar disorder, obsessive-compulsive disorder, and depression. Other characteristics of this condition may include:

- An inability to learn that cannot be justified by intellectual, sensory, or health factors
- Unsolicited inappropriate behaviors or feelings exhibited under normal circumstances
- General moodiness
- Physical symptoms or fears related to school or personal issues

- An inability to develop or maintain good interpersonal relationships with others at school

5. Hearing Impairment

This non-deaf category includes hard-of-hearing and other auditory processing disorders or impairments adversely affecting a child's educational performance.

6. Intellectual Disability

This category is characterized by significantly below-average functioning and deficits in a child's intellectual abilities and adaptive behavior simultaneously.

7. Multiple Disabilities

A child with a combination of disabilities would have severe educational needs that cannot be accommodated in the mainstream classroom environment. Examples of a child with multiple disabilities include:

- Intellectual disability and hearing-visual impairments
- Cerebral palsy and hearing impairment
- Intellectual disability and orthopedic impairment

8. Orthopedic Impairment

This includes musculoskeletal disorders or conditions that may be caused congenitally and impairments caused by severe diseases or other causes, e.g., scoliosis and bone tuberculosis.

9. Other Health Impairment

This category includes limitations in strength, vitality, or alertness (dampened or heightened) to environmental stimuli that impede educational performance significantly. These limitations may be due to chronic or acute health conditions like asthma, ADHD, diabetes, epilepsy, Tourette syndrome, or other systemic disorders.

10. Specific Learning Disability

This includes disabilities associated with basic psychological processes that involve processing or using language (spoken or written). For example, difficulties with learning may manifest as an imperfect ability to think, speak, listen, read, write, or do basic math problems. Examples include brain injury, dyslexia, auditory processing disorder, or developmental aphasia.

11. Speech or Language Impairment

This category includes communication disorders such as stuttering, language, articulation, or voice impairment.

12. Traumatic Brain Injury

This is an acquired brain injury resulting from an accident or strong physical force that induces significant brain damage, total or partial functional disability, and/or social-emotional impairment. In addition, it adversely affects the child's performance at school.

13. Visual Impairment, including Blindness

This includes vision problems that cannot be corrected by eyewear specifically. It includes both partial sight and blindness.

While the IDEA identifies 13 categories of disabilities, it leaves "adverse effect" and "education" open to interpretation. So, the eligibility meeting may also include discussions to clear the air regarding the following ambiguities:

Which category does the child fit best into concerning their challenges?

Suppose a child struggles with both dyslexia and asthma. While dyslexia is a "specific learning disability" and asthma falls under "other learning disability," the team has to decide which category to use. Some children may have more than just one learning or thinking difference. The meeting builds discussion on the child's needs to determine the needed support and services, not an isolated category or diagnosis. Therefore, the selected category should be well-suited to the challenges that impact the child's learning the most.

What does an "adverse effect" on educational performance look like?

The American Department of Education clarifies that education includes behavior, social skills, and attentiveness. Therefore, an adverse effect can be at play when children struggle with hyper-activity, impulse control, organization, attention, or social skills.

Merely doing well in school is not all that matters. Some children might score well, but only if they get ample hours at home to do their assignments or a lot of help from parents or tutors.

What qualifies as a part of the child's education?

In addition to academic performance, the team has to look into the following areas when determining the child's needs and eligibility for special education services:

- Functional performance, i.e., communication, self-care, mobility, and psycho-social skills
- Medical history
- Behavioral or emotional challenges

ELIGIBLE OR NOT ELIGIBLE

If your child is found eligible for special education services and learning support, the next step is to develop an IEP for your child. The next chapter has all you need to know to start the IEP process. Over here, we will cover the actions you can take if your child is not eligible. It can be quite upsetting, but we keep moving forward regarding processes to get where we need to. Here are options to approach this part of the eligibility process.

1. Find out the school's reasoning behind their decision
2. Contact a Parent Training and Information Center/Talk to a special education advocate
3. Review the evaluation reports
4. Submit a letter of parental concerns, i.e., an addendum page
5. Consider a 504 plan instead
6. Consider an Independent Educational Evaluation (IEE)
7. Request mediation
8. Start planning for a new evaluation

Review Box

- Remember – Students with disabilities who do not meet the eligibility criteria for special education may still be eligible for accommodations and support through a 504 Plan.
- Section 504 of the Rehabilitation Act of 1973 is a federal law that prohibits discrimination against individuals with disabilities in programs and activities that receive federal financial assistance, including public schools.
- A 504 Plan is a document that outlines the accommodations and support that a student with a disability will receive in order to have equal access to education.
- Under Section 504, a student is considered to have a disability if they have a physical or mental impairment that significantly limits one or more major life activities,

such as caring for oneself, performing manual tasks, walking, seeing, hearing, speaking, breathing, learning, and working.

Next up, we go into the nitty-gritty of the IEP. First, it is time to examine what is inside the IEP document. This document is like a roadmap for your child's education, outlining the supports and services they will receive to participate in their educational program and progress towards their goals. As a parent, it is crucial that you are an active participant in this process and have a good understanding of what is inside the IEP document, so you can use it as a tool to effectively support your child's education.

7

THE ANATOMY OF AN IEP

A re you ready to get under the hood and see what makes up an IEP document? Then, hold on to your lab coat and prepare for dissection because we're about to dive into the anatomy of an IEP. Just like the human body has a skeleton that holds everything together and allows it to function correctly, an IEP is like the foundation and framework of your child's education.

When creating an IEP, it is essential to consider the overall plan and how it will guide the child's special education and related services under IDEA. This includes understanding the goals and purpose of the IEP and the range of activities and settings it covers.

The IEP acts as a blueprint that outlines the student's special education experience across different school environments. Therefore, it should be customized to meet the child's specific needs and outline the necessary accommodations, support services, and settings in which they will be provided. It must also be reviewed on a tri-annual basis and updated to ensure that it meets the evolving needs of the student while reflecting on their progress.

By considering the "big picture" of the IEP, educators, and parents can work together to ensure that the child's needs are met and they have the best chance to succeed in school.

The two primary purposes of an IEP are:

- To establish measurable yearly goals for the child
- To define the special education services and support that the public educational agency will provide to, or on behalf of, the child

A team of the following members develops it:

- The child's parents or guardians
- At least one of the child's special education teachers or providers
- At least one of the child's subject teachers (if the student is participating in the regular education environment)
- A school district representative
- An individual who can interpret the evaluation results
- Representatives of any other agencies that may be responsible for funding or providing transition services (if the student is 16 years or, if appropriate, younger)
- The student
- Other individuals who have knowledge or special expertise regarding the child

What is the purpose and importance of an IEP?

It is difficult to see your child struggle in school as a learner, and you might wonder what more you can do as a parent to help them do better. An IEP is meant to specify the special education instructions, learning aids, and services that a student requires to do well in school. More than just a "plan," an IEP is a map that makes its way around all the obstacles a child with a disability may typically face in education.

IEP DEVELOPMENT

The 8 components of an IEP

1. Present levels of academic skill and performance

The IEP must have details of your child's current performance in school and how their disability interferes with the progress they can make in the general education system. In addition to academic areas, their motor skills, behavior, and social skills are also assessed. The IEP team needs to have all the details to know the significance of the impact your child's disability has on their learning. The IEP team collects data and information from class teachers to establish a baseline of performance, or a starting point, before devising an IEP.

2. Annual goals

One section in the IEP must outline specific, measurable, academic, and functional goals that the student can be expected to achieve. In addition, the goal must provide outcomes that support the student's growth, progress, and improvement in learning, which can be tracked. These goals must be updated at least once a year, and the child's teachers and parents must evaluate the child's performance regularly.

3. Amount and duration of services

The IEP has to include a starting and end date for any service the IEP team provides. It must also specify the frequency of use, i.e., how often and where the child will use the service.

4. Participation in mainstream classrooms (LRE)

The supporting staff and faculty at school, i.e., the IEP team, must plan to ensure that your child is educated in the least restrictive environment to the greatest extent possible. This is necessary for the plan to align with FAPE. The amount of time for which the student participates in the mainstream classroom or general education environments is stated in the plan.

5. Testing accommodations and modifications

If your child has to participate in state or local assessment tests, the IEP must specify the details of the testing accommodations that the child can use. Details of whether your child takes the local/state assessments or modified tests must be included in the IEP, along with the rationale for the decision.

6. Special education services

A description of the services, such as any programs, equipment, and teaching strategies that will be provided to the student, should be included in the IEP. These services also include faculty training.

7. Progress monitoring

The IEP must explain how your child's progress will be measured. This can be achieved by regular testing or feedback forms from teachers.

8. Transitional goals

An IEP helps your child improve and succeed in the present, but it also prepares them for the future of their education. That is why an IEP includes plans for the child's transition beyond grade school when they turn 14. For example, if your child wants to pursue further education and attend college, the IEP includes steps to help them prepare for their future environment. Transitioning includes services that provide support and instruction to help your child shift from school into vocational programs or any other program promoting an independent lifestyle.

The IEP team works in harmony and prioritizes the five following areas while developing an IEP for the child:

Student's strengths

A student's strengths can create a latticework that can support building new skills and behaviors. For example, if your child enjoys reading, perhaps their teachers can build their self-confidence by asking them to read a story aloud for the rest of the class daily.

Educational concerns of parents

The IEP team is meant to address any concerns you might have if they can impact your child's learning process, whether you are concerned that your child might be struggling with social anxiety, is being bullied, is late to understand important concepts in class, or if they are unable to submit homework on time.

Evaluation results

The results of the most recent evaluation will be considered by the IEP team (whether the original or three-year reevaluation).

Academic and functional needs

The IEP team must also take into account the most recent academic and behavioral progress reports, results of district-wide assessments, progress on goals in the existing IEP (if there is one), and a thorough discussion on the effectiveness of the accommodations and modifications that are in place with the existing IEP. Finally, through discussion with teachers, and progress reviews, the team can determine any new development or functional needs that may have come up for the child over the year.

Additional factors

- Has the child's behavior interfered negatively with their learning or the classroom environment?
- Does the child have limited English skills?
- Does the child have a visual or hearing impairment?
- Does the child have communication needs?
- Would the child need assistive technology devices and services?

IMPORTANT ELEMENTS OF AN IEP

Present Level of Performance (PLOP)

Also known as PLAAFP or PLP, a PLOP is a general overview of the child's present academic and functional achievements and provides a picture of where he or she is. It covers the child's strengths, challenges, skill levels, social skills, and behavior. The overview also includes statements about how the child's disability or impairment affects their involvement and progress in the general education classroom.

Louis is a thoughtful, caring fourth grader who persistently tries to stay on top of his work in class. He loves seeking out books related to animals and wildlife. His curiosity is an excellent drive for his learning. However, while Louis meets standard grade-level expectations in spelling and reading fluency, he shows significant difficulty grasping mathematical concepts compared to his classroom peers. Louis' challenges in mathematics seem to affect his progress in the general education curriculum by causing him to lag behind his peers.

Here's an example of an academic goal or learning objective for Louis to improve in math class:

Louis will be able to understand and explain a multiplication equation as a comparison/Give verbal statements of multiplication

For instance, interpret 15 = 5 x 3 as a statement that 15 is 5 times as many as 3 but 3 times as many as 5.

Annual Goals

Annual goals include reasonable goals for skill improvement in the academic and functional areas where the child might be lacking. *Measurable* annual goals are meant to address and meet each educational need that results from the child's disability. An ideally measurable goal would include

A timeframe (When): The amount of time in the goal period is specified as a number of weeks or a completion date.

Conditions (How): The specific resources necessary for the student to reach their goal should be mentioned. For instance, a goal related to reading skills and comprehension might require using a graphic organizer. Therefore, using a graphic organizer is the "how" or the condition.

Behavior (What): This component defines the behavior or ability that is being observed. It represents an action that can be monitored and measured.

Criterion (How Often): This identifies how often, or to what extent, the expectations must be achieved to demonstrate that the goal has been accomplished. A goal's criterion relates to how much growth is expected within a timeframe.

The IEP team reviews annual goals daily. If the goal is not met in the same year, it will stay in the plan for another year. However, if the goal has been met, you can work with the team to develop new goals for the next year.

SMART goals: Now remember that all goals to be devised must align with the child's PLOP. The goals should not be vague or generalized for students to extract maximum benefit from the IEPs. Instead, they should be 'SMART', which is short for Specific, Measurable, Attainable, Results-oriented, and Time-bound.

SMART acronym	Meaning	Examples of SMART goals
Specific	Each goal would be specific so as to name the skill or area along with the targeted goal.	By the end of the IEP cycle/ trimester, Louis will be able to use manipulative to solve a multiplication problem of a fraction and whole number with 75% accuracy on 4 out of 5 trials measured
Measurable	The goals are set so that the child's progress can be measured using curriculum-based measurements or screening.	Louis will be able to solve math problems involving the computation of fractions and decimals with 70% accuracy.
Attainable	The goal should set progress expectations that are realistic for the child	Louis will be able to write 5 sentences, each greater than 9 words, and with no more than one error in both spelling and punctuation, each
Results-oriented	There should be a clear sense of what the child would be doing to accomplish the goal.	In 4 out of 5 times, Lilliana will focus her attention toward the teacher, while she speaks to the class 95% of the time
Time-bound	The goal must include a time frame in which the child will achieve it, as well as when and how frequently progress will be measured.	By 31st March, Lilliana will be able to correctly solve an addition or subtraction math problem with 90% accuracy, in 8 out of 10 trials. Her progress will be measured weekly

Short-Term Objectives

Benchmarks of short-term objectives are intermediate objectives that mark progress toward the annual goal. They act as a means of tracking the student's progress toward reaching the annual goal in question. They are mainly prioritized for children with disabilities, who take alternate assessments to achieve alternate standards.

For instance, Lilliana's annual goal is to achieve a reading score at the 4th-grade level or above.

Her short-term objectives will be:

When given a list of 20 new words containing short vowel sounds by April, Lilliana can work them out with 90% accuracy on at least 4 out of 5 trials.

By October, Lilliana can correctly split up to 20 words by their syllables with 90% accuracy on each of the 5 trials. This will complete a learning goal related to comprehension of the rule that each syllable in a word contains a vowel.

Measuring and Reporting Progress

You don't have to wait for the annual IEP meeting to check how your child is progressing toward their IEP goals. Instead, the school should provide progress reports over the year as often as they are prepared. This should let you assess whether things are smooth sailing and the IEP in place is effective or whether you would like to forward any concerns and consider revising your child's IEP. Most examples mentioned above include a percentage of accuracy (e.g., a student may be required to perform a task with 90% accuracy). This concrete score can show the team the student's progress. Alternatively, the teacher may observe and take notes of the student's performance as they complete the assessment trials.

Parents have the right to be informed of their child's progress. In addition, they are allowed to request a review of the IEP and intervene to request adjustments if warranted.

Special education

In an IEP, special education denotes education or instruction that is individually developed to cater to *specific* needs that result from the disability of the child. Besides academic progress, special education for some students may focus primarily on speech/language development, cognitive development, motor skills, or other needs related to a physical or learning disability. For example, a personalized curriculum that differs from the mainstream general education curriculum for non-disabled individuals, teaching American Sign Language (ASL) to deaf or hard of hearing students, or teaching blind students to read and write using Braille.

Similarly, for non-disabled students, the general education curriculum can be taught with adaptations, such as accommodations or modifications for the student. For instance, a 4th grader can be taught math with assistive technology or allowed to use counting tools. Accommodations are changes that assist in overcoming or working *around* the disability while the curriculum stays the same. Modifications mean changes in *what* is being taught to the student or their goals. There's plenty more about adaptations in learning in the chapter that follows this one. Let's cover what we're on currently and see to that later.

Related services

These services are dedicated to helping children benefit from their special education program by providing additional help and support in areas of need, such as speaking, walking, or moving. Parents may not be charged for these services by the school district. Instead, they are integrated into the student's IEP. Examples of these services include:

- interpreting services
- psychological counseling
- physiotherapy
- therapeutic recreation
- disability assessment
- medical diagnostic or evaluation procedures

Supplementary aids and services

We don't have to confuse these services with those we discussed above. To clarify, here is IDEA's definition of this term (at §300.42) that reads:

"Supplementary aids and services mean aids, services, and other supports that are provided in regular education classes, other education-related settings, and in extracurricular and nonacademic settings, to enable children with disabilities to be educated with non-disabled children to the maximum extent appropriate …."

Supplementary aids and services can be but are not limited to, accommodations and modifications to the curriculum being studied at the student's grade level, the instruction being used to teach the content at hand, or how the student's progress is being monitored. These services are not entirely student-centered; they also include support and training for the school staff working with the child.

Program modifications for school staff

There is support available for the school staff to help *them* help the students be successful in special education. The IEP team decides what program modifications to avail for the staff and specifies them in the IEP. Examples of programs for the school staff include:

- attending a training program or conference related to the student's needs and disabilities,
- having a special educator in the classroom to assist, or
- providing special equipment or teaching material

The extent of the student's nonparticipation

This feature defines the extent to which the child with a disability won't be participating with their non-disabled peers in the regular classroom or the general curriculum. The reasons for nonparticipation given by the IEP team should reflect the child's special needs. The LRE (Least Restrictive Environment) principle is closely connected to this component of the IEP.

Service delivery

This component requires setting an exact date for the beginning of the modifications and services provided through the IEP and clarifying the frequency, location, and duration of those provisions.

Transition planning

For students coming of age with a transition around the corner, IDEA requires the IEP team to develop goals focusing on the world that follows secondary schooling.

Transition services include activities for the child with a disability that are coordinated and designed to follow a process focused on producing results and improving the child's academic and functional achievement. That can mean facilitating the child's transition from school to post-school learning regarding postsecondary education and leading an independent lifestyle. Transition planning protects and promotes domains of adult and independent living.

The services will be based on the child's needs, strengths, and preferences. By services, I mean:

- Individualized instructions
- "Related services"

- Community experiences
- Employment
- Developing 'adult living' goals
- If needed, help with mastering skills that are used daily and offer a functional evaluation.

Age of majority

This does not apply to all students' IEPs. Transferring rights at the age of majority means transferring rights to individuals once they reach the legally defined adult age. The age of majority does vary by state, so I would recommend you to look up yours here:

http://minors.uslegal.com/age-of-majority/

At a point between 18-21 years, some states transfer the student's educational rights from the parents to them. The transition begins at least one year before the child reaches the age of majority. It is up to the public agency to provide the necessary notice for this phase to the student and the parents.

Consent

Finally, most IEPs include a consent section where the parent/guardian can consent to implement the IEP. There is room for flexibility in an IEP because you are allowed to disagree with some parts of an IEP. You may attach an addendum that specifies parts of the IEP you agree with.

You have gotten a good understanding of the different components of an IEP in this chapter and how they work together to support your child's education. In the next chapter, we will look at the different types of accommodations, modifications, supports, and services available for your child and discuss how to advocate for and implement these strategies effectively.

8

SUPPORTS AND SERVICES

You can help your child participate in their educational program in many ways. You probably hear the words accommodations and modifications a lot. I know they've been mentioned in this book repeatedly. You might think they mean the same thing – they don't! This chapter will explore the differences between accommodations and modifications, explain why a child might refuse help, and offer tips on what you can do as a parent to support them.

First up, what is meant by *support* and *services*? What is the difference between the two? Next, the IEP outlines the appropriate support and services your child will need to enhance their learning.

Supports are general changes made to how and what a student will learn. This can mean resorting to teaching interventions and changes in instruction that would help bring the student to an equal learning level as their peers or to a level where they can exhibit significant improvement. *Services* can denote resources or learning aids that help the student in specific academic or functional areas, such as language and motor skills. Services are usually a part of the 'related services' and 'direct services' components in the IEP. They are not restricted to special education; services can also be provided in the general education curriculum.

In an IEP or 504 plan, supports include specialized instruction such as accommodations and modifications (discussed further in the chapter). Related services, on the other hand, would consist of speech therapy, occupational therapy, or learning aids such as assistive technology and staff training.

Here are specific examples of each:

Supports

Flexible timing

- Extra time on tests or class assessments
- Frequent short breaks throughout the day

Changes in environment

- Quiet spaces
- Assigned work in smaller groups
- Taking short walks to refocus

Changes in learning materials

- Provision of lecture notes
- Audiobooks

Changes in instruction

- One-on-one learning/tutoring
- Lower difficulty levels of assignments

Changes in how a student demonstrates what they've learned

- Dictating answers orally
- Typing answers instead of writing

Services and supplementary aids:

- Speech-language therapy
- Physiotherapy
- Psychological counseling
- Adaptive exercise regimens in physical education
- Social work
- Health services at school
- Assistive technology, such as speech-to-text software
- Adaptive tools and materials such as virtual reality or Q&A apps with real-time hints for answering

ACCOMMODATIONS

Accommodations are adaptations made to the learning environment and teaching instructions or material to aid students with disabilities in accessing the curriculum and demonstrating their learning. They are designed to help students with disabilities participate in learning activities and meet age-appropriate academic standards like their non-disabled peers.

They must be personalized and tailored according to the student's unique learning needs, best determined after thorough professional evaluations.

Primarily, accommodations are meant to cushion the impact of the disability on the student's learning opportunities and abilities, enabling them to participate and progress with the rest of their class. Now, accommodations do not change the curriculum being taught. Think of them as add-ons that don't alter what is taught in class but provide students with extra help to access learning. They also do not change the learning objectives or expectations for learning and assessments from the student. Accommodations address and remove learning barriers, such as loud noise, lack of instruction or structure in the presented information, or handwritten responses.

Types of accommodations

Various types of accommodations can help students access the curriculum being taught as well as demonstrate their knowledge. Some of them are as follows:

Presentation of learning material: Alternative material formats can include Braille, audio, or larger print.

Alternative response format: Typed responses on a computer or tablet, dictated answers, or multiple-choice questions.

Changes in levels of learning support: Providing one-on-one teaching and tutoring, or a class with a lesser capacity

Alternative schedules and timing: This includes extended time for tests and assessments or being given more frequent breaks during longer classwork.

Individuals with Attention-Deficit/Hyperactivity Disorder (ADHD) may have difficulty perceiving and understanding time, known as "time blindness." Students with time blindness may struggle to estimate how long it will take to complete a task, understand calendars, and allocate time for exams or assignments. Time blindness is not a behavior or a choice but a symptom that can be addressed through interventions and accommodations.

While adding extended time to accommodate a student's IEP may improve short-term outcomes, it does not address the underlying issues. To address skill deficits related to time blindness, it may be helpful to work with the student's IEP team to consider interventions such as using a kitchen timer or visual task timer to make the time more concrete.

As a parent, it is crucial to communicate with your child's education providers to ensure that your child, with time blindness, is not penalized or excluded from school activities due to their inability to complete tasks within a specific time frame. For example, it is not appropriate to restrict access to recess, or class parties, due to a child's difficulty in keeping up with work or participating at the same level as their peers.

Examples of accommodations

- Visually impaired students can be accommodated by providing braille materials, text-to-speech software, or large-font prints.
- Students suffering from an orthopedic impairment may have poor motor skills and face difficulty with handwriting. They may use a word processor or notes app to type their answers and class notes or dictate answers.
- Some students struggle with inattention or hyperactivity. They can be provided with sensory or fidget tools to release energy quietly. They can also be provided seating closer to the teacher or a spot where they can learn best, such as a quiet spot or somewhere close to helpful learning charts and posters.
- Additional examples of IEP accommodations can also include:

  ○ Visual guides, such as charts, schedules, and cues on classroom desks or for directions in the hallways
  ○ Noise-canceling headphones
  ○ Emotions cards
  ○ Pass cards for students who need to leave the class frequently for movement breaks

MODIFICATIONS

Modifications are changes to the curriculum, content being taught, and what is expected from a student. School can be challenging for students living with disabilities. The purpose of IEPs and 504 plans is to break down barriers that can get in the way of learning and work around obstacles to improve access to learning for those kids. Modifications are related to changes in instruction or assessment. For instance, a student can be graded using the pass/no pass option rather than letter grades or percentages with more restrictions. Further examples of modifications can include:

- Readjusted pace or duration of instruction
- Allowing the use of assistive technology
- Provision of additional instructional resources during both learning and testing
- Assigning less homework
- Easier assignments
- Questions reworded in simpler, straightforward language

Now, how are accommodations and modifications any different?

Accommodations allow students to learn and be tested on the same material as their peers. At the same time, modifications involve changing the expectations or content of a task to meet the student's abilities better.

Students who need help learning the same material as their peers to meet the same expectations and learning objectives can benefit from accommodations. Accommodations change *how* a student learns. For instance, a student with dyslexia can listen to the audio version of the same book that the rest of the class is reading to follow along. On the other hand, some students consistently fall far behind their peers and may benefit from modifications. For example, they may be assigned homework assignments of a reduced difficulty level that differ from what the rest of the class receives. In addition, modifications can allow students to use a calculator in their exams.

Regarding classroom tests, accommodations *don't* change what the student is being tested on. For instance, students with poor muscle control may be allowed extra time to complete their tests or type their answers out instead of handwriting them.

Students who receive modifications are learning lesser material or material that is simpler. Therefore, they will be tested along with the provision of appropriate modifications. Modifications can change *what* the student has to demonstrate or what they are tested on. For instance, if the class has to solve a test including 30 math problems, a student with modifications might have to solve only 15 problems. Or they might have a different test syllabus from the rest of the class. Modifications can also change the grading system used for certain students who receive them, such as a pass/no pass.

Before agreeing to implement a modification or an accommodation, you should carefully consider whether it is the most appropriate support strategy for the child. Especially with modifications, your child would be learning less than other students. With modifications, learning less and knowing less is a significant disadvantage in the long run, particularly if your child is getting modified learning throughout their school life. Many places require a high school exam to graduate. A student who has sat through modified learning for their entire school life might have the cards stacked against them when it comes to passing this exam. Modifications can limit options for future education, which can go on to impact career options and employment in adulthood.

Of course, modifications for some students, who significantly struggle in some academic areas, are warranted. For example, children with dyslexia can struggle with spelling for their entire life. IEP teams can decide that the child won't be able to progress if they spend far too much time on spelling. A modification in this particular student's IEP can include letting the student learn fewer words to spell and use spellcheck to keep things moving instead.

Before going along with modifications, consider making changes to instruction that suit the child's learning style better, i.e., accommodations. Requesting a modification when an accommodation would be sufficient can cause the following:

- This may create an inaccurate perception of the student's abilities and have unintended consequences, such as limiting their ability to be mainstream or increasing their time in special education classes.
- The false sense of the student's abilities may not adequately challenge or prepare them for the demands of college or the workforce.

Reasons your child may refuse support

Both you and the school are motivated to improve your child's learning experience. However, if you have arranged for your child to receive accommodations through their IEP but refuse to use them, it is common to feel confused and concerned. Therefore, weighing in on your child's words and approaching the situation accordingly is important. Unfortunately, it is quite common for kids to refuse IEP or 504 plan accommodations.

One of the children's most common concerns is feeling or looking different from their peers. Children are driven to feel like they belong at school and be friends with their peers. Some special education services can require your child to be pulled from class to visit a resource room or separate classroom for instruction. They might fear looking like the odd one out and even prefer to struggle in class. They worry about what other kids might say. Kids don't hold back, you know? Your child might worry that their friends think they are "cheating" or that they will get made fun of for "being special."

In other cases, when children are not fully involved in choosing the accommodations or explained they are being chosen, they may not understand the purpose behind them. This can prevent them from fully utilizing their accommodations. In addition, they need a few weeks to get comfortable asking for and using them.

Children are not born with an innate skill for self-advocacy. Therefore, it is an important skill to build for students who learn differently. Self-advocacy begins by asking for what one needs. Not all children know how or when to ask, but you can ensure your child has picked up the language and skills to ask to use an accommodation politely.

One of the most difficult challenges is when your child needs accommodations to learn but refuses to accept that they need help. It is rather complex. A simpler way to look at it is that they are only human for wanting to show everyone that they are self-sufficient and don't require help. They are more likely to refuse help if they are uncomfortable with opening up about their problems and find it difficult to ask for help. It can be a matter of low self-esteem or hyper-independence as well. Each case of this reasoning should examine the child's input and understand *their origin*.

WHAT CAN YOU DO AS A PARENT WHEN FACED WITH THIS SITUATION?

If your child refuses to help for any of the reasons discussed previously or otherwise, there are a few strategies you can try out to approach this situation.

The first step is always creating a steady and level ground of understanding. Please help your child understand their disability. Since disabilities or impairments significantly impact one's life for a long time, talking to your child about their disability is a conversation you will have with them often. As your child sees and experiences more of the world, they will have many new questions or even feel confused regarding their disability. How you respond to your child in these conversations is important for how they view themselves and their ability to achieve new goals.

You don't have to fear bringing up the topic of their disability, thinking that it'll make them feel unhappy or bad about themselves. Dismissing this topic has many consequences in one's young life and childhood. It can confuse the child as to why their peers do well in class but do not struggle to maintain relationships or care for themselves.

Whether sensory-related, emotional, physical, or learning, the kind of disability your child has and when it starts affecting their life will play a major role. Providing age-appropriate information about their disability can help your child better understand themselves and their needs, thus, the purpose of accommodations. While being honest is important, you also have to keep it child-friendly. If you are explaining to your 5-year-old about a condition they have congenitally, they wouldn't nearly begin to grasp the works of the science and research behind it or why they struggle with it in particular, unlike most other people. You can help them understand what happens in their condition matter-of-factly, such as "Your muscles have not always been very strong. It is okay to need help with some difficulties at school so that you can learn like everyone else." Talk to your child about how the people involved, including yourself, look out for them and are happy to help them and be on their team.

If your child resists using accommodations for fear of standing out or being singled out, try to address these concerns and reassure them that accommodations are a normal and necessary part of their education. It is expected that many people and children at school or in the community may turn their heads to ask your child questions about their disability or why they are getting extra help. No one owes anyone an explanation for why they need help or are struggling, especially not your child. But helping your child be prepared to respond to questions like these can help them feel more comfortable at school and around other people in general. Of course, it is up to your child whether they want to answer other people.

Most of all, show your child the positive side of things. Tell your child and other people you meet that they are great at drawing/coloring, wonderful storytellers, or excellent at math. Let them know that their disability does not have to stop them from progressing in school. They'll feel more confident and motivated to learn and demonstrate their knowledge and abilities. What parent does not want to see their kid shine? You can also help your child feel inspired by telling them about famous personalities who may be struggling with the same disability or condition as them. Praise them for using their accommodations and make an effort to highlight their strengths and successes. This can help to build their confidence and self-esteem.

If your child dislikes being pulled from class to the resource room, help put things into perspective by explaining what they can get help with, such as tutoring or time management skills. Tell them about the importance of extra support solely being provided to help them achieve their goals. Resource rooms are usually temporary and only last until your child has achieved their goals. You can tell them they won't have to keep going to the resource room once their goals have been reached. If your child resists using a particular accommodation from the start, consider trying it out for a limited period and reevaluating its effectiveness. This can help to ease your child into using the accommodation and may make them more willing to continue using it. If your child is beyond frustrated or upset, consider seeking support from the school or a mental health professional. They may be able to offer additional strategies and resources to help your child understand and accept their accommodations. If your child feels particularly self-conscious about being singled out, you can ask the teachers to find a more subtle method that your child can alert them that they need assistance. Please encourage your child to actively participate in the IEP process and involve them in decisions about their accommodations. How would you feel if a group met regularly to discuss your school life and how you would spend your time in class without including yourself? Kids, especially teens, will be curious and ask many questions as they age. It is only fair to involve them in transition planning regarding what classes they will take in their high school years, what they will do for work over the summer, what colleges they can apply to and attend, etc. It is important to hear them out and include their visions for *their* future. But it is not all about the planning. Children and youth in special education programs should be informed about advocacy and feel welcome and motivated to be involved with their team members. After all, the IDEA does count the student as a part of the IEP team.

Now you are ready for the IEP meeting itself. The IEP meeting is an important opportunity for you, as a parent, to participate in the decision-making process and advocate for your child's needs. But with so much on the line, it is natural to feel slightly nervous and unsure of what to expect. So in the next chapter, we will provide some tips and strategies for what to do before, during, and after the IEP meeting to help you feel more prepared and confident as you advocate for your child's education.

'On feeling like a cheater.'

Being dyslexic is tough. You can't read or spell the same words that others find simple. I felt too dumb to even try on most days. I only managed to do well in English when I started getting accommodations, such as using spell check, audiobooks, having the test read to me, and answering verbally. Eventually, I started to feel a little at ease as my grades started to improve. The words on the pages and screens did not seem so daunting anymore. Unfortunately, this relief was short-lived because as I started to get better, the real shame and self-doubt started to creep in. Was I an imposter?

I knew I couldn't be as good of a writer as the other kids in class, but I found ways to produce quality work that I could be proud of. People find whatever works for them and stick to it, right? I felt ashamed when my classmates would ask me how I was managing to pass my tests when I was dyslexic or why I got extra time to write my tests, but they did not. A self-shaming voice in my head all the time was quite troubling.

But there can't be just one single way to write. Everyone is a different kind of learner. It does not mean I've cheated because I found a way to rise above my defeats and overcome my learning barriers. I have real ideas and words in my head that I enjoy sharing, but I could use a little help from external resources to get them down on a medium. I learned that I deserve respect from myself like I respect other people for their differences. My dyslexia made working hard enough. I wasn't going to let others get in the way too. I appreciate my parents for seeing my learning differences and striving to get me the accommodations and support I needed in class, and I have started to own my efforts in school.

9

THE ART OF THE IEP MEETING

L ike most parents, you are probably feeling a little bit like a deer in headlights at the thought of sitting down with a room full of educators and discussing your child's education. But, not to worry, I've got your back. In this chapter, I'll provide tips and strategies for what to do before, during, and after the IEP meeting to help you feel more prepared and confident as you advocate for your child's needs. These strategies will help you navigate the nerve-wracking IEP meeting and emerge victorious.

What exactly *is* all the planning we have been discussing so far? What happens at an IEP meeting? Let's decode that.

The first official IEP meeting occurs within a month (30 days, to be precise) after the school has determined that your child is eligible for services and support. First, it gets the IEP up and running. Then, annual meetings take place, as mandated by IDEA, to review elements of the IEP each year. You will revisit your child's plan, goals, and components for the next year each year. The meeting will especially involve looking at your child's progress over the previous year and what adjustments should be made to the goals and resources for the year to follow.

At the meeting, you can expect to see the rest of the IEP team members, of course. Your child's teachers will be present. A person from the school district who can approve the support and services in the plan will be there, along with someone to present and interpret the evaluation results. One of the team members at school will play the role of your child's case manager, supervising the process and answering any concerns and questions you might have. When your child turns 14, they can join the team meetings to draft and discuss the transition planning with everyone else.

While there are certain bases to cover, there is no predetermined or concrete way the meeting *must* be run.

Whether the IEP meeting is in person or virtually, the school must inform the parents of the meeting's time and place/platform beforehand. The notice will contain all the information on who will attend the meeting and the meeting agenda. It should take a convenient time for the parents to attend. The IEP meeting notice should be sent to you 10 days before the meeting is due.

Here's a look at an IEP meeting's agenda.

- **Introductions:** The meeting begins by reviewing introductions from the attendees, including parents and other family members, teachers, and specialists.
- **Present Levels of Performance (PLOP):** The student's academic and functional behavior and progress made is

reviewed. Input relates to how the student is performing at home or in class and how the disability has been affecting the student's ability to make progress in the general education classroom. The child's strengths and weaknesses are discussed and used as leverage throughout to make plans.

- **Goals and objectives:** Annual and SMART goals and objectives are revised, and new ones are set based on the student's needs and PLOP.
- **Services**:

1. What measures will be taken to help the child reach their goals?
2. Who will be providing the special education services?
3. What accommodations can be provided? Inquire about time, frequency, placement, and LRE.
4. How will the school help the student participate in classes and extracurricular activities?

- **Monitoring of progress:** Methods of tracking and reporting progress to the student's parents
- **Other items of discussion:**

  ○ Transfer of rights, transition, and graduation planning
  ○ Testing protocol (in-class, state, and standardized assessments)
  ○ Behavior intervention plans
  ○ Extended School Year (ESY)
  ○ Addressing questions and additional input
  ○ Meeting notes and decisions

o Next steps; revise the roles and responsibilities of all the involved team members for implementing the IEP

WHAT TO DO:

Before the meeting

- **Prepare questions and recommendations**

While I've taken the liberty to a few important ones, reflect and note down any questions you have to clear the air completely before the meeting. Because of your child's needs, strengths, and weaknesses, be prepared to share any concerns you may have and recommendations for improvement. What new challenges in your child's life and learning career must be noted and shared?

- **Review your child's records**

Make sure you have the following information filed and ready:

- The current IEP (if your child has one)
- Progress reports on annual goals
- Accommodations and services your child currently has on their IEP
- Work samples (preferably recent work)
- Performance reports on assessments
- Evaluation results
- Student records

- Correspondence with teachers, the school, or other outside professionals (e.g., therapists, pediatricians, neurologists, physiotherapists, etc.)
- If your child is employed, include letters or reviews from their supervisor

- **Invite people on your side**

You are free to invite someone to join you if you need support. It could be a close friend, family member, or professional advocate. You must inform the team beforehand of the people accompanying you to the meeting. Explain their role and how they can help in a courtesy notice you can send to the school. You can prepare your meeting points with them, share your concerns, think out loud, and get their take on matters. It generally helps to have an extra set of eyes and ears in case you lose track of the meeting or need someone to take notes to double-check in case you have missed the point afterward. Most importantly, having emotional support with you at the meeting will help calm the nerves.

- **Review Case Conference**

Look at the notice sent to you by the school and make sure the time and date work for you and anyone attending the meeting with you. For example, if your child is coming of age and their transition is approaching, ensure that representatives from transition agencies attend the meeting.

Go over the school staff members who will be attending. You can contact the school to ask to enlist other school personnel you feel should attend the meeting. While reviewing the attendee's list, ensure that at least one person from the school/district attending is specifically authorized to allocate funds.

- **Review your rights and procedural safeguards as the parent/caregiver of your child (You may revisit Chapter 2 for this step)**
- **Know all about the IEP form**

Familiarize yourself with the IEP form's structure, elements, and order of contents. The meeting should follow the IEP form in that very order. Some states offer addendum forms to the IEP plan (e.g., behavior intervention plans, communication plans), so you might want to check if yours does in case it is an option you might want to consider.

- **Request a draft of the IEP**

An important step you would like to cover is to call the school at least 10 days before the meeting and ask about the IEP draft for your child. If a draft is being prepared, request a copy at least 5 days before the meeting. With an early look at the draft, you can judge whether parts of it need improvement or make suggestions. The draft can give you an idea about how the annual goals will be designed, and you can comment on intervention strategies you think may work for your child, for instance. Any suggestions, feedback, and additions to the draft can be submitted in advance or brought to the meeting for discussion.

If the documents seem confusing at first, flip to the last page of the IEP to check for the summary. Usually, the summary is written succinctly and contains recommendations, so it is more to the point. You won't find it so daunting after getting a basic idea of what the IEP contains.

- **Prepare a parent report or vision statement**

Prepare and share a report with the school before the IEP meeting. The information you include here can be drafted into the next IEP if they decide to make a redo. Here's what you can include in the report:

- The goals you have in mind for your child's progress
- Your take on strategies that may or may not be working
- Your child's strengths and weakness
- Your child's educational, functional, and social needs
- What *do you* think your child would benefit from
- Share your child's learning style and preferences

- **Relax**

Once everything's been prepared and looked after, try to relax. Spend some time with your child and reflect on their strengths and interests. Talk to them about what they like or don't like about school and learning. Get to know them because kids can be wondrous.

Remember, you know your child better than anyone on the team. Therefore, you can project strength and confidence and share your insights at the meeting as much as anyone else.

Questions to ask:

- What are we hoping to achieve in this IEP meeting?
- May I have a copy of my child's IEP document to follow during our discussion?
- Can I have prior access to copies of the notes/reports that we will be looking at?
- Who will interpret the results of my child's evaluations at the meeting?

During the meeting

- **Arrive early to the meeting**

Not only does punctuality have a good impression, but it will also allow you time to settle in before the meeting starts. You can share copies of your parent report or other discussion material with the participating team members.

If your child is present at the meeting, allow them to arrive later and leave earlier to avoid stressing them out.

- **Ask for members to be introduced**

It would help to know who's who and what their role is. You can know whom to look at during different parts of the meeting and share input that concerns them and their role.

If your child is attending the meeting with you, have them prepare a way to introduce staff members. They can share how they interact with that person daily or weekly. Again, the student's perspective is important because the goals of the meeting concern them.

You are not limited to strictly discussing the technical stuff or details concerning academics. Talk to the team about your child's bright areas, strengths, and personality.

- **Be a team member, not a spectator**

Special education laws and evaluation report jargon can be complicated. Even if you have covered everything to prepare, there might still be a new term or concept here and there. You have the right to be well-acquainted with all the details and decisions going into the building and finalizing the plan. Remember, no questions are stupid. Practice interrupting *politely* to ask your questions or wait for someone to finish speaking to ask for something to be clarified. By this point in the book, you have covered a major chunk of all you need to know about the IEP process. So, trust me when I say that I think it is only fair for you to trust *yourself* now. You know what to talk about.

- **Finalize the IEP**

Toward the end of the meeting, ensure you have voiced everything, from expectations to goals, for your child. Leave no doubt or question hanging and no concern unaddressed. Suggest any changes you thought about while the IEP was being discussed.

Share your concerns if any gray areas or some part of the IEP does not add up to you.

A copy of the final IEP should be sent to you within 2 weeks. It is important to get back to the school personnel regarding the IEP. If you disagree with the IEP, ignoring it will not have a good impression. A lack of response can say that you either agreed with the recommendations or no longer have interest in the process. Your signature on the IEP will indicate whether you have consented to or partially agreed to the plan. You can still disagree with some parts of the IEP while agreeing with other parts. You don't have to decide then and there. If you would like time to review the IEP and share it with someone to discuss it, you can ask to take a copy home. However, you must respond within 10 days with your concerns or any requests for changes, a finalized agreement and signature, or your refusal. If you refuse the IEP, you can follow up by requesting an additional meeting or mediation.

- **Remain calm**

You are not alone in this process. It is okay not to know what to expect or not know what is happening at the meeting entirely. You are working with others, and others are working with you and *for* you. Remember to be polite and respectful. Agreeing to disagree is always an option, but honesty is also important. Share your appreciation for the school personnel, other professionals, and advocates, and thank them for their time and effort in supporting your child.

Questions to ask during the meeting:

- What training or experience does the staff have in the IEP planning process or generally in special education?
- Could you tell me more about how my child's day is scheduled?
- Can you tell me what observations you have made about my child that makes them different from the other children in the class?
- Can we discuss the IEP plan step by step?
- Please share what data or information you used to make this decision.
- Would the team like to recommend any changes?
- While it holds importance nonetheless, is this a SMART goal?
- Can you explain more about the methods that will be used to monitor and note down the progress of my child's goals?
- Who will be working with my child? When? How often and where?
- What would this particular intervention or accommodation look like in the class setting?
- What can I do at home with my child to help them work towards their IEP goals?
- When can I see a copy of the finalized IEP before agreeing to the suggested changes?
- Can we ease my child into their IEP accommodations and changes?
- If I would like to know further about the rights I've been given regarding my child's rights, whom can I speak to?

- How can I schedule another meeting down the line, if needed?

After the meeting

- **Go over the IEP with your child at home**

Explain to your child their goals and how they are to help them progress in class. You should also discuss who will meet with them to help them, when, where, and how. If it helps, you can write down the names and roles of the teachers or instructors assigned to your child and give them the list to refer to, e.g., Mrs. Harrison will be helping you with math.

Discuss with your child what you will start working on with them at home to make progress. Overall, it paints a picture of growth and improvement for them. It might help to motivate them by setting up a rewards system for when they make progress. Remind them that you are there for them and would like them to tell you about their day at school or how they like it in class.

- **Share your notes from the meeting**

Consider sending an email, letter, or fax to the IEP case manager that includes a summary of the decisions and questions resulting from the meeting. This will help bring everyone to the same page and start planning the next steps.

- **Review and sign the final IEP**

As mentioned previously, the IEP discussed at the meeting is a draft. The school or district is responsible for finalizing and sending over the official IEP after the meeting. Remember to get back to them before the deadline. Before signing an IEP, it is important to ensure all the information is correct and accurate. Even if your state does not require you to re-sign the IEP after a meeting (unless there are any changes to the services provided), double-checking the document is always a good idea. Discuss the important elements you need to check before giving consent. Review the IEP page-by-page. If needed, ask for an additional meeting to cover any concerns.

You are allowed to consent to some parts of an IEP while excluding others. For example, the regulations for IDEA say that a school district:

[M]ay not use a parent's refusal to consent to one service or activity ... to deny the parent or child any other service, benefit, or activity...

You cannot partially consent to the IEP or change your mind *after* the IEP services have been initiated. That would cancel the entire IEP, and your child would fall back into general education. However, you can still use dispute resolution to *request* changes to the same IEP you already consented to.

Partial consent to an IEP needs to be done in writing. One way to do this is to note on the IEP signature page that you consent partially and attach an additional document that explains the reasons for your disagreement. Alternatively, you may add mark-up changes as notes in the margins of the parts of the IEP you would like to disagree with, along with your signature.

- **Update your IEP binder at home**

Arrange the documents you received before, during, and after the meeting into your child's files at home, along with the new IEP.

- **Keep up with the updates on your child's progress**

Maintain correspondence with your child's teachers and school personnel and ensure you regularly receive progress reports. Updates on progress can include report cards and assessment data from tests or trials that have been conducted.

SHOULD YOUR CHILD ATTEND THE IEP MEETING?

Under IDEA, a student of age 14 or older is required to be *invited* to attend their IEP meeting. Students in high school are expected to participate in IEP meetings to discuss their transition plans for the future. However, even younger students may benefit from the involvement and contribute a fair amount of valuable input.

If an IEP is yet to be agreed upon and the student is new to the process, they can participate in the meeting by elaborating on their strengths, weaknesses, and what they could use as accommodations to help them at school. If there is an IEP in place or it is being reviewed, the student can talk about what is worked for them, what hasn't worked for them, and what other services they think they could benefit from. Teachers and parents can collaborate to help the child prepare for the IEP meeting. They can also reassure the child that they will be there to support him and help them out. It is important to help younger children feel safe and reassure them that the process is not judgmental or a form of punishment. It is only to help them succeed. With this opportunity, you can help your child build functional performance, including social skills, communication, behavior, and self-determination, which is extremely important for accomplishing future IEP goals.

For children in elementary school, you may consider discussing the following questions with them:

- What do you like about school?
- What do you enjoy doing?
- What do you think you are good at?
- What do you like about being in class?
- What do you want to work on getting better at?

Use positive reinforcement to encourage the child and credit them for being present. The IEP team should be informed of the child's attendance beforehand and how they will participate in the meeting. If the child shows interest or willingness to contribute at the meeting, compliment them for their willingness and input. This will help boost their self-confidence and encourage a sense of self-advocacy and better self-understanding. In case other members of the team seem too "targetting" or interrogating the child, you can step in and redirect the line of discussion. In addition to the previous questions, parents and teachers can both ask the student:

- What do you think makes learning in class difficult?
- Do you ask for help from your teachers when you need it? If not, why not?

Let your child showcase their determination and express their wants at the meeting. On the other hand, if things don't go according to plan (say, your child has an emotional meltdown or throws a tantrum), that's okay too. What matters is giving your child the opportunity to have them seen and heard and to see others involved in the IEP process.

IEP meeting Do's and Don'ts

Do: Express your concerns and any information that could be helpful

Don't: Withhold information, i.e., external evaluation results, medical information

Do: Ask questions if you do not understand or have suggestions

Don't: Assume you understand everything because you are too afraid to ask questions

Do: Be respectful, especially of the team's time

Don't: Be late and unprepared

Do: Be respectful and trust that the team is there to help your child

Don't: Get defensive when discussing your child's behaviors and struggles

Do: Revise and read the reports sent by the school before the meeting thoroughly

Don't: Act as the education expert

You have mastered the art of the IEP meeting and feel more prepared and confident as you advocate for your child's needs. Finally, you are ready to move on to the next stage: IEP implementation and review. This is where the rubber hits the road, and you will see the results of all your hard work. But what happens if things don't go as planned? What if you disagree with the school about your child's IEP? In the next chapter, we will discuss the IEP implementation and review process and provide options for resolving special education disputes.

IMPLEMENTATION AND RESOLUTION

I t can be a source of concern for parents when they are not at school to see firsthand whether the IEP is being implemented as planned. So how can you ensure the school follows through on its commitments and provides your child with the support and services outlined in the IEP? Ahead, I have provided an overview of the IEP implementation and review process and discussed some options for resolving any special education disputes that may come up. You will also read some tips and strategies for staying informed about your child's progress and advocating effectively for their education, even when you are not at school.

IEP IMPLEMENTATION

The implementation stage of the IEP process involves providing the student with the services and supports outlined in their IEP. To ensure this is done effectively, the school administrator should involve the student's parents and establish that school personnel has the necessary skills and training to deliver the support and services outlined in the IEP. In addition, it is important to monitor and assess the IEP's effectiveness regularly. You should track whether the school provides all the services and supports outlined in the plan and consider whether these adequately address your child's needs.

Here are some tips to keep in mind as you monitor your child's IEP implementation:

1. Stay in touch with your child's teacher and check in regularly
2. If the IEP is not being followed correctly, contact your case manager or the IEP leader to clear up any misunderstandings and make any corrections
3. If there are no signs of improvement, request an additional IEP team meeting
4. Know your child's special educators, what special education services they will receive, how frequently, and for what duration.
5. Read the progress reports
6. Watch your child's grades, test scores, and how consistent they are with homework
7. Remember to speak positively about the school and its staff around your child

RESOLVING DISPUTES

Even if you have a good relationship with the school, you may disagree with them about your child's IEP. For example, these disagreements could be related to the types or amount of services included in the IEP or your child's placement. Fortunately, the Individuals with Disabilities Education Act (IDEA) provides several options for resolving these disputes.

Firstly, let's discuss an informal approach to resolving disputes. The IEP is reviewed annually. After the first IEP meeting or annual IEP review meeting, parents may have concerns about their child's progress rate, suitability of the services provided to the child, or their placement. It is all right to return and request the IEP team to reconvene. At the additional meeting, the school can collaboratively discuss the parent's concerns and work toward an agreeable solution. To avoid a repetitive back-and-forth between the parents and the school and constant review meetings, the IEP teams can agree on a temporary solution.

For instance, an intervention or teaching plan can be substituted for another for a certain period during the child's IEP. By the end of the period, the school can check on the child's progress and meet with the team to discuss the child's progress with the temporary solution and the next step. This can be a trial period for figuring out what works for the child, and many parents are quite comfortable with reaching an agreement in this manner. IEP meetings can also be conducted with an impartial facilitator who ensures the IEP team *focuses* on building up the child's IEP *and* catering to the parent's concerns. The facilitator is not a member of the IEP team. They are unbiased and work to address conflicts as they arise during the meeting. This can help establish a true middle ground for all parties to participate equally. The facilitator does not impose any decisions. Instead, they ensure effective listening and communication for all the team members. In conflict or disagreement, the facilitator intervenes and encourages the members to explore alternative options. To talk a bit about disputes with the school, which can be either "procedural" or "substantive."

Procedural disputes concern the detailed, more technical aspects of the IEP or evaluation processes. Substantive disputes, however, concern your child's legal right to an "appropriate education," as protected by IDEA.

Let's go over the six options for resolving disputes in special education more formally now.

Negotiation

Since you can request an IEP meeting at any time, you can call a meeting with the team to discuss problems. You would meet with your child's teachers, the school district, and advocates to discuss the issues you have noticed and propose solutions. This is another friendlier, less complicated avenue that lightens each party's perspective. When, or if, an agreement is reached, it is documented in writing, and the student's IEP can be updated to include the agreed-upon amendments, i.e., additional services or accommodations.

Mediation

This option is similar to a facilitated IEP meeting involving a mediator and an impartial third party. The mediator joins the parents and school staff in the mediation session and assists with open and respectful communication to resolve all the differences between the two parties. As a result, parents and school personnel can try to reach a compromise while the mediator makes decisions for the parties.

IDEA requires the following conditions to be met:

- The decision to conduct a mediation session must be mutual on the part of both parties
- The school cannot use mediation to deny or delay the parent's right to a due process hearing, or any other right
- The state must select mediators for the session on an impartial or random basis
- The state will fund the mediation process
- The discussion taking place during mediation must remain confidential
- The agreement reached by the parties has to be presented in an official written mediation agreement.

Due process hearing

At a glance, a due process hearing is similar to a courtroom trial. However, in a due process hearing, parents and the school personnel will present evidence and witnesses before an impartial third party member, a hearing officer. It is up to the hearing officer to decide how the problem will be resolved based on the evidence provided and the IDEA's requirements. Due process is a relatively serious and rather complicated legal process. Consult a special education advocate before considering this particular option.

The first step in this file is a due process complaint, including the child's profile, a description of the dispute or complaint, and a proposed resolution of the conflict. The complaint has to include a violation of IDEA to be registered. After the complaint application has been filed against the suit, you and the school will attend a *resolution session*, where both parties will attempt to reach an agreement before proceeding. You and the school must agree to waive this meeting or attempt mediation.

If an agreement is not possible, a due process hearing is conducted. The due process hearing is similar to a civil courtroom hearing in that evidence is presented to the hearing officer, and witnesses are there to speak. The case is in the hearing officer's hands, and the decision they go on to make can be challenged further.

Due process is not the go-to option for just any dispute. Under IDEA, to be precise, you can file a due process complaint for a dispute when it comes to *"identification, evaluation, or educational placement of [a child with a disability], or the provision of a free appropriate public education [FAPE]."*

This entails that due process is specifically for special education-related disputes. A due process hearing related to whether your child is receiving a FAPE or not has to be based on substantive issues. Your complaint should relate to your child's right to a FAPE, not technical issues, i.e., procedural dispute.

However, exceptions may include faults on the school's part that impacted your child's access to education, e.g., the school failed to forward you a written notice (procedural error) which consequently had an impact on your child's right to an (appropriate) education (substantive error). Additionally, if you were deliberately excluded from an IEP meeting, for instance, you were not allowed to participate, which can be a reason to file a complaint.

Note the following time limits set on the different stages of the due process (fixed by IDEA but susceptible to variations between different states)

- The due process complaint must be filed within two years of learning about the action you are complaining about against the school
- The school must hold a resolution session with you within 15 days of receiving the due process complaint. This is followed by a 30-day period where both parties can attempt to reach an agreement.
- Once it has been decided that there will be no resolution agreement, the Department of Education will have 45 days to ensure that the follow-up due process hearing takes place and a decision is reached.
- You will have 90 days following the due process decision to file a lawsuit

Lawsuit

You can file a lawsuit in state or federal court if unsuccessful at the due process hearing. This is no small deal regarding legal matters, and you would require a lawyer. A civil lawsuit can only follow after you have gone through the due process option.

State complaint

You can file a state complaint against the school if any part of IDEA has been violated on their end. This complaint has to be filed within one year of the violation, and you can request the State Department of Education to intervene and investigate the matter. A state file complaint can be filed by groups of parents or organizations, especially if the school affects more than one child. After the complaint has been filed, it is in the state's hands to decide if the school violates IDEA. You can gain further insight by reviewing your state's rules and regulations on resolving these complaints.

Office for Civil Rights Complaint (OCR)

We discussed how Section 504 of the Rehabilitation Act protects students from harassment in the IEP system. Section 504 also allows you to file a complaint to the Office for Civil Rights. You can file a complaint with the Office for Civil Rights (OCR), under the federal Department of Education, against the school/district if you believe the team members or staff have discriminated against your child or you. This complaint should be filed within 180 days of the school's violation. Discrimination can be based on race, color, sex (including gender identity and sexuality), or *disability*. Your child should not be bullied, harassed, discriminated against, or made unsafe at school because of who they are.

The complaint will not need to be processed by the school. Instead, you may file it directly with the OCR if it comes down to this option. Similar to the way a state complaint is handled, the OCR would be in charge of leading an investigation of the school.

IEP REVIEW

When an IEP has been established for a student with a disability, it must be reviewed at least once annually. In addition to the routine review that is conducted yearly, an IEP can be reviewed at any time if the parent or teacher feels that the services or instruction are not fit or insufficient to meet the child's needs. The IEP team meets to review the existing IEP and determine whether efforts are adding up to meet the child's goals and objectives.

Changes and amendments to an IEP are called for when or if:

- The child is not making progress towards their goals and objectives
- All the present goals have been achieved, and the child needs updated ones to resume progress
- You have received new information about your child's diagnosis or condition from their provider, including necessary suggestions or recommendations

To drive changes in the IEP, the IEP team members, including the special education and general education teachers, counselor, school district representative, case manager, and parents, work collaboratively to discuss student needs changes. For instance, a child with dyslexia, who's been receiving services, may later be diagnosed with ADHD. This would require updated additional services to accommodate the student. In another case, parents can request changes with recommendations from their child's health or service provider, e.g., an audiologist might recommend an additional modification to a classroom environment to help a child with hearing loss.

Before any changes are implemented, the IEP team and parents must mutually agree on those proposed changes. You can propose changes to your child's IEP by forwarding a written request to the IEP team or your case manager. In the application, it would be ideal to mention the reasons for proposing the changes you would like in as much detail as possible. In case you have word or recommendations from a special education advocate or your child's service provider, provide the specific details of your conversation with them or attach an addendum that includes their recommendations written under their name.

If the school refuses to implement the proposed changes, you can request an IEP meeting at any time of the year (whether or not the annual review has occurred). The meeting is not meant to be quarrelsome. Instead, the spirit of teamwork can be maintained as the focus is fixed on catering to the child's learning needs. To work through tough blocks, you may call in your child's specialist or a special education advocate to help build your case. They can explain to the school district representatives, establish your case, and help them understand how the proposed amendments or changes to the IEP would be productive and beneficial for your child.

Phew. We have come to the end of our journey. By now, you should have a solid understanding of the special education process and feel more prepared and empowered to advocate for your child. But this is just the beginning. The real work starts now.

CONCLUSION

In this book, we covered all there is to know before stepping into the world of advocating for your child's special needs at school:

1. We visited multiple aspects of the legal system and were familiarized with special education laws.
2. Of course, we took ourselves to dust every corner of the IEP and 504 Plan while looking at how they work and how to attain them.
3. We simplified the work of the nerve-wracking referral and evaluation processes and how to prepare for them, followed by the eligibility determination meetings.

We dove into the IEP meetings and their framework, the hot talk about accommodations and modifications, and what to do when things don't go your way. We have covered it all.

I still remember when my daughter started first grade. I immediately broke ground and started working with the school to develop an IEP meeting her needs. I knew she needed one. I stayed on my feet and involved myself in every stage of the process as much as possible, attending every IEP meeting and advocating, to the best of my knowledge and will, for the support and services she needed. Of course, I faced a fair share of resistance from the school initially, but I kept my head up and refused to back down. It was never a race but a marathon.

I knew my daughter needed accommodations and modifications to have fair access to the curriculum and make progress, the same as her peers. I couldn't bear imagining her struggling and falling behind in school – a place where a child is meant to thrive, build their hopes and dreams and learn about and experience this spectacular world we live in. Nonetheless, I worked relentlessly to get my points and concerns across to the school board's IEP team to ensure they understood the gravity of addressing my daughter's needs. Finally, after months of hard work, determination, sleepless nights, and worrying, I managed to secure an effective IEP plan that was set to work in my daughter's favor.

I was utterly grateful for the end of a long and complicated process. I felt accomplished, and it was all thanks to this fierce sense of advocacy and sheer determination. I pat myself on the back for getting through a long and challenging process like this. What is the result? My daughter came home with a beaming smile, telling me how much she loved her class. I have seen my daughter make great strides in her education. The most delightful part of this for me was getting to see her enjoy school for the first time. The progress reports and updates from the school were self-explanatory; my daughter was making consistent progress, and I couldn't be more proud.

As a parent of a child with a disability, it can be easy to feel like you are constantly fighting for your child's needs to be met and that you are constantly at odds with the school or other professionals. However, it is important to remember that advocating for your child is not about putting yourself against others or creating an "us vs. them" dynamic.

Instead, it is about working together as a team to ensure that your child has the resources and support they need to succeed. Think of advocacy as a collaborative process rather than a combative one. It is about finding common ground and working towards a shared goal: to support your child and help them reach their full potential. This may require compromise and cooperation on both sides, but the ultimate goal is to create a positive and supportive environment for your child.

Remember that everyone involved wants what is best for your child and that you can achieve great things that will benefit your child by coming together and working as a team. Don't be afraid to speak up and advocate for your child, but try to do so respectfully and collaboratively. By approaching advocacy in this way, you can create a positive and supportive environment for your child and help them succeed.

So, here's my advice:

- Keep learning and stay informed about your child's rights and the laws and regulations that govern special education.

- Join a support group or network with other parents of children with disabilities. Having a support system can do wonders. Remember that you are not alone in this journey. Many people, resources, and support systems are available to help you along the way.
- Don't be afraid to speak up and advocate for your child's needs.
- Remember, you are your child's biggest advocate! Know your rights and dispute resolution options if you disagree with the school or district.
- Keep a positive attitude, and don't give up! You can help your child achieve their full potential with determination and perseverance.
- An IEP is not a set-it-and-forget-it process. Constant monitoring and progress reports should ensure you can correct course when necessary.

Thank you so much for reading this book about advocating for your child and getting them the support they need. I genuinely hope that you found the information helpful. If you have a moment, I would appreciate it if you could leave a review on the platform where you purchased this book. Your feedback is incredibly valuable, and it can help others discover this resource and learn more about advocating for their children. I wish you the best of luck, and more power to you!

A SHINING OPPORTUNITY TO HELP
ANOTHER PARENT

You're doing a remarkable thing, and everything you've learned here will make your journey that little bit easier. Now you have the perfect opportunity to give that chance to other parents!

Simply by leaving your honest opinion of this book on Amazon, you'll show new readers where they can find the guidance they're looking for – no matter how little time they have.

WANT TO HELP OTHERS?

Thank you for your support. The parenting journey can feel terribly isolating at times... but when we share information, we see that none of us are really alone.

If you are in the UK, please scan the QR code to leave your review.

If you are in the US, please scan the QR code to leave your review.

REFERENCES

https://www.parentingspecialneeds.org/article/advocating-for-your-child/

https://www.pacer.org/parent/php/PHP-c226.pdf

https://www.readingrockets.org/article/how-parents-can-be-advocates-their-children

https://www.verywellfamily.com/parental-importance-special-education-2162701

https://www.understood.org/en/articles/parent-advocacy-steps

https://www.cbc.ca/parents/learning/view/10-things-to-remember-when-advocating-for-your-special-needs-child

https://www.understood.org/en/articles/understanding-special-education

https://www.parentcenterhub.org/iep-specialeducation/

https://www.allisonacademy.com/students/learning/learning-disabilities/importance-of-special-education/

https://www.talentedladiesclub.com/articles/five-reasons-why-special-education-is-important-in-early-childhood/

https://educationtoday.org.in/2022/04/07/importance-of-special-education-for-special-children/

https://www.verywellfamily.com/what-is-idea-3106870

https://www.understood.org/en/articles/individuals-with-disabilities-education-act-idea-what-you-need-to-know

https://sites.ed.gov/idea/about-idea/

https://www.smartkidswithld.org/getting-help/know-your-childs-rights/your-childs-rights-6-principles-of-idea

https://www.askresource.org/resources/six-principles-of-idea

https://www.smartkidswithld.org/getting-help/know-your-childs-rights/childs-rights-appropriate-education-child-ld/

https://www.understood.org/en/articles/finding-out-if-your-child-is-eligible-for-special-education

https://www.understood.org/en/articles/section-504-of-the-rehabilitation-act-of-1973-what-you-need-to-know

https://www.verywellfamily.com/top-comparative-points-between-section-504-and-idea-2162070

https://www.cmcss.net/wp-content/uploads/2021/06/Understanding-the-Differences-between-IDEA-and-Section-504.pdf

https://www.northcollins.com/departments/special_education_department/what_is_a_504_plan_/what_is_the_difference_between_section_504_and_i_d

https://dredf.org/special-education/special-education-resources/special-education-acronyms-and-glossary/

https://www.sfusd.edu/sped/special-education-acronyms-and-glossary-terms-and-definitions

https://www.verywellfamily.com/what-is-a-504-plan-3104706

https://www.understood.org/en/articles/what-is-a-504-plan

https://www.pvsd.net/departments/student_services/special_education_services/504_plan

https://kidshealth.org/en/parents/504-plans.html

https://www.understood.org/en/articles/504-plans-and-your-child-a-guide-for-families

https://www.understood.org/en/articles/myths-about-504-plans

https://www.understood.org/en/articles/504-plans-5-common-pitfalls

https://www.understood.org/en/articles/7-tips-for-developing-a-good-504-plan

https://www.washington.edu/accesscomputing/what-individualized-education-plan

https://www.understood.org/en/articles/what-is-an-iep

https://www.verywellfamily.com/when-to-ask-for-an-iep-2601418

https://www.theintentionaliep.com/why-ieps-important

https://www.understood.org/en/articles/understanding-the-iep-process

https://www.smartkidswithld.org/getting-help/the-abcs-of-ieps/ieps-5-mistakes-parents-make/

https://onevoiceillinois.com/2016/01/12/10-common-mistakes-parents-make-during-the-iep-process/

http://www.projectidealonline.org/v/special-education-referral-process/

https://www.greatschools.org/gk/articles/pre-referral/

https://iris.peabody.vanderbilt.edu/module/preref/cresource/q2/p03/#content

https://www.verywellfamily.com/what-is-a-developmental-delay-2162164

https://www.greatschools.org/gk/articles/obtain-your-childs-school-records/

https://www.understood.org/en/articles/steps-for-requesting-your-childs-school-records

https://assets.ctfassets.net/p0qf7j048i0q/9ab5413c4fff4bfeb7c7cfe
fc9fcd9f9_en-US/420818cc50fa4da2f9f754792ee4fc2e/
2_Request_a_Copy_of_Your_Childs_Records.pdf

https://www.csnlg.com/what-to-ask-your-special-education-consultant/

https://soeonline.american.edu/blog/special-education-advocate/

https://dredf.org/special-education/special-education-resources/sample-
letter-referral-for-special-education/

https://www.verywellfamily.com/making-a-special-education-referral-for-test
ing-2162690

https://adanc.org/wp-content/uploads/2018/08/IEP-Referral-Process.pdf

https://www.npaschools.org/special-education-referral-and-evaluation

https://iris.peabody.vanderbilt.edu/module/iep01/cresource/q2/p04/#content

https://www.understood.org/en/articles/evaluation-rights-what-you-need-to-
know

https://www.google.com/url?q=https://www.understood.org/en/articles/the-
benefits-of-getting-your-child-evaluated&sa=D&source=docs&ust=
1679490567279157&usg=AOvVaw1aeP7FsDfvWAobHzV5qKfd

https://www.understood.org/en/articles/the-evaluation-process-what-to-
expect#Getting_consent_to_do_the_evaluation

https://www.advocatesforchildren.org/sites/default/files/library/sp_ed_evalua
tions.pdf?pt=1

https://www.understood.org/en/articles/deciding-on-an-evaluation

https://www.understood.org/en/articles/understanding-evaluation-results-
and-next-steps

https://www.understood.org/en/articles/the-evaluation-process-what-to-
expect

https://www.understood.org/en/articles/what-special-education-testing-evalu
ations-results-mean

https://www.ascendlearningcenter.com/blog-highlights/how-do-i-make-
sense-of-iep-evaluation-or-private-testing-data

https://www.smartkidswithld.org/first-steps/evaluating-your-child/making-
sense-of-evaluation-results/

https://behavioralinspiredgrowth.com/special-ed-resources/categories-disabil
ity-idea-law/

https://www.understood.org/en/articles/conditions-covered-under-idea

https://www.understood.org/en/articles/what-to-expect-at-an-iep-eligibility-
meeting

https://www.understood.org/en/articles/what-to-expect-at-an-iep-eligibility-meeting

https://www.understood.org/en/articles/9-steps-to-take-if-the-iep-eligibility-meeting-doesnt-work-out

https://www.understood.org/en/articles/10-steps-to-take-if-your-child-is-denied-services

https://www.pacer.org/parent/php/PHP-a58.pdf

https://www.pacer.org/parent/iep/guide-to-iep/development-of-iep.asp

https://www.understood.org/en/articles/setting-annual-iep-goals-what-you-need-to-know

https://www.understood.org/en/articles/how-to-tell-if-your-childs-iep-goals-are-smart

https://www.parentcenterhub.org

https://tea.texas.gov/sites/default/files/FinalAccessibleIEPDevelopment-July%202020_website_locked.pdf

https://www.understood.org/en/articles/the-difference-between-services-and-supports-for-kids-with-learning-and-thinking-differences

https://www.understood.org/en/articles/modifications-what-you-need-to-know

https://www.understood.org/en/articles/the-difference-between-accommodations-and-modifications

https://www.understood.org/en/articles/common-classroom-accommodations-and-modifications

https://iris.peabody.vanderbilt.edu/module/tran-scp/cresource/q1/p01/

https://www.verywellfamily.com/talk-to-your-child-about-his-or-her-disability-4142685

https://www.understood.org/en/articles/my-child-is-embarrassed-to-go-to-the-resource-room-what-can-i-do

https://www.understood.org/en/articles/am-i-cheating-the-shame-i-felt-using-accommodations-for-dyslexia

https://www.understood.org/en/articles/5-important-things-to-do-before-an-iep-meeting

https://handsandvoices.org/IEPmeetingplanner/iepmeetingplanner.pdf

https://www.understood.org/en/articles/questions-to-ask-before-and-during-your-childs-iep-meeting

https://www.understood.org/en/articles/navigating-iep-meetings

https://dpi.wi.gov/sites/default/files/imce/sped/pdf/agmt-iep-agenda.pdf

https://www.understood.org/en/articles/5-important-things-to-do-during-an-iep-meeting

https://www.smartkidswithld.org/getting-help/the-abcs-of-ieps/iep-meeting-6-tips-parents/

https://handsandvoices.org/IEPmeetingplanner/iepmeetingplanner.pdf

https://www.understood.org/en/articles/5-important-things-to-do-before-an-iep-meeting

https://www.understood.org/en/articles/how-to-consent-to-some-parts-of-an-iep-and-not-others

https://www.understood.org/en/articles/5-important-things-to-do-after-an-iep-meeting

https://handsandvoices.org/IEPmeetingplanner/iepmeetingplanner.pdf

https://www.parentingspecialneeds.org/article/child-attend-iep-meeting/

https://chadd.org/adhd-weekly/should-students-attend-their-iep-meeting/

https://www.brightspottherapy.com/dos-and-donts-as-you-navigate-the-iep-process/

https://www.understood.org/en/articles/6-tips-to-make-sure-your-childs-iep-is-implemented-properly

https://prntexas.org/wp-content/uploads/2021/04/IEP-Implementation-Monitoring_Tips-for-Parents.pdf

https://www.parentcenterhub.org/disputes-overview/

https://www.brainbalancecenters.com/blog/amending-an-iep-how-can-i-get-my-childs-iep-changed

https://www.myschoolmyrights.com/rights/file-a-complaint-with-office-for-civil-rights/

https://www2.ed.gov/about/offices/list/ocr/docs/howto.html

https://www.understood.org/en/articles/6-options-for-resolving-an-iep-dispute

https://www.understood.org/articles/due-process-rights-what-you-need-to-know

https://www.understood.org/articles/what-to-expect-at-a-due-process-hearing

https://www.smartkidswithld.org/getting-help/know-your-childs-rights/resolving-special-education-disputes/

Free for you!

As a thank you for reading this book, download this BONUS GUIDE to teach your child how to keep their room tidy and functional in 7 steps!

Check out my other books and follow me on Amazon to get updates of when I have new publications! Click here to Follow Me Rose Lyons Author Page